The Rise of the Far Right in Europe

Gabriella Lazaridis • Giovanna Campani • Annie Benveniste
Editors

The Rise of the Far Right in Europe

Populist Shifts and 'Othering'

Editors
Gabriella Lazaridis
School of Social Sciences
University of Leicester
United Kingdom

Annie Benveniste
Department of Educational Science
University of Paris8
France

Giovanna Campani
Dipartimento di Scienze della Formazione e
Psicologia
Università degli Studi di Firenze
Italy

ISBN 978-1-137-55678-3   ISBN 978-1-137-55679-0   (eBook)
DOI 10.1057/978-1-137-55679-0

Library of Congress Control Number: 2016938058

© The Editor(s) (if applicable) and The Author(s) 2016
The author(s) has/have asserted their right(s) to be identified as the author(s) of this work in accordance with the Copyright, Designs and Patents Act 1988.
This work is subject to copyright. All rights are solely and exclusively licensed by the Publisher, whether the whole or part of the material is concerned, specifically the rights of translation, reprinting, reuse of illustrations, recitation, broadcasting, reproduction on microfilms or in any other physical way, and transmission or information storage and retrieval, electronic adaptation, computer software, or by similar or dissimilar methodology now known or hereafter developed.
The use of general descriptive names, registered names, trademarks, service marks, etc. in this publication does not imply, even in the absence of a specific statement, that such names are exempt from the relevant protective laws and regulations and therefore free for general use.
The publisher, the authors and the editors are safe to assume that the advice and information in this book are believed to be true and accurate at the date of publication. Neither the publisher nor the authors or the editors give a warranty, express or implied, with respect to the material contained herein or for any errors or omissions that may have been made.

Printed on acid-free paper

This Palgrave Macmillan imprint is published by Springer Nature
The registered company is Macmillan Publishers Ltd. London

To the refugees who die to reach Europe and to the 3000 people who committed suicide in Greece because of the austerity policies

Contents

Authors' Biographies

Edma Ajanovic, junior researcher and Ph.D. student at the Department of Political Science, University of Vienna, Austria, currently works on the project 'RAGE—Hate Speech and Populist Othering in Europe' and is writing her Ph.D. thesis on the issue of racist discourses and practices. Her research interests are migration, racism, right-wing extremism, intersectionality and transnationalism. Contact: edma.ajanovic@univie.ac.at

Annie Benveniste is an anthropologist and Professor in the Department of Educational Sciences and on the Masters programme in Gender Studies at the University of Paris VIII, France. She has conducted many studies in the fields of migration, ethnicisation of social relations, ethnicisation of religion and discrimination, including research in Soweto on violence against women in the post-apartheid context. She is currently involved in other European projects (SPRINGARAB, GENDERCIT). She is a past president of the Association Française des Anthropologues and is currently a member of the publishing committee of *Le Journal des anthropologues*.

She has coordinated many issues of this review, including on the concepts of 'Sexe and Gender' 2011, and on 'Norms and Ethics', 2014. Other recent publications are 'Racialisation et ethnicisation de la religion' in *Dictionnaire des faits religieux*, Paris 2010; *Se Faire Violence. Analyse des coulisses de la recherche*, 2013; and a forthcoming article in a collected volume *Women and religion; comparison Jews and Muslims*.

Giovanna Campani is Professor of Intercultural Education, Gender Anthropology and Intercultural Communication in the Department of Education and Psychology, University of Florence. She earned a Ph.D. in Ethnology from the University of Nice with a thesis titled 'Family, Village and Regional Networks of Italian Immigrants in France' and a Master of Philosophy from the University of Pisa with a thesis on 'History, Science and Sociology in Max Weber's Thought'. Her research interests have included social movements, social inclusion, comparative education, the sociology of migration and gender issues. The intersectionality of gender with class and ethnicity has become her main field of study during the last ten years. She has been principal coordinator of the Italian team on numerous EU projects and has coordinated EU projects in the field of migration and gender.

Her most recent publications are: *I populism nella crisi europea* (with Giovanni Stanghellini), Pacini Editore, Pisa 2014; *Madri Sole*, Rosenberg and Sellier, Turin 2012; *Precarious migrant work in Europe* (with Mojca Painik), Mirodvni Institute, Ljubljana 2011; *Genere e globalizzazione*, Pisa 2010: ETS; *Dalle minoranze agli immigrati: la questione del pluralismo culturale e religioso in Italia*, Milano 2008: Unicopli; *Migranti nel mondo globale*, Roma 2007: Sinnos.

Anna Krasteva is full professor at the Department of Political Sciences at the New Bulgarian University and doctor honoris causa of the University of Lille III, France. She has authored and edited 29 books and published numerous articles in Bulgaria, the USA, France, the UK, Belgium, Russia, Switzerland, Germany, FYROM, Slovakia, Greece, Serbia, Turkey, Italy, the Netherlands and Romania. She has been visiting professor and lecturer at numerous universities, as well as a fellow of the Institute for Advanced Studies in Nantes, France. Her main fields of research are migration and ethnic politics and policies, populism, border politics, digital democracy, and e-citizenship. Her recent publications are: La rue et l'-e-rue (co-ed) Paris, 2015, From migration to mobility: policies and roads, Sofia, 2015, Elastic (post)secularism, e-book 2014; Migrants and refugees. Equitable education for displaced populations (co-ed.) Charlotte, NY, USA, 2013), E-citoyennetes (ed.), Paris 2013; Migration from and to Southeastern Europe (co-ed.), Ravenna, 2010. She is editor-in-chief of the international journal Southeastern Europe and a member of the editorial board of Nationalism and Ethnic Politics (Routledge). She has been a board member of a number of international academic institutions, including the Institute of Central, Eastern and

Balkan Europe at the University of Bologna, the Reseau des Maisons des Sciences de l'Homme in France (2008–2012), Association International des Sociologies de Langue Française (1996–2004), and an evaluator for the European Commission and Fonds de recherche du Québec - Société et Culture. She has been awarded the Palmes Académiques of France and is president of Amopa-Bulgarie (Association of the members of the Palmes Académiques). She is a member of the Board of the Diplomatic Institute, vice-president for international relations of the Bulgarian Political Sciences Association and member of the board of the Balkan Political Science Association.

Roman Kuhar is an Associate Professor of sociology at the University of Ljubljana (Faculty of Arts, Department of Sociology) and researcher at the Peace Institute, Ljubljana. His research interests include GLBT/queer topics, intolerance and equality, media, citizenship and sexuality. He is the author of several books, including *Media Construction of Homosexuality* (2003, MediaWatch, Ljubljana), *At the Crossroads of Discrimination* (2009, Peace Institute, Ljubljana), co-author (with A. Švab) of *The Unbearable Comfort of Privacy* (2005, Peace Institute, Ljubljana) and co-editor (with J. Takács) of *Beyond The Pink Curtain: Everyday life of LGBT people in Eastern Europe* (2007, Peace Institute, Ljubljana) and *Doing Families: Gay and Lesbian Family Practices* (2011, Peace Institute, Ljubljana).

Gabriella Lazaridis is Senior Lecturer at the University of Leicester, UK. She has published more than 60 papers and has edited/co-edited several books in the fields of ethnicity, migration, racism, citizenship, social inclusion/exclusion, gender, and 'othering' and pro- and anti-migrant mobilisation. Her latest work has been on the rise of the far right in Europe and 'othering', and she was the principal investigator and over-all coordinator of the recent nine-country comparative project, 'RAGE—Hate Speech and Populist Othering in Europe', funded by the EU's Justice and Home Affairs. Her latest books, *International Migration in Europe: from Subjects to Abjects* (monograph), and *Securitization of Migration in the EU: debates after 9/11* (co-edited with Khursheed Wadia) were both published in 2015 by Palgrave.

Susi Meret is an Associate Professor at the Department of Culture and Global Studies, Aalborg University, Denmark. She is affiliated to the research group COMID, Center for the Studies of Migration and Diversity. She is the main coordinator of a research network on Nordic Populism, financed by NordForsk, and a partner in the NORDCORP project 'Ideological transformations, organizational development and mainstream reactions. A comparison of populist parties in four Nordic countries'. She has published on right-wing populist parties, populist ideology and voters, anti-immigration attitudes and Islamophobia. For her recent publications and work, see http://personprofil.aau.dk/100658?lang=en.

Mojca Pajnik is Senior Research Associate at the Peace Institute, Institute for Contemporary Social and Political Studies in Ljubljana and lecturer at the Faculty of Social Sciences, University of Ljubljana. Her research is related to issues of citizenship, migration, integration, multiculturalism, the politics of inclusion/exclusion, gender inequality and the media. Her recent books include *Contesting integration, engendering migration: Theory and practice*, co-edited with F. Anthias (Palgrave, 2014); *Work and the challenges of belonging: Migrants in globalizing economies*, co-edited with F. Anthias (Cambridge Scholars, 2014); *Precarious migrant labour across Europe*, co-edited with G. Campani (Peace Institute, 2011); and *Prostitution and human trafficking: Perspectives of gender, labour and migration* (Peace Institute, 2008).

Etienne Pingaud is a post-doctoral researcher at the University of Paris VIII. He holds a Ph.D. in sociology from the School for Advanced Studies in Social Sciences, Paris. His main research fields are the development of Islam and the related rise of Islamophobia; the identitarian; transformations of the far right; and the political construction of cultural identities generally. Recently published articles and chapters on these topics are: 'Les temporalités de la lutte. Evénement, urgence et changements de rythme dans une mobilisation locale pour la Palestine', *Politix*, 2014; and 'La costruzione del nazional-populismo', in Campani, 2014). He has presented his work at a number of international conferences, including the ISA World Congress of Sociology and the International Society of Sociology of Religions Congress in Turku.

Birgit Sauer is Professor of Political Science in the Department of Political Science, University of Vienna. She is one of the founders of the Gender and Politics section of the German Political Science Association and Convenor the research network Gender and Agency at the University of Vienna. She was the co-director of the EU's VEIL project on the regulation of Muslim body covering and Austrian director of the Research Network on Gender, Politics and the State. Her research interests include gender and governance, comparative gender policies, migration, affective politics and populism.

Birte Siim is a political scientist and Professor of Gender Research in the Social Sciences in the Department of Culture and Global Studies at Aalborg University (AAU), Denmark. She was Research Director of FREIA, the Gender Research Centre, AAU and Danish coordinator for several EUprojects on European citizenship, diversity, hate speech, racism, and intersectionality (bEUcitizen, RAGE, RECODE, EUROSPHERE and VEIL). She has published on intersectionality, citizenship, democracy, migration, ethnicity and the welfare state. Recent publications are: 'Gender Diversities—Practicing Intersectionality in the European Union' (with L.Rolandsen Agustin), *Ethnicities* (2014); *Negotiating Gender and Diversity in an Emergent European Public Sphere* (with M. Mokre) (2013); and 'Citizenship' in *The Oxford Handbook on Gender and Politics* (2013).

Iztok Šori, Ph.D. is a Researcher at the Peace Institute, Institute for Contemporary Social and Political Studies in Ljubljana. His research experience and bibliography include issues of populism, migration, prostitution, human trafficking, gender equality, political representation, reconciliation of private and professional life, and being single as a lifestyle. In recent years his main research focus has been on populism based on othering and racist exclusion.

Vasiliki Tsagkroni completed her Ph.D. in Political Sciences at Queen Mary University of London. Her area of research is political communication and the use of marketing and branding in politics, and she is investigating the interaction between communication strategies and political parties with a particular focus on parties of the far right. She has experience in a wide range of research, organisational and managerial positions, including at Keele University and the National Hellenic Research Foundation, and has developed her teaching skills in an academic environment as a teaching associate at Queen Mary University of London. She is currently working as a research associate at the University of Leicester on RAGE, a comparative project which examines 'populist' political discourse and its effect on those 'othered' by such discourse. The project is funded by the EU's DG Justice, Fundamental Rights and Citizenship Programme.

List of Figures

List of Table

1

Introduction
Populism: The Concept and Its Definitions

Annie Benveniste, Giovanna Campani,
and Gabriella Lazaridis

The most recent European elections in 2014 saw the rise of parties labelled 'populist' across the European Union (EU). The prominence in Denmark of Dansk Folkeparti (Danish People's Party), in Slovenia of Slovenska Demokratska Stranka (Slovenian Democratic Partry), of Front National

This publication has been produced with financial support from the Fundamental Rights and Citizenship Programme of the European Union through the EU's Justice and Home Affairs for the project 'Hate Speech and Populist Othering in Europe through the Racism, Age, Gender Looking Glass' (Grant Number Just/2012/FRAC/AG/2861) and from the EU's Daphne initiative for a project on E-Engagement Against Violence (Grant Number JUST/2011/DAP/AG/3195). The contents of this publication are the sole responsibility of the authors and can in no way be taken to reflect the views of the European Commission. We would like to thank the RAGE and E-EAV teams for their work and support for this book.

A. Benveniste (✉)
Department of Educational Science, University of Paris VIII,
Saint-Denis, France

G. Campani
Department of Education and Psychology, University of Florence,
Florence, Italy

G. Lazaridis
University of Leicester, Leicester, UK

© The Editor(s) (if applicable) and The Author(s) 2016
G. Lazaridis et al. (eds.), *The Rise of the Far Right in Europe*,
DOI 10.1057/978-1-137-55679-0_1

1

in France,[1] the high scores of the United Kingdom Independence Party (UKIP) and Beppe Grillo's Movimento Cinque Stelle (Five-Star Movement) in Italy, the new MEP seats won by the Freiheitliche Partei Österreichs (FPÖ, Freedom Party of Austria) have all been perceived as turning points that are changing the face of the European Parliament, and challenging at some level the hegemony of the 'big four' well-established European political forces leading the Strasbourg assembly (ALDE, EPP, S&D, Greens/European Free Alliance).[2] In this context, the surprisingly weak performance of the Dutch PVV (Partij voor de Vrijheid or Party for Freedom) appears to be the single exception to the visible trend of EU political life: 'populism' has become a major issue in many countries of the European Union. A ghost is haunting Europe, the ghost of 'populism'.

It is hard to identify many characteristics these figures of contemporary populism have in common. Can Marine Le Pen and Beppe Grillo really be united under the same political banner? Does it make sense to compare gay rights supporter Geert Wilders, the Catholic Conservative Timo Soini and the neo-Nazi Michaloliakos, or to associate the Cinque Stelle with the anti-immigration Dansk Folkeparti? Even if we focus on the organisations traditionally considered radical right or far right, the difficulties of contracting alliances and building a parliamentary group to gain influence show that their links are not obvious: a far cry from the idea of similarity suggested by an umbrella concept such as 'populism'. For example, Front National and Lega Nord are rejected by UKIP, Front National rejects Golden Dawn, the Five-Star Movement denounces the fascist threat represented by far-right parties such as Front National or Jobbik in Hungary.

This book aims to provide a critical understanding of current European trends and considers the complex phenomena covered by the notion of populism, focusing especially on right-wing populism. It also recommends ways these can be challenged both in theory and in practice by using the gender–race–ethnicity–sexual orientation intersectionality approach.

---

[1] Dansk Folkeparti won 26.6 per cent of the vote and 4 MEPs (on 13), Slovenska Demokratska Stranka 24.9 per cent and 3 MPs (on 8), while the Front National gained 24 seats (24.85 per cent). 26.6 per cent was won by UKIP (24 MPs), 21.16 per cent by Beppe Grillo's M5S (17 MEPs); the FPÖ won 2 more MEPs than In 2009.

[2] ALDE (Alliance of Liberals and Democrats for Europe); EPP (European People's Party); S&D (Socialists and Democrats).

The book explores how we can make 'populism' a tangible concept. What is it supposed to express: a value system, an ideology, a political style or a way of using narratives? Populism does not actually appear to fit into any classical classification of political parties, which challenges its intelligibility. To avoid the temptation of using it, depending on the context, as a synonym for 'nationalism', 'racism', 'euroscepticism' or sometimes even 'anti-establishment', we first question the concept itself, aiming to deconstruct it and go beyond (Wittgenstein 1953).

In exploring the literature on populism, we face the same complexity. The sheer variety of political parties and movements labelled 'populist' has led some scholars to call the phenomenon itself a 'chameleon'. Karin Priester, for instance, chose the subtitle 'approaching a chameleon' for the 2012 book in which she references Paul Taggart (2000), who writes of the 'chameleon-like quality' and the 'empty heart' of populism. The complexity is increased by the assertion of authors such as Margaret Canovan (1982) or Pierre-André Taguieff (1984, 1997) that fieldwork offers a definition rather than the theoretical baseline. An empirical grounded approach seeks to overcome the fluidity of the definitions by providing many ethnographic heuristic texts about populist formations all across Europe, even if these contain no references to theory. This book is an empirical study exploring the flexible application of the meaning of 'populism' in eight different countries in Europe (Austria, Bulgaria, Denmark, France, Greece, Italy, Slovenia and the UK) with diverse historical trajectories and various political party systems, each with its own rules, languages and political games.

Populism: A Problematic Concept

The term 'populism' has become a common way to describe many very different movements in politics both in Europe and outside the European continent. Since the 1980s, it has been used to evoke the transformation of political ideology and practices with rhetoric, style or 'narratives' designed to conquer electoral audiences.

In Europe, the contemporary success of this notion is linked to the rise of new kinds of far-right movements in the 1980s and the emergence of leaders as Jean-Marie Le Pen (Taguieff 1984), Jörg Haider or Umberto

Bossi. In the 1990s, it was used to describe the rise of Latin American leaders claiming to oppose neoliberalism, such as Hugo Chavez in Venezuela or Evo Morales in Bolivia. Mudde and Kalwasser (2013) speak of inclusionary populism in Latin America, as opposed to exclusionary populism in Europe. It is now a common way of speaking about European radical left forces as Oskar Lafontaine's Die Linke in Germany or Jean-Luc Mélanchon (Front de Gauche) in France, or Alexis Tsipras (SYRIZA) in Greece. And populism is no longer associated solely with parties situated in the periphery of the main positions of power: even the mainstream party leaders are facing the risk of being discredited by the label 'populists'.

At the intersection of the media and academia, 'populism' quickly invaded the political field and in certain electoral circumstances was used as a pejorative term. Because of its wide-ranging application and its common meaning, the technical content of the notion seems to be problematic. It is difficult to agree on a consensual definition of 'populism'. In addition to ideological issues, several historical references position various kinds of movements in a situation of conceptual uncertainty that has been summed up by Diamanti (2010):

> Populism is one of the words that appear the most (…) in the political discourse for some time now. Without much difference, however, between the scientific environment, public, political and everyday life. Indeed, it is a fascinating concept, able to "suggest" without imposing too much precise and definitive meaning. In fact, it does not define, but evokes. (Diamanti 2010)

The invasive and normative extension of the concept tends to obscure its theoritical value. How can 'populism' become an heuristic notion under these conditions? Nowadays, it seems to be impossible to completely avoid the term, but the disparity of the contexts makes it hard to agree on a common definition that transcends borders and national peculiarities. Several authors such as Margaret Canovan (1999) give preference to empirical classifications; others (Zaslove 2008) define populism by its emphasis on the people and the elite, a supposedly homogeneous people standing against an elite, not only within a particular country but also on the EU and global levels (financial capitals) and against 'others' defined by race, religion, ethnic origin or sexuality. As Pelinka (2013: 9) writes, contemporary populism is directed 'against elites who have opened the doors to foreign influence and to foreigners'. But as an ideology, populism does not tell us who the elite and the people are, what they do and what they think; so it can be found in many forms, contingent on the existing relationships between government and society. The widespread acceptance and the 'populist' label given to many organisations not only contributes to the inflation of neologism around populism already pointed out by Dezé (2004)—neopopulism, national populism, euro-populism, modern populism, new populism—it also explains the profusion of definitions available in the literature. Nowadays, there is a common diffusion that creates a singular situation: it seems to be impossible to completely avoid the term, but the disparity of the contexts makes really hard to arrive at a common definition that can cross borders and national particularities. It also explains the profusion of definitions available in the literature, each author often having their own.

The concept is so frequently used that studies already exist which begin with a review of the scientific literature about the issue (Canovan 1999): indeed it would be possible to assemble a review of the reviews.

In some cases, 'populism' does not fit into the political situation. In several countries, it needs to be divided into different categories to make it suitable for academic research. In these cases the concept 'populism' makes sense as a way of distinguishing between several forces. In Denmark, the Dansk Folkeparti, now the third largest party in the country, illustrates pragmatic and 'respectable' populism far from the radical anti-Islamic views diffused by networks and 'right' groups as the Free Press Society. In Bulgaria, 'soft populism' is used in connection with the comeback of the former king, Simeon Saxcoburgotski, who won an election by capitalising on his own name and personal resources, while 'hard populism' is symbolized by the organisation Ataka, producer of hate speeches and supporter of discrimination against 'others'.

The wide range of populism definitions makes it hard to express all the criteria that are considered essential to a firm explanation of the concept, except that populism has always been used in a negative sense by governing elites to characterise any form of opposition that claims to represent the 'people's voice' without basing its policy declarations on real facts and viable solutions to actual problems (Liakos 1989; Mouselis et al. 1989; Pappas 2013). All definitions show the constitutive ambiguity of the concept, while scholars tend to regard it as a style of political argument that can be found in virtually all parties. Whatever the case, Pels (2012: 31ff) argues that it would be dangerous to reduce new right-wing populism to a 'frivolity of form, pose and style' and 'to think that there is no substance between its political style' (ibid.: 32). Hence, the fundamental question remains: what is populism? How, can we make 'populism' a solid concept? What situations can it explain? What is it supposed to express: a system of values, an ideology, a political style or a way to use narratives? How far is 'populism' from fascism, for example, in all its aspects? In this book, the Italian chapter presents the academic debates around the connections that can be made between fascism and populism. Is fascism populism? Is 'populism' a modern acceptable term to evoke similar issues and evolution? Even if it is more localised in the countries which have known fascist or Nazi regimes, the reference to the ideologies of the 1930s appears to be omnipresent in academic debate.

What is populism supposed to characterizse? Should populism be considered an ideology? An individual political style? Does the concept more usefully describe a certain position inside politics? Many theoreticians of the field raise all these dimensions. Karin Priester (2012) organises definitions of populism into three groups according to whether it is understood as an ideology, a strategy to attain and stay in power or a discursive practice, but without attempting an overarching definition. This is also true of Smilov and Krastev (2008); the criteria they use for 'populism' are: the appeal to the 'people as a whole' as opposed to 'corrupt' and 'impotent' political elites; opposition to the key idea of liberal democracy (that the political majority should be limited in important ways by constitutional constraints); and the rejection of the 'political correctness' of liberalism, meaning a challenge to at least some elements that are seen as the 'liberal consensus' of the transition period—market-oriented reforms, integration in Euro-Atlantic organisations, rejection of nationalistic language and behaviour.

Clarification is important here. Depending on the category 'populism' fits into, it can be linked to certain conceptual channels. If 'populism' is an *ideology*, it belongs in the system of values it aims to defend. What are the foundations of this ideological trend? In this case, the differences between 'populism' and other classical and historical ideological standpoints of the radical right must be questioned. How far is, for example, 'populism' from racism, in all its aspects? Big differences on the issue can be seen between countries, and most of the time between different organisations and case studies presented by the same country. The biggest parties and structures (e.g. FPÖ, Front National, Danske Folkeparti, UKIP) usually tend to avoid visible direct racist speeches, whereas the smaller groups, which often remain on the edge of institutional politics (like the Italian Forza Nuova), are more radical. But most of them, even when they eliminate classical racist vocabulary, defend nationalist ideas and values.

By the same logic, in Italy academic debates around the connections that can be made between fascism and populism appear in the *Treccani Encyclopedia of Social Sciences* (Bongiovanni 1996). Is far-right 'populism' an acceptable modern term to describe similar issues and evolution? Even if it is more localised in countries that have known fascist or Nazi regimes (e.g., Italy, Austria), reference to the ideologies of the 1930s appears to be omnipresent (Sternhell 2012; Winock 1990). But the most obvious link for the vast majority of organisations described as populist is with 'nationalism'[3]

How does 'populism' combine with 'nationalism'? A rich and interesting literature states that *populism*, with its naturalistic, essentialist and restrictive depiction of the people[4] is a by-product of the re-affirmation of a 'deeply, culturally ingrained perception of social belonging, and of the foundations of the polity, in which the social whole is considered prior to the individual' (Blokker 2005: 371), and thus is linked to *nationalism.*

The Herderian concept is of the nation as a naturally ordained and homogeneous whole, a national individuality (Blokker 2005: 382) with specific and unique characteristics that supplies its members with norms of behaviour as well as forms of identity. This understanding of nationalism clearly discloses its exclusivist features and the essentialisation and naturalisation of the nation results in the construction of the nation's non-members as undesirable others. Within this framework, boundaries are defined ethnically. Therefore, whether as an 'imagined'

---

[3] Of course there also are strong populist organisations working in a regional tropism, the most famous case being the Lega Nord in Italy.
[4] For an analysis of the connection between nation, nationalism and populism in both Eastern and Western Europe, see Blokker (2005).

(Anderson 1991) or 'invented' (Gellner 1983) national identity, or as the privileging of a 'natural' community (Smith 1991), the promotion of a monolithic homogeneous group legitimises a sense of territoriality within the polity's borders.

The nationalist interpretation of populism equates the people with the ethnic nation (Canovan 2002) and thus strengthens the eternal value of the organic community and reinforces its exclusionary nature (Canovan 2002: 34; Mudde 2007: 546). Analyses of such populist manifestations underline the marginalisation of those not belonging to the majority group, which can easily lead to ethnic cleansing, 'a latent possibility once the discursive construction of the community proceeds along purely ethnic lines' (Laclau 2005: 197). In other words, in order to safeguard internal cohesion, populist nationalism not only excludes others, but in fact rejects all forms of pluralism and difference in the community of the people, relegating all uncertainties or conflicts beyond the borders of the nation state (Chiantera-Stutte and Petö 2003). Given the diversity of populist forces present in Europe, the term 'the people' does not coincide with the nation as bounded by the territory of the nation state.

In order to shed light on the connection between populism and nationalism, the chapters in this book go beyond the state of the art on populism, taking into account theoretical approaches from research on 'race', ethnicity and ethnic boundaries. Furthermore, since the symbolic construction of ethnic and national identities can be compared with the symbolic references employed by populists in this context, the question that arises is what imagined roots populists attribute to themselves and how they compare to national myths and officially endorsed histories? This is of crucial importance for the populist manifestations that can be labelled as 'populist nationalist', involving the 'race'/ethnicity aspect in the definition of their movement or party identity (e.g. Lega Nord in Italy, the Front National in France, Golden Dawn and LAOS in Greece etc.). Since Taguieff's work (1984), 'national populism' has been a label commonly used to describe the modern far right. For other authors as Germani (1975), every populism (even those in Latin American countries) is nationalist. As the chapters in this group show, in many cases ethnic considerations prevail. In other cases, opposition to immigration is the first criterion, and the definition of 'nationals' is close to the official administrative one (citizens), leaving the ethnic aspects in the background. And sometimes, as for UKIP, the anti-EU rhetoric directly builds on the core of national views about sovereignty.

Behind the construction of nationalism, a system of gender relations is implicitly put in place; any analysis of the populist phenomenon is enhanced by attention to the role of gender (see chapters in this book). Scholars have consistently and convincingly argued that the national community is envisioned as gendered in a heteropatriarchal construction of *the people is a family*, a sort of 'metaphoric kinship' (Smith 1991: 79) or, in other words, as a 'family-writ-large' (Golden 2003). Indeed, the metaphor of the family is indispensable to nationalism. 'The nation is depicted as one great family, the members as brothers and sisters of the motherland or fatherland, speaking their mother tongue. In this way the family of the nation overrides and replaces the individual's family but evokes similarly strong loyalties and vivid attachment' (Smith 1991: 79). However, feminist scholars argue that such an interpretation suggests that the nation is founded on gender bias and inequality and does not allocate sufficient weight or salience to gender in the construction of identities. Rather, populist parties are characterised at their core by gender differences which are not 'automatically enabling' (Einhorn 2009: 8).

Finally, 'populism' as an ideology questions the strength of conservative values in European societies. Once again, the appropriation and demonstration of the issues can vary a lot according to the organisations in the countries examined in this book. Some of them claim their modernity, defending it against new threats, and especially the rise of Islam (Free Press Society in Denmark, English Defence League in the UK, Activists against Islamization in France). Many of these forces claim their religious affiliation as key to their fight. Catholicism in Slovenia, France or Italy, and the Orthodox religion in Bulgaria and Greece (the Greek LAOS explicitly mixes an Orthodox Christian religious identity with a radically nationalist political identity) are among the main basic identities proposed by populists. In political and ideological terms, it usually goes with strong opposition to women's rights or sometimes to abortion, LGBT rights or homosexuality itself.

In the light of these issues—in front of nationalist visions and conservative values—we should wonder whether 'populism' constitues a
new phenomenon. In other words, its recent rise and dispersion across
Europe could be, at some levels, the renewal of old ideas and propositions
now translated into the language of modern political contests, finding an
incarnation in a new style of politician that is immediately recognisable
and gives 'populist' organisations in the different countries some 'family resemblance'. Mudde (2007: 115) distinguishes between populism as
ideology and populism as style. He states categorically that despite the
greater visibility of the former, the key challenge comes from the latter:
'In my view, even though populism as ideology is theoretically considered
as the principal danger, in actuality the main threat in Europe today is
populism as style'.

If populism is considered as an individual *political style*, its modernity
and its foundations deserve to be analysed. As shown in this book, not all
populist leaders act in the same way, but they manage to be distinguished
from the classical figures of established politicians. Being considered populists means introducing discontinuities in common behaviours, acting
differently from the rest of the politicians. This perspective emphasises
the role of personality in the current 'populism' wave. All the organisations discussed in the book are associated with one or a small number
of strong leaders who can be at the same time spokesmen, leaders and
in some cases founders of their party, movement or network. The most
famous of them, from Jean-Marie Le Pen to Nigel Farage, from Jörg
Haider to Pia Kjaersgaard, have all accumulated these different functions.
It also questions the importance of the media (especially television) in
the production of 'others', the enemy, a phenomenon which according
to Wodak (2015: 2) manifests itself as 'politics of fear'. Sometimes the
scapegoats are Jews, sometimes Muslims, sometimes ethnic minorities,
women, anarchists, homosexuals and so on. As Wodak (2015: 4) writes,

the discursive strategies of 'victim-perpetrator reversal', 'scapegoating' and
the 'construction of conspiracy theories' ... belong to the necessary 'toolkit'
of right-wing populist rhetoric. In short, anybody can potentially be constructed as dangerous 'Other', should it become expedient for specific strategic and manipulative purposes.

It is difficult to describe the main aspects of a 'populist' style. Some authors such as Crick (2002) have suggessted descriptions: 'a style of politics and rhetoric that seeks to arouse a majority, or at least what their leaders passionately believe is a majority … who are, have been, or think themselves to be outside the polity, scorned and despised by an educated establishment'. At a more general level, it can be seen as an illustration of what Albert Hirschman (1970) calls *voice* in his famous triptych of protestation. 'Populism' is always a form of protest against the establishment, loudly expressed in a way that encourages large audiences. At least two characteristics of this style are commonly described in the literature.

The Charisma of the Leaders

The role of this particularly rare virtue is always hard to analyse in a mass-media society, because since Max Weber it has been understood that 'charisma' cannot be intelligible without the specific bonds linking the leader to their public. But the specific properties of certain personalities are undoubtedly of decisive importance considering the 'symbolic capital' (Bourdieu 1972) they accumulate and the opportunities it offers them. The Bulgarian case in this book underlines, for example, the central function of charisma in the soft populism exemplified by the surprising comeback of the former king in the early 2000s. Meanwhile the French case shows the importance of Marine Le Pen's charisma in the Front National's new lease of life in recent years. For Martin Reisigl (2002: 159), this charismatic dimension is even one of the main characteristic of populism, with this 'focus on a strong leader while in contrast a homogeneous collective identity—that is often linked to racism and xenophobia—is being invoked.'

The Use of Specific Rhetoric

Rhetoric is at the heart of the literature on populist issues (where discourse analysis have become a common way to approach the topics), as Margaret Canovan (2004: 243) says: '…more recent studies tend to focus on populist discourse, a rhetoric of appeals to "the people"'. If the narratives can be really different in relation to the various national contexts, there is a resemblance in the way 'the people' is loudly invoked against the establishment, to denounce the failure of mainstream organisations or to combine classical left-wing issues with conservative or nationalist ones. A famous example is the 'village idiot' of the historical leader of Lega Nord, Umberto Bossi. But the key condition seems to be the ability to play on the emotional register, to use speeches and arguments to raise the affects of the people and arouse their immediate feelings. This affective dimension crops up in all the country cases.

Finally, populism is often used as a keyword to express a certain *position in the political field*, depending on the kind of populist organisations that are competing in certain countries. In this logic it is the topographic semantics that must be considered to make 'populism' understandable. In some countries, organisations described as figures of 'populism' can be classified without any discussion as far right, because they hold extreme or outrageous points of views which are far more radical than those of all the government or mainstream parties: examples include Ataka in Bulgaria, English Defence League in the UK, Forza Nuova in Italy, Golden Dawn in Greece. All these organiations are sometimes claimed with pride by some activists to belong to this category.

But in other cases, 'populism' is used to cover another scenario. The concept is today probably mainly used to describe a modernised far right that is avoiding extremism, presenting realistic propositions, cleansing the internal membership to expel the more radical members, and thus more openly joining the democratic competition for power. Consider Lega Nord or Freiheitliche Partei Österreichs (FPÖ) who have recently been part of national governments. The Dansk Folkeparti, UKIP or Marine Le Pen's new-look Front National, have all spent time disciplining their ranks, and training all the intermediary leaders and executives. They try to expel the more extreme elements, to control the Facebook pages, Twitter accounts or personal blogs of the members and activists. The shift is important because these organisations are seeking respectability and rejecting other small far-right groups or splinter groups now considered people to be avoided. On some level they are seeking a new political position somewhere between right wing and far right. Priester (2012) positions populism between the parliamentary and the extra-parliamentary right wing. In her view it is 'neither right-wing extremism nor conservative, but an amalgam of the two'. That is why links with mainstream right-wing parties have been built in several countries (Italy, Austria, Denmark). This is also the reason for the 'mainstreaming' of certain far-right ideas which are now expanding inside right-wing parties in government, as in the French case where the trend named 'the strong right' is in a leading position within the right-wing party Les Républicains.

To conclude, the impossibility of reaching a valuable definition of 'populism' is linked to the catch-all aspect of the term, to the normative content it is supposed to evoke, and to the multiple dimensions, sometimes weirdly mixed, that are included in the academic uses of the term. We could of course add the question of the 'translation' and adaptation of the term to each national political situation, always redefined to be meaningful in the specific context of the country. In all of the countries studied in this book, there is a central organisation that figures as paradigmatic of populism, and that broadly defines what academics talk about when they discuss 'populism'. In Austria for example, the FPÖ is the key example for an understanding of the phenomenon. In France Jean-Marie Le Pen's Front National is at the heart of all discussions on the far right, extremism, populism and even racism. In Finland (not examined in this book) True Finns represent the axial model, with political movements especially relevant to the Finnish case, such as that envisaged by Voitto Helander (1971), which is characterised by the idealisation of the simple, rural life and ordinary people, emerges in crisis or transition periods and aims to return power to the people by, for example, favouring small entrepreneurs instead of international corporations and opposing bureaucrats.

This book aims to:

1. shed light on a field of study characterized by highly uncertain theoretical frames, and redefine and assess the typologies and characters attributed to populist parties and forces in the countries under study;
2. clarify and highlight the differences between populist experiences in the Central and Eastern, and Western parts of the EU member states covered in the book;

3. bring new elements to the understanding of continuities and discontinuities with the authoritarian experiences of the past, and with nationalism;
4. explore the relationship between populism, on one hand, democracy and power, on the other, through the intersectionality approach;
5. link populism to sexism and racism substantively and theoretically, investigating the articulation between various, sometimes contradictory, political positions in policy domains of direct importance;
6. analyse how populist rhetoric influences the political arena and mainstream culture;
7. clarify the impact of populist parties on the anti-discrimination and gender-equality agenda promoted by the EU in those countries where they have been, or are, in power;
8. provide tools for policy makers to promote a peace and gender-equality culture, questioning the boundaries and borders that are essentialised by populism, but are also legitimised by mainstream political culture.

Chapter 2 explores the link between neo-fascism and populism in Italian political history. Neo-fascism represents a political movement—deeply rooted in Italian history—dating back to the end of the 1940s; over the years, it has produced various expressions, some of which have been incorporated into parliamentary dynamics, while some have chosen the anti-system path. Both trends have preserved traditional elements and, at the same time, re-adapted traditional messages (including anti-Semitism, anti-capitalism and anti-Americanism).

In this chapter Campani looks at the political dynamics surrounding the evolution of neo-fascism and neo-fascist groups and parties in post-war Italy up to the present day and then concentrates on two neo-fascist organisations formed in the 1990s, Forza Nuova and Casa Pound. She analyses their symbols, values, beliefs and forms of 'othering'—marking the division between us and the others. An in-depth understanding of the history, the manifestos and the political activities of the two organisations informs the outline of the differences between neo-fascism and neopopulism. While neo-fascism has a strong ideological dimension, neopopulism is a chameleon-like trend spreading across a great number of EU countries and responding to various challenges (globalisation, post-industrial economic conditions, immigration and European Union constraints). In Italy, it is mainly represented by the Northern League. Campani shows how neo-fascism and neopopulism overlap in targeting some topics, such as hostility to immigration, and how they both tend to oppose 'the system'—the corrupt politics, the financial capitalism, an EU that is an instrument of financial capitalism and has deprived Italy of sovereignty. But, although they may combine in some cases, populism and neo-fascism are distinct phenomena. The concepts of people and of the role of the state are very different in populism and neo-fascism. The last section of the chapter looks at the victims of neo-fascist organisations and the resistance to them that has been established by organisations like ANPI (National Association of Italian Partisans).

The third chapter presents an in-depth study of the French Front National and of anti-Islam networks, focusing on the reasons for the growing influence of far-right ideas in France and the weakening of anti-racist and anti-discrimination movements despite their historical presence. Front National is described through its ideological production and its evolution, its conception of the 'other' and the links with other organisations or institutions whose intellectual work can build political and ideological cleavages. The analysis of data collected from interviewees who were all strong Marine Le Pen supporters illustrates the party's new recruitment strategy and the new orientation it seeks to adopt to become a 'regular' political party. Benveniste and Pingaud also explore the latest French far-right trend that has emerged in the 2000s and situates Islam as the principal enemy. These individual activists, linked to the international anti-Islam or counter-Jihad network that is being built in Europe, have developed a new way of observing French society through the lens of Islamic issues. The chapter ends with an analysis of the role played by anti-far right organisations in combating hate speech and crime against the 'other'.

Chapter 4 focuses on Austria, one of the first European countries with a successful right-wing extremist party—the Freedom Party Austria (FPÖ). This chapter aims to answer the question why right-wing extremism has been successful and why it is therefore difficult for anti-racist movements to counter FPÖ's discourses. Sauer and Ajanovic approach this question by analysing, first, the discursive strategies of the party, second, the resonance of these policies in right-wing populist movements such as the Viennese anti-mosque movement (the former BPÖ/Bewegung pro Österreich/ Pro- Austria Movement) and third, counter-strategies to these discriminatory and racist discourses in Austria.

The chapter shows how right-wing populist groups in Austria construct binary groups of 'us' and 'the others', as well as gender binaries, as these strategies successfully create societal problems, enemies who cause them and victims who are affected by them. An 'us' group thus comes to be represented by right-wing extremist groups. The chapter also deconstructs strategies of consensus building and hegemony around migration issues. The article begins with a context section, which outlines the rise of the populist right wing in Austria starting with the transformation of the FPÖ under Jörg Haider's leadership in the late 1980s. This section contextualises the early emergence of right-wing populism in Austria's political establishment as well as in the neoliberal transformations of the country after its EU accession, and explains the role of other right-wing and anti-migrant actors in the country. The chapter then illustrates metaphors, symbols and narratives as well as framing their use by right-wing extremist parties and groups—especially when referring to the 'problems' of migration, Islam, the EU and (changing) gender relations. These chains of equivalents create a hegemonic discourse of inequality and hence exclusion. The second part of the analysis outlines strategies within civil society fighting racism and 'othering' on the grounds of ethnicity, nationality, gender or sexuality by Austrian right-wing groups and seeks to establish whether these counter-strategies are adequate.

Chapter 5 looks at right-wing populism in Denmark. Scholars suggest that Danish and Scandinavian welfare and gender regimes have influenced the way populism has emerged, developed and been consolidated in the past half century. It has been argued that Scandinavia developed a form of 'welfare nationalism' that since the late 1960s has linked national, social and democratic issues with social equality, democracy and gender equality in the construction of 'national belonging and identity'. Since the 1990s mainstream political parties have been reframing the relationship between national, democratic and social questions. Siim and Meret suggest that the Danish understanding of the nation and the people has been re-interpreted by the populist right. The chapter presents the results of two case studies of contemporary right-wing populism, the Danish People's Party (DPP, Dansk Folkeparti) and the Free Press Society (Trykkefrihedsselskabet), and focuses on the heritage, shifts and variations in the ideology of the populist right. The findings suggest that constructions of the nation, the people and the other by radical right-wing populist actors are diverse: the DPP claims to address the problems and concerns of the 'common man'—a native Dane—and aims to defend 'the people's interests against immigration and against the elites damaging national sovereignty, culture and identity. This contrasts with the Free Press Society which has developed a rhetoric and discourse aimed at mobilising the intellectual elites against the dangers of Islam, framing itself as the defender of the universal value of free speech in the Western world. Finally the chapter presents some of the counter-strategies to the 'politics of fear' fostered by the populist right, referring to interviews with victims' organisations and democratic antibodies engaged in strategies for the rights of migrants, asylum seekers, refugees and the LGBT community. This leads to a discussion of the strengths and weaknesses of the Danish approach to counter-strategies against hate speech, othering and racism.

Chapter 6 looks at how the political shifts in the post-1989 period in Central and Eastern Europe and the military conflicts in the Balkans have intensified (ethnic) nationalism in these societies, but have at the same time given rise to populist discourses by the extreme right and consequently to intolerance, hatred, othering and true national values allegedly suppressed by the communist regime. As one of the former Yugoslav republics, Slovenia was no exception: the rise of the right in the Slovenian context meant the rise of a mixture of authoritarianism, traditionalism, religion and nativism. Populist re-traditionalisation of post-socialist Slovenia found its new enemies in various groups of 'others' who were imagined as endangering the future of the nation and its people. Pajnik, Kuhar and Šori suggest that the process of establishing independent statehood brought about two types of populist discourse: ethno-nationalist and ethno-religious populism. The former is linked to attempts to differentiate Slovenian national identity from anything regarded as Balkan, which became a metaphor for backward and primitive, while the latter came about through the onset of re-traditionalisation of Slovenian society, with conservative and religious actors regaining power after years of repression under the previous political system. The chapter analyses the two contexts through two case studies: the right-wing Slovenian Democratic Party and the Catholic Church-based Civil Initiative for the Family and the Rights of Children. The chapter also reflects, first, on the consequences of populist exclusion, and specifically on the effects on the victims or target groups of such anti-politics, and second, on anti-populism, anti-racism and anti-sexism initiatives that counteract populist exclusion and provide space for the practice of alternative politics.

Chapter 7 looks at Bulgarian national populism. During the first decade of its democratic transition, Bulgaria enjoyed a 'shy' nationalism; once democracy was consolidated, radical national populism emerged. Several aspects of the latter are analysed by Anna Krasteva. The first puts the spotlight on Ataka in a case study of this first and most emblematic national populist party in Bulgaria. It is 'left wing, right wing, everything' (Ghodsee). If Ataka occupies such an eclectic position along the classical socio-economic and political cleavages, it is because the party seeks to position itself along a new type of cleavage—it is transitioning from party politics to symbolic politics, from ideological to identity politics, from socio-economic and political to cultural cleavages. The second—party—perspective verifies, in the case of Bulgaria, the perspective of Eastern Europe as backsliding and the 'usual suspect' for every kind of extremist nationalism. The genesis and rise of national populism is studied in regard to the diversification of its actors who are compared in terms of agency, politics and power. The third perspective reconstructs the symbolic cartography and maps the three poles of identitarianism (the politics of fear and overproduction of othering), post-secularism (the religionisation of politics, exemplified by 'Orthodox solidarity', and statism (the politics of sovereignty versus nationalism). Far-right populism is—and often wants to be—a paradoxical phenomenon. The concluding section looks at emerging anti-bodies against this phenomenon.

Chapter 8 examines the case of far-right populism in three political parties in Greece: Golden Dawn, LAOS and ANEL. Since 2007 different forms of far-right populist parties have achieved not only parliamentary representation but also participation in coalition governments. With a realignment of the electorate away from the established political parties, far-right populism has prodcuced a strong impact with its rhetoric of nationalism, extremism, xenophobia and racism. The analysis follows the road that led to the support of such parties with a challenging level of legitimacy, seeking a wider understanding of collective identity and the popularised version of hate crimes in a profoundly entangled country struggling to overcome a period of economic and socio-political crisis.

Chapter 9 examines the role of 'identitarian populism' in 'othering' and hate incidents, with a focus on three 'populist' groups in Britain, the United Kingdom Independence Party (UKIP), the British National Party (BNP) and the English Defence League (EDL). Evidence suggest that the leadership of UKIP, BNP and EDL recognise the importance of a more popularised rhetoric to attracting the attention of the public. UKIP's position on EU migration and homophobic sentiments, and similarly, EDL's Islamophobic tactics, place the 'other' at the centre of their discourse. With the victim representatives arguing that mainstream culture and politics have the greatest impact on for example, hate speech and hate crime in general, the chapter concludes that the violent activities of the EDL, the rhetoric of UKIP and BNP, and the inconsistent media coverage create a breeding ground for the politics of fear.

In applying content analysis and frame analysis tools, the main aim of this book was to identify how right-wing populist groups construct binary groups of 'us' and the 'others' as well as gender binaries, as these strategies succeed in creating societal problems, enemies who cause them and victims who are affected by them, thus constructing an 'us' group represented by right-wing extremist groups in Europe was gathered during a major comparative research project on 'Hate Speech and Populist Othering in Europe through the Racism, Age, Gender Looking Glass', directed by Gabriella Lazaridis and funded by the EU's Justice and Home Affairs (Just/2012/FRAC/AG/2861). The fieldwork was conducted in eight member states of the EU; the data is drawn from interviews with members of the relevant right-wing parties, organisations and groups, and with representatives of NGOs engaged in fighting racism and discrimination, and was gathered through an integrated multi-method approach (content analysis, focus groups, in-depth open-ended interviews, online media analysis, etc.). This method combines the advantages of extensive transnational comparative data analysis and the maximisation of interpretive depth research at the discursive, attitudinal and behavioural levels. The eight studies situating 'populism' within the specific national contexts where it is developing and growing represent a rich resource. The detailed exploration of the entire available literature, which of course includes many field studies, enables us to evaluate how the different aspects and manifestations of far-right populism come together in these countries in a complex combination of national social situations, the state of the political 'offering', realignments in politics, and the international circulation of references and models.

Systematic analyses of populist parties and movements that are not only challenging the EU project and EU policies but also fighting to be represented at EU level, are still lacking in the European and international contexts. As this book shows, European populism finds a source of inspiration in opposition to the EU's aims—by confronting directly the EU construction, and sometimes exploiting political and economic advantages (such as the economic crisis and participation in the European Parliament).

Further research is needed to look in particular at how the construction of an essentialised, homogeneous people affects *the idea of Europe*. The various interpretations of the collective identities and boundaries produced by populist movements in relation to the nation presented in this book are an important starting point, but they only touch upon the European dimension (which means a rejection of the EU and a different idea of Europe). The rejection of the supra-national EU concept of governance is justified by the evocation of collective identifications of the *homeland* representing 'a more potent and durable influence than any other collective cultural identities which is likely to continue to command humanity's allegiance for a long time to come, even when other larger-scale but looser forms of collective identity emerge alongside national one' (Smith 1991: 175–176). It is clear from the material presented in this book that national populism challenges affiliation to a post-nationalist project such as the EU, and the EU project of 'unity in diversity'.

Populist parties and forces need to be analysed in the crucial area of *divergent opposition to the EU project*: how the EU model as a voluntary union of nations, deciding on common policies and based on representative democracy, is being attacked because of its alleged inefficiency and its distance from 'authentic' European traditions and the *European people*. The idea of a 'stable' national identity implies not merely the refusal of the idea of a common Europe, but the construction of a Europe of Homelands. The idea of Europe is of course linked to a common European identity and to a common memory. The questions that arise are: what are the positions of populists in relation to a common European historical memory, when viewed against the background of totalitarianism and authoritarianism? How does this affect attitudes to the Russian Federation, which is also affected by the growing phenomenon of populism? How do populist parties and movements oppose the actions that aim to make the EU a multilayered, multicultural democracy that is based on mutual respect for its diverse peoples and cultures, values diversity and inclusion, and runs decidedly counter to hierarchies, inequalities and exclusion? How do they erect obstacles on the road to establishing European citizenship through the overcoming of racism and sexism? How are these forces and parties, while vociferously opposing the European project and the EU, becoming increasingly involved in various types of transnational and international relations, i.e., bilateral contacts and representation in the European Parliament?

References

Anderson, B. (1991). *Imagined communities. Reflections on the origin and spread of nationalism*. London: Verso.

Blokker, P. (2005). Populist nationalism, anti-Europeanism, post-nationalism, and the East-West distinction. *German Law Journal, 6*(2), 371–389.

Bongiovanni, B. (1996). Retrieved from http://www.treccani.it/enciclopedia/populismo_(Enciclopedia-delle-Scienze-Sociali)/

Bourdieu, P. (1972). *Esquisse d'une théorie de la pratique*. Genève, Switzerland: Librairie Droz.

Canovan, M. (1982). Two strategies for the study of populism. *Political Studies, 30*(4), 544–552.

Canovan, M. (1999). Trust the people! Populism and the two faces of democracy. *Political Studies, 47*(1), 2–16.

Canovan, M. (2002). Taking politics to the people: Populism as the ideology of democracy. In Y. Mény & Y. Surel (Eds.), *Democracies and the populist challenge* (pp. 25–44). Gordonsville, VA: Palgrave Macmillan.

Canovan, M. (2004). Populism for political theorists? *Journal of Political Ideologies, 9*(3), 241–252.

Chiantera-Stutte, P., & Petö, A. (2003). Cultures of populism and the political right in Central Europe. *CLCWeb: Comparative Literature and Culture, 5*(4), 2–10.

Crick, B. (2002). *Democracy: A very short introduction.* Oxford, England: Oxford University Press.

Deze, A. (2004). Lectures critiques. *Revue française de science politique, 54*(1), 179–199.

Diamanti, I. (2010). Italianieuropei, Giovedì 14 Ottobre 4, online version. Retrieved from http://www.italianieuropei.it/it/la-rivista/ultimo-numero/itemlist/user/984-ilvodiamanti.html

Einhorn, B. (2009). *European citizenship or narrow nationalisms? The challenge of gender* (ISET Working Paper 10). Unpublished working paper, London Metropolitan University.

Gellner, J. (1983). *Nations and nationalism.* Oxford, England: Blackwell.

Germani, G. (1975). Authoritarianism, fascism, and national populism. *American Journal of Sociology, 119*(2), 590–596.

Golden, D. (2003). A national cautionary tale: Russian women newcomers to Israel portrayed. *Nations and Nationalisms, 9*(1), 83–104.

Helander, V. (1971). Populismi ja populistiset liikkeet. In V. Helander (Ed.), *Vennamolaisuus populistisena joukkoliikkeenä* (pp. 12–21). Finland, Helsinki: Hämeenlinna.

Hirschman, A. (1970). *Exit, voice, and loyalty: Responses to decline in firms, organizations, and states.* Cambridge, MA: Harvard University Press.

Laclau, E. (2005). *On populist reason.* London: Verso.

Liakos, A. (1989). Peri laikismou [On populism]. *Historica, 10,* 13–28.

Mouselis, N, Lopowatz, T., & Spourdalakis, M. (1989). *Laikismos kai Politiki* [Populism and politics]. Athens, Greek: Gnosi (in Greek).

Mudde, C. (2007). Популисткият Zeitgeist в днешна Европа [The populist Zeitgeist in today's Europe]. *Critique and Humanism Journal, 23,* 115–119.

Mudde, C., & Rovira Kalwasser, C. (2013). Exclusionary vs. inclusionary populism: Comparing contemporary Europe and Latin America title. *Government and Opposition, 48*(2), 147–174.

Pappas, T. S. (2013). Populist democracies: Post-authoritarian Greece and populist Hungary. *Government and Opposition, 49*(1), 1–23.

Pelinka, A, (2013) 'Eight-wing populism: concept and typology' in Wodak, R. , KhosraviNic, M. and Mral, B. (eds) Right-wing populism in Europe, London: Bloomsbury.

Pels, D. (2012). The new national individualism—Populism is here to stay. In E. Meijrs (Ed.), *Populism in Europe* (pp. 25–46). Linz, Austria: Planet.

Priester, K. (2012). *Rechter und linker Populismus. Annäherung an ein Chamäleon.* Frankfurt, Germany: Campus.

Reisigl, M. (2002). "Dem Volk aufs Maul schauen, nach dem Mund reden und Angst und Bange machen". Von populistischen Anrufungen, Anbiederungen und Agitiationsweisen in der Sprache österreichischer PolitikerInnen. In W. Eismann (Ed.), *Rechtspopulismus* (pp. 149–198). Wien, Austria: Czernin.

Smilov, D., & Krastev, I. (2008). The rise of populism in Eastern Europe: Policy paper. In G. Mesežnikov, O. Gyárfášová, & D. Smilov (Eds.), *Populist politics and liberal democracy in Central and Eastern Europe* (pp. 7–13). Bratislava, Slovakia: Institute for Public Affairs.

Smith, A. D. (1991). *National identity.* London: Penguin.

Sternhell, Z. (2012). *Ni droite ni gauche, l'idéologie fasciste en France [Neither right nor left: Fascist ideology in France]* (Folio histoire no. 203). Paris: Gallimard Collection.

Taggart, P. A. (2000). *Populism 1.* Buckingham, England: Open University Press.

Taguieff, P.-A. (1984). La rhétorique du national-populisme. *Mots, 9,* 113–139.

Taguieff, P.-A. (1997). Le populisme et la science politique : du mirage conceptuel aux vrais problèmes. *Vingtième siècle, 56,* 4–33.

Winock, M. (1990). *Nationalisme, antisémitisme et fascisme en France.* Paris: Editions du Seuil.

Wittgenstein, L. (1953). *Philosophical investigations.* Oxford, England: Blackwell.

Wodak, R. (2015) The Politics of Fear: What right-wing populist discourses mean, London: Sage

Zaslove, A. (2008). Here to stay? Populism as a new party type. *European Review, 16*(3), 319–336.

2

Neo-fascism from the Twentieth Century to the Third Millennium: The Case of Italy

Giovanna Campani

Introduction

Italian political history over the last 100 years offers a unique opportunity to analyse the relationships between fascism and populism. Fascism—an ideology and a totalitarian way of organising society—is an Italian invention. It emerged as an unexpected political change following the crisis of the parliamentary system shaken by class conflicts during the troubled years after World War I. Created in Italy, fascism was copied and re-adapted to national contexts in other European countries—from Nazi Germany to Franco's Spain.[1]

---

[1] In Portugal, Salazar's Estado Novo was a corporate state that had some similarities to Italian fascism, but also exhibited considerable differences from Mussolini's fascism. Salazarism was strongly inspired by Catholicism. The papal encyclical *Rerum Novarum* (from its first two words, Latin for 'of revolutionary change' [n 1]), or *Rights and Duties of Capital and Labor*, was issued by Pope Leo XIII on 15 May 1891 (Wiarda 1977). Moreover, Salazarist nationalism was not grounded in race or biology.

G. Campani
Department of Education and Psychology, University of Florence,
Florence, Italy

© The Editor(s) (if applicable) and The Author(s) 2016
G. Lazaridis et al. (eds.), *The Rise of the Far Right in Europe*,
DOI 10.1057/978-1-137-55679-0_2

25

The Italian fascist regime lasted for 20 years. In 1943, the military defeat of Italy, allied with Nazi Germany in World War II, provoked its fall. A popular reaction—the Resistance—battled at the same time against the brutal German occupation and the criminal Nazi collaborationist regime of the Salo[2] Republic led by Benito Mussolini. The Resistance represents the re-foundation of the Italian nation.

In spite of the disastrous outcomes of fascism—the huge sufferings provoked by the war, the military defeat, the participation in Germany's crimes against humanity during the persecution of the Jews, the perpetration of war crimes in Slovenia and Croatia[3]—a minority of Italians—both for personal and political reasons—remained faithful to the fascist ideology. As for the majority, elements of fascism remained in their worldview, everyday practices and mentality.

The political and cultural legacy of fascism was not erased by a limited de-fascistisation (Dondi 1999). A profound mistrust of liberal democracy and the party system survived in the mentality that was shaped during fascism. It is no coincidence that the DNA of the two dominant parties after the war—the Christian Democrats[4] and the Communists—contained no liberal democracy and they endorsed it only during the 1960s and 1970s, with various caveats.[5]

The rejection of liberal democracy and of the party system led to the success of a curious post-war movement—l'Uomo Qualunque (The Ordinary Man), gathered around a satirical magazine founded by Guglielmo Giannini in 1944, when the Allied forces were still in charge of the country and the political parties in the process of reorganising. Attacking the elite, opposing the professionalism of politicians and

---

[2] Small town by Lake Garda in Lombardy, capital of a fascist republic supported by the Germans.
[3] See the BBC documentary *Fascist Legacy*.
[4] The Christian Democrats had no liberal-democratic roots. After the unification of Italy (1861) the Vatican rejected an Italian nation state and prohibited Catholics from playing any part in it (including voting). It was only after World War that the Pope supported a party uniting peasants and the lower middle class, the Partito Popolare, founded by a priest, Don Sturzo. The Partito Popolare functioned within a system whose legitimacy the Church continued to reject. For the Popolari, the term 'democrat' went beyond signalling the acceptance of representative democracy,— meaning working for ordinary people.
[5] The Communist Party became a major force in Italy after World War II; until the 1990s it was the biggest Western European Communist party.

resisting taxes, Uomo Qualunque aimed to represent the ordinary man against negatively depicted politicians. Defined as a 'populist'[6] movement, it differed considerably from fascism: for example, it supported a 'small' state, exactly the opposite of the totalitarian idea of the fascist state. Moreover, the satirical magazine called Mussolini 'the clown of Predappio'.[7] When Uomo Qualunque was dissolved in 1948, many of its voters probably turned to the new neo-fascist party the MSI (Movimento Sociale Italiano, Italian Social Movement), founded in late 1946 despite the fact that the Italian Constitution prohibited the re-establishment of the Fascist party (Transitory and Final provision XII)[8]—which had nothing to do with ideological similarities, but was a consequence of mistrust of the parliamentary regime.

While the Uomo Qualunque had a short life, the MSI—although it represented a minority of Italians (in the first national elections it achieved 2 per cent of the vote and its highest tally over the years was 8.6 per cent, with an average of 5–6 per cent) and had no hope of becoming an hegemonic political force—cast a long shadow over the political landscape.

The MSI maintained elements of the fascist tradition (fidelity to Mussolini, the idea of a strong and authoritarian state, a sense of hierarchy) while constantly re-adapting its traditional messages (including anti-Semitism, anti-capitalism and anti-Americanism) to the changing context. This binary process—preservation and adaptation—was marked by frequent divisions between the two 'souls' of the MSI, two dimensions defined by the historian Renzo De Felice (1996, 1997, 2002) as 'fascism as a movement' and 'fascism as a regime'. Tension between the search for respectability in the parliamentary system and violent revolutionary action characterised the MSI and produced a scattered neo-fascist archipelago far beyond the party's structure.

---

[6] The Fronte dell' Uomo Qualunque stood in the 1946 election for the Constituent Assembly and won seats for 30 deputies. In 1948, when the Cold War polarised the elections, it only had 19 deputies, who transferred to the Liberal Party during the parliamentary term.

[7] The town where Mussolini was born.

[8] The June 1946 amnesties for crimes committed during the period of the Civil War (1943–1945) probably encouraged the foundation of the MSI. http://www.tuttostoria.net/storia-contemporanea.aspx?code=680.

Caught in a 'third position' between Anglo-American capitalism and communism, neo-fascism—of both respectable and revolutionary kinds—finally chose to target communism as its main enemy, but lost part of its *raison d'être* after the fall of the Berlin Wall in a rapidly changing world that no longer corresponded to the old political categories.

New right-wing movements and parties such as the Northern League—offering responses to globalisation, post-industrial economic conditions, immigration and European Union constraints, with the consequent loss of sovereignty—challenged the old nationalistic fascist ideology with new narratives focusing on identity politics, emphasising strong polarisations (elite/people, immigrants/natives) and defining new far more motivating priorities—taxes, political corruption and immigration.

Confronted by new political competitors, neo-fascists were forced to redefine their place in the political landscape. While 'respectable' neo-fascism decided to definitively abandon the fascist legacy and to ally with the mainstream 'liberal' right-wing party of Silvio Berlusconi, the 'revolutionary' component tried to re-adapt the fascist identity to the new millennium, redefining targets, re-thinking political communication and incorporating youth cultures.

This new phase of neo-fascism shares political themes and mass movements against globalisation, immigration, multiculturalism and the EU with parties that, like the Northern League, are generically defined as 'populist'. Convergences should not, however, hide multiple differences between neo-fascism, the so-called 'populisms' and a far-right extremism that is not embedded in the fascist tradition—occurring relatively rarely in Italy, but frequently in the rest of Europe.[9]

During the 1970s, Gino Germani, an anti-fascist exiled in Argentina, compared European fascism and Latin American populism. Having experienced fascism and the rise of Peronism, Germani became aware of the contradictions that existed in contexts where a liberal economy and formal democracy are perceived as expressions of an oligarchy ultimately allied with foreign imperialist powers that has failed to provide

---

[9] In Italy, for example, Militia Christi—an extreme-right Catholic fundamentalist party without references to fascist legacies. Many countries have parties (such as UKIP in the UK) whose far-right extremism is not connected with fascism in any way.

a model for modernisation, social justice and effective participation. In *Authoritarianism, Fascism, and National Populism*, published in 1975, Germani describes the general theory of authoritarianism in modern society and applies it to authoritarian movements and regimes likely to emerge from the social mobility of the middle and lower classes together with the aim of promoting modernisation. Germani takes into account political, economic and class dimensions. Nowadays, the Italian academic literature on neo-fascism, right-wing extremism and populism— developed by scholars such as Pietro Ignazi (2000), Marco Tarchi (2003) and Ilvio Diamanti (2010)—offers interesting analytical tools that break with the generic notion of populism and take account of the socio-economic and socio-political structures as the social blocs behind one or other of the political movements and parties labelled 'populist'.

This chapter looks at the political dynamics surrounding the evolution of neo-fascism and neo-fascist groups and parties in post-war Italy up to the present day and then focuses on Casa Pound and Forza Nuova, their symbols, values, beliefs and 'othering'. As this chapter shows, migration is far from the central issue of their political message; instead, their main opponent now is 'the "system"—corrupt politics, financial capitalism, the European Union which is an instrument of financial capitalism and has deprived Italy of sovereignty. The last section looks at the victims of neo-fascist organisations and resistance to them established by organisations like ANPI.

Neo-Fascism in Post-War Italy: Legacy of the Past; Adapting to Changing Post-War Contexts

The founders of MSI—most of them active in the fascist party and the Salo Republic—aimed to reunite the different 'souls' of the 'fascism movement' and the 'fascist regime' (De Felice 1996, 1997, 2002): (1) the intransigent, revolutionary, socialistic, anti-capitalist, anti-American, anti-Semitic 'soul', representing the initial period (1919–1928) and the end of fascism (1943–1945); and (2) the right-minded, traditionalist 'soul' favouring order and authority representing the period of the fascist government (1928–1943). The two 'souls' joined forces to revive Mussolini's fascism, to indicate a third way, between Anglo-American capitalism and communism, to overcome the corrupt and inept democracy, and re-establish the authoritarian state.

They accepted the parliamentary system in order to push the country's political axis towards the right. In the name of the anti-communist fight, they accepted—tactically—pro-Atlanticism (the NATO choice), despite rejecting consumerist values and the American way of life[10] (Germinario 2002).

The compromises between the 'souls' seem to have been difficult over the years. In 1956, the moderate line chosen by the majority of the MSI pushed some opponents out of the party. They founded the Centro Studi Ordine Nuovo (New Order), which became a point of reference for neo-fascist extremism. Ordine Nuovo enhanced the anti-parliamentarian tone, launched a process of redefinition of the fascist doctrine and supported a campaign of assaults and provocation against individual opponents and organisations. Violent militancy became an important dimension of neo-fascism, ideologically justified by Mussolini's postulate on the primacy of direct action.

In 1960, a new division inside Ordine Nuovo led to the foundation of Avanguardia Nazionale (National Vanguard), whose symbol was the Odal, a letter of the ancient Runic alphabet, positioned at the centre of a white circle surrounded by red, exactly like the flag of the Third Reich. From the 1960s onwards, influences coming directly from the neo-Nazi world, like the Odal or the Celtic cross, the symbol of an SS division, started to fascinate the youngest component of Italian neo-fascism. Introducing these symbols signified a detachment from Italian fascism and a new interest in Nazism and Eastern European fascism. The Romanian Codreanu and the Belgian Degrelle became reference points, together with Julius Evola, whose vision of the 'tradition' as a timeless entity running through the history of ancient times led to the discovery of the Nordic sagas (and also indirectly to Tolkien's *Lord of the Rings*).[11] The training

[10] The MSI remained always faithful to the idea of fascism as a 'third way' between communism and Anglo-Saxon capitalism, showing strong elements of anti-Americanism.
[11] Traditionally, fascist narratives were inspired by Roman mythology; the discovery of the Nordic saga is part of the Europeanization of Italian neo-fascism.

camps organised for neo-fascist militants were called 'Hobbit Camps' (Fasanella and Grippo 2009).

Avanguardia Nazionale established links with European neo-fascism in the form of the French institute (Groupement de Recherche et d'Études pour la Civilisation) (the New Right), joining a project that bypassed individual nationalisms in favour of a 'European nationalism' able to release the old continent from the logic of the Cold War between the United States and the USSR and to pursue a re-foundation of fascist Europe, recovering the design of the New European Order developed by the Nazis.[12] The opening towards Europe was seen positively by militants who felt marginalised by the left-oriented Italian mainstream culture, as a Tuscan neo-fascist militant recalls:

> The symbolism that refers to *The Lord of the Rings* and *The Hobbit* comes from the culture of the 1970s ... the new right ... at that time the right was ghettoized, attacked; it was an attempt to find in fantasy world the answers that reality did not give, to build a parallel universe like Tolkien's Middle Earth. Of course there are also the deep meanings in *The Lord of the Rings* ... respect for nature, the ethical warrior. (Interview with a militant from Casaggi[13])

While looking towards Europe, Italian neo-fascism continued to demonstrate specific characteristics: the legacy of the 20-year-long fascist regime meant that neo-fascism had a more significant presence than in other European countries—in spite of relatively low electoral success and the perceived marginalisation spoken of by the militant interviewed. Excluded from official political power (the so-called Constitutional Arch), because of the anti-fascist foundations of the Republic, the MSI developed local sports associations, youth organisations, a trade union (the CISNAL), associations of fascist veterans, and magazines and the party's daily newspaper, *Il Secolo d'Italia (The century of Italy)* (Ignazi 1994).

---

[12] In 1963 former Belgian SS member Jean Thiriart founded Jeune Europe, inaugurating neo-fascism in solidarity with Arab nationalism against US imperialism and Zionism. In Italy, a group close to Ordine Nuovo, the Young Nation, was associated with Jeune Europe (Tarchi 2010).

[13] Florentine right-wing cultural and youth centre close to Fratelli d'Italia (see page 36).

After the loss of the representation monopoly by the MSI, various neo-fascist organisations could mobilise different population groups. The older militants of the MSI, nostalgic for the benefits that the strong fascist state brought to the lower-middle class, were in favour of the 'law and order' model represented by the MSI; younger people, keen on the rebellion that exploded in the 1968 movements, found their way in extra-parliamentary militancy.

In the troubled 1960s and 1970s, neo-fascism—mainly its extra-parliamentary component—was part of a process defined as the 'strategy of tension'—a plan elaborated by a few heads of the army and intelligence services, who did not reject terrorist actions in order to avoid the country turning to communism. The strategy of tension developed in different forms: attempts to induce the public to identify the struggles of students and workers as a danger to 'public order'; blaming bombings on left-wing organisations as protagonists of those struggles; hypothesis of a coup (*golpe*)—in the authoritarian sense, inspired by the model of the Greek colonels or of the Latin American examples, such as Chile.

A few neo-fascists leaders associated with the strategy of tension tried to develop their own strategy in order to gain power through subversion. Some of the subversive strategies, everyday violence in streets, schools, universities, factories, against left-oriented political and cultural centres, against left militants, reminded the practices of the squads of the 1920s in continuity with the legacy of 'revolutionary fascism': '... the violence finds its place as a dynamic that responds to the logic of the political action that funds the neo-fascist paradigm' (Bartolini 2010). Violence may, incidentally, be a criterion determining whether a neo-fascist group belongs to the extreme right or not, in opposition to the democratic system.

Orphans of the Cold War: From MSI to Fiamma Tricolore and Forza Nuova

On 2 August 1980, tension reached its highest point in the massacre at Bologna railway station, where a bomb killed 85 people. Responsibility for this act of terrorism was attributed to neo-fascist militants, members of the Nuclei Armati Rivoluzionari, (NAR, Revolutionary Armed

Nuclei).[14] The subsequent dismantling by the police of the largest extra-parliamentary neo-fascist organisations meant a period of exile or low profile for many militants.

In the meantime, the global context was radically changing: the fall of the Berlin Wall in 1989 marked the end of the Cold War; neoliberalism was the new triumphant model; while the nation state was weakening, the European Union was becoming a crucial political and institutional actor. In 1991, the Italian Communist Party changed its name and strategy. The same year, a new party, the Lega Nord (Northern League), created from scratch, introduced identity politics to the Italian political debate, invented the land of Padania and the Padan People, reproduced supposed Celtic rituals and invited the masses to Pontida to celebrate Alberto da Giussano, hero of a 1000-year-old battle (Diamanti 1993, 1996).

The confrontation between communists and fascists lost direction. 'The century of ideologies is ending' declared the MSI secretary, Gianfranco Fini, at the Party's congress at Fiuggi in 1995, encouraging the delegates to abandon the fascist legacy. 'It [the century] buries the totalitarian temptations that have marked it, with its contradictions and its fierce clashes (…) The Third Millennium masses will be protagonists of history, citizens aware of their role … no one will question the notion of freedom as a supreme value …'

Fini asked the MSI militants to fully accept liberal democracy, to renounce to the old project of remaining faithful to the fascist legacy and to become a modern European democratic right. The new context favoured ending the political marginalisation of MSI. Christian Democrats and Socialists collapsed in 1993–1994 under the weight of corruption. A brand new party, Forza Italia (Force for Italy), emerged and its leader, Silvio Berlusconi, was prepared to legitimise the MSI as a political partner in order to have a sufficient electoral majority.

The transformation of the MSI into a democratic European conservative party, Alleanza Nazionale (National Alliance), allied with Berlusconi's openly liberal party, could not be approved by many MSI activists, such as Pino Rauti, who considered Gianfranco Fini a traitor. Breaking with him, they founded the Fiamma Tricolore (Tricolored Flame). While proudly defending the fascist legacy, Pino Rauti positioned the Fiamma Tricolore

---

[14] The NAR were active from 1977 to 1981.

in a strong social and popular space, supporting the lower-middle and the working classes against globalisation and neoliberalism. The choice of social fascism answered the demands of MSI voters, mainly from the lower-middle and working classes.

The Fiamma Tricolore quickly lost the monopoly of neo-fascist representation. In 1997, Roberto Fiore, a former member of the NAR, having escaped to London to avoid jail after the Bologna massacre,[15] came back to Italy, and together with Massimo Morsello,[16] former activist of Avanguardia Nazionale, founded the party of Forza Nuova (FN, New Force). The new party aimed to compete with the Fiamma Tricolore for hegemony on the far right. The competition was mainly not about the elections (extreme neo-fascism gets less than 3 per cent at national level), but about direct activism (organising street protests, demonstrations and marches, and political campaigns) that continued the neo-fascist movements of the 1970s.

To expand the party base, Roberto Fiore, applying tactics learned in Britain, developed the strategy of recruiting among radical soccer clubs. FN quickly took over right-wing clubs like Lazio FC, but also traditionally left-wing clubs such as Roma AC. Today, FN controls most Italian teams' fan clubs. Its leaders, who belong to an older generation, have successfully attracted young people by establishing special relationships with the skinhead movement, which originally represented a music style and British working-class urban culture and had nothing to do with fascism. According to the few studies on the topic (Cadalanu 1994; Sabatini 2010), the years 1982–1983 marked the Italian explosion of Oi!, a sub-genre of punk music[17] representing the anarchist or apolitical skinheads. While in most cities, like Bologna, Genoa and Pisa, the skinhead movement was in line with the original assumptions of Oi!, in Milan and in the Veneto region, it was monopolised by neo-fascism through

---

[15] Roberto Fiore was involved in terrorist activities in the 1980s and sentenced to five years' imprisonment for organising terrorist groups (*banda armata*). He escaped to London but returned to Italy after being granted amnesty for his crimes. It seems that, during his stay in the UK, Fiore was in touch with the National Front and created Terza Posizione Internazionale (International Third Position).

[16] For the biography of Massimo Morsello, see Telese (2006).

[17] Oi! developed originally in London and derived from the early skinhead movement. It tends to have more melody than other forms of punk and more choruses, in which the word oi! is repeated.

the activism of the militants of the Movimento Politico Occidentale (Western Political Movement), founded in 1984 by Maurizio Boccacci in an attempt to reconstruct neo-fascism after the dismantling of the largest extra-parliamentary organisations following the Bologna massacre. The skinheads' incorporation into neo-fascism was reinforced in the years between 1985 and 1990 when football became one of their central interests and they joined fan clubs controlled by FN, which sought to 'domesticate' them while cultivating their radical (and violent) action on specific occasions (such as Gay Pride events). The relationships with fan clubs and skinheads, who are, at the same time, kept at a certain distance to be used at crucial moments, reveals FN's 'double dealing'— 'respectable' political party and 'revolutionary' violent movement—and continues the neo-fascist tradition in Italy.

The Scattered Archipelago of Italian Neo-Fascism in the New Millennium

In the global world of triumphant neoliberalism, the distinction between moderate and revolutionary components remains the principal characteristic of a neo-fascist archipelago in search of a new narrative. This division is crossed by other multiple divisions that concern both the Finians— the group that gave birth to the 'post-fascist' democratic party, Alleanza Nazionale, and was ready to abandon most of the fascist legacy—and those faithful to the fascist legacy, initially reunited in the Fiamma Tricolore.

Gianfranco Fini's experiment—building a conservative party out of neo-fascism—quickly failed. Fiamma Tricolore was just the first of several divisions: in 2004, it was the turn of Alessandra Mussolini, Benito Mussolini's grand-daughter, to leave Alleanza Nazionale and create a new group, Alternativa Sociale (Social Alternative). In 2007, the Lazio Region's President, Francesco Storace, left Alleanza Nazionale to form La Destra (The Right). These small neo-fascist parties—the moderate and parliamentarian part of neo-fascism—were short-lived, and in order to survive, were sooner or later forced to make alliances with Silvio Berlusconi in local or national elections.

Weakened by the scissions, in 2008 Alleanza Nazionale joined with Berlusconi's party, the PDL (Popolo della Libertà, Freedom's People).[18] In 2012, a group of former members of Alleanza Nazionale, who had entered the PDL, created a new neo-fascist party, Fratelli d'Italia (Italy's Brothers), which is today active present in Italian politics with 3–4 per cent of the vote. Its political message is close to that of the French National Front: an end to massive immigration; a return to national sovereignty, reduction of EU power; rejection of the austerity measures imposed by the EU.

In spite of its different sensibilities, the neo-fascist element that went through the experience of Alleanza Nazionale and has been active—with various responsibilities—in Italian politics during the Berlusconi governments, has completely absorbed the idea of liberal democracy and the parliamentary system. On the other hand, acceptance of the rules of liberal democracy does not accord with the deep convictions of many militants in the 'revolutionary' component, for whom the temptation to reject 'the system' as a whole is always there. As a FN militant from Venice explains,

for us democracy can be a value, but only if it is true … If it is a simulacrum … then I can only say no … what they are offering is demagoguery, circumlocution for the gullible, oligarchy … We are in a state that is definitely not democratic, in a Europe that is not democratic, that does not listen to her citizens … There are other ways of doing democracy, which is a more direct democracy, where the citizens must be informed. So democracy, but not this one.

For him, as for many others, the electoral rituals of liberal democracy are less important than direct activism (organising street protests, marches and demonstrations, and political campaigns). As a Tuscan FN militant observes, "Being a social force, we will never accept going with a strong liberal party like the PDL".[19]

In spite of their common rejection of 'the system'—globalisation, the neoliberal model, EU consensus—their differing views on priorities and strategies produce divisions within the revolutionary element of

---

[18] Gianfranco Fini had a disagreement with Silvio Berlusconi and was completely marginalized from Italian politics.

[19] Berlusconi's party.

neo-fascism. As we have seen, FN was founded to contest the hegemony of the Fiamma Tricolore, whose unity lasted a few years: in 2008, Gianluca Iannone, a former singer and football fan, and Maurizio Boccacci, former leader of Movimento Politico Occidentale at the junction between neo-fascism and skinheads, left. Boccacci founded a neo-Nazi anti-Semitic organisation, Militia (the name comes from the book by Degrelle, a main point of reference for European right-wing extremism), a marginal group which had many problems with the law. Gianluca Iannone created the national structure of Casa Pound, a youth cultural centre opened in 2003 by militants in an occupied building in the Esquilino area of Rome (Di Tullio 2010; Di Nunzio and Toscano 2011).

Militia demonstrates that anti-Semitism is still extremely strong in the neo-fascist Italian area, at least on the most extreme fringes: 'The Judeo-Masonic conspiracy is no longer a maybe; it's a matter of fact: I invite you all to look at all the economic leaders of Wall Street, name by name, from Madoff to the Italian De Benedetti. They are all people of Jewish faith, and it was them who created the international crisis we are experiencing today!' (interview with a Militia militant, Rome). With its strong focus on anti-Semitism and Holocaust denial Militia is close to neo-Nazi ideology. Fiercely anti-Zionist, they are openly pro-Palestinian.

Casa Pound (CP, after the American poet Ezra Pound)—the Fascists of the Third Millennium, as they call themselves—represents the most original expression of neo-fascism, having a very strong social dimension (they fight for the right to public housing for all) and at the same time a very innovative political language close to youth cultures.[20] Casa Pound activists produce alternative music, (the *Zetazeroalfa*), they have a streaming radio station, Radio Bandiera Nera "Black Flag"—a reference both to fascism and to pirates—(their slogan is 'free beautiful rebels'), a film club, magazines and a newsletter. They run various fashionable websites frequented by young people, and use Myspace and Facebook. They have launched new types of activity called 'futurist or squads media', such as the attack on the home of the popular TV show

---

[20] The symbols that are referenced by Casa Pound are innovative connections with the imagery of piracy, using icons of cartoon characters familiar to young people who grew up from the 1970s onwards (Di Nunzio and Toscano 2011).

The Loft (symbol of the alienation mainstream media imposes on youth). They have around 5,000 official members (interview with CP militant, Florence), with many more sympathisers.

Casa Pound and Forza Nuova: Different Symbols and Values

Both CP and FN reject 'fascism nostalgia', intend to adapt fascism to the new millenium and aim to approach youth cultures; the differences between them are, however, important.

> The term fascists of the Third Millennium means to assume a heritage of values, ideas, roots, traditions and bring it into the third millennium, updating it; this is the reason why Casa Pound was born; because we believe that the core fascist values—the state, social welfare, identity—are the best to oppose globalisation, capitalism and modern society as it is being established and built. (Interview with CP militant, Florence)

Rejecting the label 'nostalgic for fascism', FN militants explain that today there is no decent social policy as there was during the fascist years:

> For many of our opponents, we are seen as nostalgic for fascism, frankly we do not long for somebody speaking from the balcony of a square [Mussolini] ... what we miss is the most advanced social state fascism had implemented, do not forget that in fascist times, social laws, social measures were at the forefront. (Interview with FN militant, Florence)

FN's web page, publications and electoral leaflets show few clear symbols of Italian fascism—no images of Mussolini, no 'fasces'. The Celtic cross—in red and black—predominates.Casa Pound has completely different symbols and criticises the use of the Celtic cross:

> in our symbolism, in the slogans, it seems clear even to a superficial observer that we don't want to follow antiquated traditions ... we use the tortoise rather than the flames, the Celtic cross and so on ... the previous generation

took them to the streets, kept them in the heart ... but in our opinion they are no longer suitable for the Third Millennium or for the political or social reality of the country today. (Interview with CP militant, Florence)

The symbol of the *tortoise* is explained thus:

The first battle of Casa Pound is that of the house ... the tortoise is the animal that carries its home on its back, therefore what better symbol for the battle for the house than the tortoise? In addition, the tortoise is an animal that lives long, this gives the idea of something lasting over the years ... solid ... The four arrows pointing towards a single centre represent the centrality that Casa Pound wants to represent, the centre of the national revival, the national revolution. (Interview with CP militant, Florence)

As a matter of fact, many Italian political forces and Prime Minister Renzi evoke the need for a national revival in the face of the crisis and decay that characterises Italy today. One step in this direction is to change the Italian political class, whose are widely rejected, and political practices. Still, while other forces—such as the Five Stars movement of Beppe Grillo or the leftist element of the mainstream Democratic Party see the solution as introducing greater democracy, participation and control over politics by citizens, Casa Pound and FN support the idea of politics based on 'spiritual values' and of militancy as moral commitment. Some militants quote past models such as ancient Sparta. The two organisations have, however, a quite different idea of the spiritual values that should sustain politics. Inspired by Julius Evola's philosophy (1963), the FN ideology venerates a tradition that represents the overlap between spiritual values and roots, both transmitted from one generation to the other, inside a specific community considered as an organic body:

The values, the eternal community values are important, tradition is important ... certainly it must be renewed, but the cornerstones of tradition can give us answers, those who stray too far from the tree of tradition and its roots are lost, break down, remain confused. (Interview with FN militant, Venice)

FN identifies spiritual values with the Roman Catholic tradition, transforming the Celtic cross into a Christian symbol: "The Celtic cross represents Catholicism, the European tradition" (interview with FN militant, Milan). According to an FN militant from Rome, the Celtic cross has a double meaning:

> it represents the intersection of spiritual values and the material world, the first dominating the second. The Celtic cross is the intersection of a vertical view of the world acting on horizontality which is daily life, material life … it means the spiritual principle that intersects with life; the 'circularity' represents other aspects. Moreover, it is a symbol that also refers to the Christian cross.

The combination of fundamentalist Catholicism and the neo-fascist tradition is peculiar to FN and is expressed by other Christian symbols: 'Archangel Michael is FN's protector. FN was founded on 29 September, the day of St. Michael Archangel. He is the prince of the heavenly army, who led the revolt against the army of Satan, and the symbol of the good that, armed, defeats evil …' (interview with FN militant, Milan). Casa Pound also wants to introduce spiritual values into politics, but it does not think that these spiritual values should be religious. On the contrary, they should be secular—in continuity with the Hegelian fascist idea of the state. Casa Pound is very critical of what they consider 'nonsense'—a political proposal that would support a sort of Pope King (the reference to FN is clear even if not explicit):

> Casa Pound defends the idea of the state of historical fascism. State is a value, the ultimate goal of all, of the people who join in the state. No other institution should impose its dogmas, as does the church, because even those who are not, unfortunately, or fortunately, believers, have to collide economically, socially, culturally with the dictates of the Catholic Church, which I think absolutely unfair. (Interview with CP militant, Florence)

Casa Pound is in favour of a secular and non-confessional state where no religion should have an advantage over others, but it does not oppose the building of mosques. The militants interviewed insist that Casa Pound is not Islamophobic; they have Syrian militants; they have

Syrian flags in demonstrations and they recall that Mussolini received the sword of Islam.

This difference in attitude to religion between FN and Casa Pound affects family policies and gender relations. FN is obsessive in its opposition to abortion and gay marriage, tolerated by Casa Pound. The old slogan of the French Vichy government—*Dieu, Patrie, Famille* (God, Fatherland, Family)—has been revitalized by FN who are building their value system around it: 'A link between earth, family, social group, forming a nation, an organic construction of the social fabric, for us is always present: God, fatherland and family' (interview with FN militant, Rome).

The same slogan—God, Fatherland, Family—is accepted by Casa Pound, but it has a completely different meaning: 'We can use it, but without Catholic implications. God is the spiritual dimension; family is the large family of brothers, which is your people, your country ...' (Interview with CP militant, Florence).

From Tradition to the Organic Nation: Opposition to Multiculturalism and Globalisation

For FN, 'tradition' is connected to an 'organic' idea of the nation, in the continuum from earth through family to society: 'Nation is identity and belonging, opposed to "bourgeois nationalism", that is a society divided in social classes, where big capitalists and corrupt politicians use nationalism for their interest (as the present European leaders do)' (interview with FN militant, Rome). The FN idea of nation corresponds to a 'people' held together by common values and by solidarity among all the members of the society/community (the two concepts overlap). In practice, people's cohesion and solidarity is ensured by a particular idea of 'race' as a biological concept—even if this is denied by most FN militants interviewed. The genetic 'racialisation' of the nation is explicitly expressed by one militant: 'We are loyal to the principle that is also genetic, of the blood, of the soil'. Not all interviewees mention the concept of biological race, and it is always a question of identity and culture, yet behind the fierce opposition to 'hybridisation' and to mixed marriages lies a racial principle:

> There may have been in the history of some peoples a mixing with other peoples, but the best thing is to have an area for each people to grow and to develop as one people. There are people who are mixed creating intermediate people, there are people like this in Africa, in Ethiopia you see that they are not entirely Bantu nor totally white Arabic, they were born from the mixing and a new people has emerged; however, they have developed in their territory, where they have been able to create their own culture, to live their lives, they are not a guest in other people's homes ... that is too humiliating, it is certainly not beautiful. (Interview with FN militant, Pisa)

Whereas FN goes back to some form of biological racism, Casa Pound insists on cultural differences marking the borders of nations and groups:

> Casa Pound loves difference, Casa Pound wants to preserve difference, Casa Pound advocates a different world that is the opposite of rejection or hatred of other cultures or races, or of other ethnic groups ... on the contrary, we believe it is a form of violence that is preached by the left, that is, forced inclusion, integration. Integration is violence, if you look at it from a certain point of view. (Interview with CP militant, Florence)

They express, moreover, an ideological universalism, rejecting biological racism:

> [T]alking about spirit and race, I can tell you that Casa Pound coined this slogan: our race is the spirit. In this sense I think an Ascaro[21] who fought with fascism in Africa in 1936 is more my brother than an Italian partisan. He is my brother, fought for my national idea, for the imperial idea, for an idea of social justice. He is much more my brother, I repeat, than a partisan who sold our home to an invading foreigner[22] and today we are paying the consequences. So our race is not a biological discourse, it is a spiritual discourse. (Interview with CP militant, Florence)

---

[21] A special military corps of Black people in the Italian army.
[22] That is, the Anglo-Americans.

Leaving aside an interpretation of history that completely denies the foundations of the Italian Republic, this Casa Pound militant suggests an idea of 'ideological brotherhood' that goes beyond race—a sort of international fascism that brings together blacks and whites (Bulli et al. 2015).

Nation, Globalisation and Immigration

FN and Casa Pound justify their opposition to immigration with their idea of an organic nation/society/community, referring either to a biological idea of race or to an homogeneous cultural/ideological identity, and with a critical analysis of globalisation and the neoliberal capitalist domination that deliberately provokes migration.

Both FN and Casa Pound are against globalisation, the aim of which, as they see it, is to destroy differences between peoples and to produce homogenisation:

[L]ook, I see the differences as I travel. If I make the whole world alike—uniform, standardised—it becomes a monster, and who is this uniform world good for? For consumers, capitalists and those who have to sell products, because they can standardise them ... the economy is simple: standardising everything to sell all over the world, transforming everyone into identical consumers to destroy individuality. I'm willing to go to the stake for this. The end of individuality is the end of the meaning of life, if I lose that I lose the very reason why we are in the world, this is what I think of it. (Interview with FN militant, Pisa)

Behind globalisation lie the forces of capitalism and of finance. These same forces are also behind uncontrolled migration, as an FN militant from Rome explains:

Immigration is the fault of the capitalist system, the multinationals that exploit third-world countries, forcing these people to emigrate, and then exploiting them. These people represent a workforce that is more exploitable than Italian workers, creating competition among Italian workers.

Another militant clarifies FN's position on immigration:

> Our discourse on immigration is broad … we think that migration flows have been caused by a specific liberal policy, and in combination with the Mafia, in the sense that having people in slavery … cheap workforce coming from desperate situations, whom does it suit? The entrepreneurs who pay them informally and the mafias … we do not attack immigrants arriving by boat, because they are obviously desperate … we are Christians … we could not say … we will bomb them into the sea (as the League sometimes does) that's vulgar, we say something else … we have to help them in their own country.

Casa Pound also links the growth of immigration to the various underground organisations that the corrupt system does not really want to destroy. The slogan 'against immigration, but not against migrants' summarises the FN and Casa Pound arguments on migration policies. Immigration is regarded as a consequence of globalisation, impoverishing the countries of origin and creating tensions in the countries of destination. Both FN and Casa Pound believe in developing the countries of origin through international cooperation (Casa Pound has an NGO for cooperation in Kenya). Both organisations believe that Italy cannot support current numbers of immigrants for economic and social reasons.On the basis of this analysis, the FN's political agenda is a total ban on immigration and encouragement of repatriation:

> As far as immigration goes, we have always been clear: a total ban is our recipe, and a humanitarian repatriation of those who are illegally on our national territory. Look, we don't like being labelled racist or xenophobic. The word xenophobia literally means fear of the foreigner, we are not afraid of the others … but, for example, in a city like Florence, we see illegal immigrants living without dignity … crammed into cardboard shacks under a bridge. We say that an immigrant who comes to Italy should live with dignity, and we figure we cannot afford it, because at this moment in time Italy doesn't even have work for Italians. (Interview with FN militant, Florence)

Casa Pound's proposals are similar:

> We want a total end to immigration now, because Italy can neither economically, nor socially, nor culturally withstand such large migration flows

on its territory. Of course we are against the forced return of people who are already here, because now, unfortunately or fortunately, depending on your point of view, they are already ... not Italian, but Italianised, and so it would be violence to forcibly send them back to their own country, but we believe in a total end to future flows. (Interview with a CP militant, Florence)

The Issue of the *Jus Soli*

Militants within FN are more insistent on 'privileged' status of immigrants than those in Casa Pound:

we have nothing against immigrants, because, let's face it, immigrants who are offered rights or privileges, it is logical that they accept them ... the blame lies with the institutions that favour them at the expense of Italians, and even at their own expense, because then there are families who stop voting Democratic Party or PRC (Communist) for this reason. (Interview with an FN militant, Pisa)

This argument—immigrants are more privileged than Italians—justifies the FN slogan, *Prima gli italiani* (Italians first):

We are for the 'national preference'. This discourse is often misunderstood: we are accused of racism, but in reality what we say is different ... given equal conditions and equal needs, we prefer Italians. For example, if we have five families in need, and there is an Italian family, the house or the help should be given first to the Italian one as a matter of identity and also out of respect for ourselves, our fathers have created what we have here ... this is not a discourse of exclusion, we do not have a conflicting relationship, we prefer to help the Italians, our activities refer to the Italian cause ... it is a matter of identity. (Interview with FN militant, Rome)

Despite the reassuring words of this militant, the idea of a rift between 'us'/Italians and 'the others'/immigrants has been translated into racist slogans, demonstrations against reception centres for immigrants and even attacks on immigrants. It must, however, be stressed that the main victims of violent attacks by FN and Casa Pound militants are not immigrants but left-wing activists.

FN and Casa Pound support a ban on immigration and are opposed to the introduction of elements of *jus soli* in Italian law. The battle started a few years ago, but it has been reinforced during the appointment of a Congolese, Cecile Kyenge, as Minister for Integration. 'Kyenge back to Congo' is one of the slogans used by Forza Nuova militants. 'Congolese and bankers … Italy is dying' combines the xenophobic and anti-capitalist attitudes of the FN militants.

For FN, opposition to *jus soli* corresponds to an idea of national identity that is 'quasi-biological':

> we think that the *jus soli* is a form of violence, what does it mean that if you are born in Italy, you are necessarily Italian … Italian by force … we speak of *jus sanguinis*, not in the racist, biological sense, but in the sense of the right to be born from cultural and identity seeds … and to belong to that identity. (Interview with FN militant, Rome)

Casa Pound is more moderate, but it also opposes *jus soli* and is in favour of the status quo.

> We think the system that exists now is correct. We believe it is neither too harsh nor too soft, it is simply a normal law. There is no need for any further restriction, nor of any enlargement of citizenship, or *jus soli* … Categorically, the *jus soli* is rather aberrant, we stick to this position … we hope that those who are on our territory, will not be westernized by force. I do not think that we live in a civilisation 'so superior' to that which these people come from … we are not used to assessing the civilisation of a people, the 'superiority' of one model over another. (Interview with CP militant, Florence)

The Casa Pound cultural relativist approach has been criticised by more extreme neo-fascist groups: 'You know, the site recently closed by the state police, Stormfront … they have repeatedly called us "cuddle niggers" … I do not cuddle anybody … I don't cuddle them, I don't beat them, let them be, "each to his own"' (Interview with CP militant, Florence).

We can conclude that immigration is an important issue in the political message of these two neo-fascist organisations; its ideological role reveals their ideas of nation and identity and can easily be used to exploit and mobilise xenophobic and racist 'us' against 'them/foreigners' feelings. Immigration is also a key issue for the Northern League which, at least in some areas of the country, competes in the neo-fascist arena. The Northern League—in government between 2001 and 2006, and between 2008 and 2011—is the political party that has most exploited the migration issue (and continues to do so). The other parties of the centre-right government led by Silvio Berlusconi until 2011 have also often used anti-immigrant rhetoric for electoral purposes.

As for Forza Nuova and Casa Pound, migration is far from their central political message: remaining faithful to the fascist ideology, re-adapted to the new context, means fighting for a certain idea of a state, a strong authoritarian state that organises people's lives and is responsible for social problems. Even though they still have violent conflicts with far-left militants (sometimes leading to fatalities), neo-fascists are deprived of the communist enemy. Consequently their main opponent now is 'the system'—corrupt politics, financial capitalism, the European Union as an instrument of financial capitalism that has deprived Italy of its sovereignty (Caldiron 2013).

Direct Activism and Violence: Reaction and Resistance

In recent years, the militancy model of direct activism has degenerated for both Forza Nuova and Casa Pound into cases of violence against militants of the far left, against Roma and against migrants. Official representatives of the two organisations tend to justify and even support collective protests—such as marches at Roma camps—even when some violence is involved, but to distance themselves from the most violent events. They generally condemn individual attacks on migrants as the actions of isolated individuals.

Casa Pound leaders denied responsibility for the shocking events of 13 December 2011, when Gianluca Casseri, a 50-year-old extreme-right militant who used to attend Casa Pound events, killed two Senegalese and wounded three others in Florence. He then shot himself in the head during a shoot-out with police, and died shortly afterwards. 'Casseri was not a militant of our association, he just attended—sometimes—a few activities in Pistoia and we have no reason to conceal that' declared the leader of Casa Pound in Florence. 'Today a tragedy of madness was consumed, and four people died for no reason, but if it happened we should remember that this is also because the state is not able to provide any protection and assistance to its weaker children.' The Casa Pound spokesman in Pistoia, Casseri's home town, denied any responsibility, stating: 'He had come a few times in our circle to talk about his book *The Keys of Chaos*, but we knew that he just was a very closed person that gave no confidence."

There is no doubt, however, that Gianluca Casseri identified himself as neo-fascist and followed some of the activities of the neo-fascist organisation Casa Pound. The leader of the Senegalese community in Florence, Pap Deaw, supported by the ANPI (Associazione Nazionale Partigiani d'Italia, National Association of Italian Partisans),[23] demanded the closure of Casa Pound. His request was rejected. In our interview with him three years after the event, he declared:

> One of the first things we asked for, supported by the ANPI, was the closure of those places (the headquarters of the neo-fascist groups), because they are places where people are taught to hate, and also there is a law, the Mancino Law, that should prosecute these groups for the crime of reconstructing fascism. But, as they say in Italy: once the law is passed, they find a way to break it.[24]

According to Pap Deaw, the Mancino Law, which bans the re-building of fascist organisations and is harshly criticised by the neo-fascist movements, is not really enforced. Both Pap Deaw and the president of the ANPI believed their request had been rejected because Casa Pound

---

[23] Italian Resistance fighters during World War II.

[24] At the time of the murder of the Senegalese, Pap Deaw declared: 'We call on all political forcesto seek to reduce social tension and even to send a real message with the closure of Casa Pound in Italy, beginning in Tuscany.'

enjoyed support or were at least tolerated among the centre-right government led by Berlusconi that was in power at the time of the tragedy. Both denounced the centre-right government's role in legitimising fascism, racism and hate speech. The ANPI representative even described the government as 'populist', in a clear reference to the theories of national populism.

> We as an association [ANPI] we are very concerned about the situation that has arisen, but not now … for ten years, because with this populist government, fascist symbols, gestures and attitudes are legitimised … We are opposing groups that are increasingly organised, there are thousands of associations with different names that have the same neo-fascist ideology. They have the media and they have the economic means to support the venues that we are asking be closed down. (Interview with Alessandro Pini, president of the ANPI in Florence)

The president of the ANPI makes two arguments that are important for understanding the interaction between the centre-right governments and neo-fascism. One is that the centre-right government has produced a political discourse legitimising fascism as a historical experience and an ideology; the other is that it has offered neo-fascist organisations the economic means for expansion. This point of view is shared by militants from left-wing social centres who are also often victims of attacks by neo-fascists, as happened to Dax, a left-wing militant from Milan who was attacked by three fascist sympathisers and died from his wounds in 2003. The speaker for the Dax Association (set up in memory of the victim) makes a clear link between legitimation of fascism and the development of racist ideas, supported by the government:

> In the case of Dax, the murderers were just three children of the fascist intolerance … children of the various speeches you could have heard in recent years from the various Bossi (Northern League), Fini (National Alliance) … when the representatives of the Northern League say: If you see an immigrant, grab a gun and shoot at the boat …? Then … why wouldn't someone who really has a weapon do it? The blame in my opinion lies with the politicians who make these kinds of speeches … who—because it is easy, they say that there are no jobs because there are immigrants, and

then blame the immigrants, the homosexuals … these discourses of racial hatred, hatred towards the other, can take root in people who may be a little less aware, from the cultural point of view, or are psychologically weak. (Interview with militant, the Dax Association)

In its fight against neo-fascism and neo-fascist ideas, the ANPI, to which surviving partisans belong, is now open to young people who share Resistance values and want to show their opposition to fascism.

Our association made a very radical change to its statutes in 2005, the association was previously only for those who had actually been partisans during World War II; since 2005 we have changed the rules and we have allowed all anti-fascists, if adult, to be members of the ANPI, because, otherwise, we would have encountered the same problems as many veterans' associations, such as … those who took part in the liberation of Florence … the members are 92, 93 years old … they are too old for activities … without young people we risked disappearing. (Interview with ANPI President, Florence)

Conclusions: Neo-Fascism and Populism

The use of the term 'populism' to describe a number of political forces that are critical of the mainstream parties or the management of the EU crisis does not clarify the political dynamics in Europe—nor those in Italy. The historical presence of neo-fascism in Italy has avoided a simplistic inclusion of all 'anti-system' political forces in the category of populism. Moreover, the simplistic use of the term 'populist' has been challenged by the fact that the centre-right government of Forza Italia, Berlusconi's party, and the Northern League has often been defined as 'populist' by mainstream European media. Does populism then represent Italy's political mainstream?

As Marco Tarchi (2002, 2003), one of the most prominent Italian political scientists has recently declared in an interview:

Although they may be in admixture in some cases, populism and the extreme right are distinct phenomena. The ambiguity of the concepts that define them has led most observers to confuse them—in order to disqualify both—but if we take a scientific approach it is clear that there exist and have existed movements and populist politicians who have nothing to do with the extreme right (for example Hugo Chavez) and movements and politicians of the extreme right who have nothing to do with populism (in the case of all those who turn to conservatism and statism). To define how the former and the latter use the term 'people' an article of several dozen pages would not be enough. (Tarchi 2013)[25]

Tarchi (2013) defines populists' idea of the people thus: 'the depository of civic virtues and the true ruler of the "polis", the only source of legitimacy of the institutions, starting from those based on representative elections'. In the hierarchy of the far right, on the contrary: 'it is the state, not the people that leads. The state transforms the people from a raw mass through the cultural and ethnic melting pot of the nation, and makes it governable (in the interest of the people)' (Tarchi 2013). This idea of the state, as it happens, forms part of European political history embedded in visions inspired by European philosophers such as the German Friederich Hegel or the Italian Giovanni Gentile[26] (Haddock and Wakefield 2014). Fascist ideology is not an alien political product: it is part of Europe's political history; today's neo-fascist presence is inscribed in political and social dynamics very different from those that characterised Europe until the fall of the Berlin Wall. The Treaty of Maastricht, the enforcement of neoliberalism in the economies, the Schengen agreement, increasing migration, the introduction of the euro and the management of the economic crisis with the imposition of austerity policies, all these factors lie at the heart of two political phenomena: the formation of new political forces that have been defined as neopopulist, and the adaptation of neo-fascist aims and strategies to the new context.

The social and cultural tensions provoked by globalisation and Europeanisation have led to a focus on immigration that has concerned both neopopulists and neo-fascists. Anti-immigrant discourses have shifted

---

[25] Diorama Letterario, 312. http://www.diorama.it/index.php?option=com_content&task=view&id=233&Itemid=48.
[26] Giovanni Gentile (1875–1944) described himself as 'the philosopher of Fascism'. He ghostwrote *A Doctrine of Fascism* (1930) for his country's prime minister, Benito Mussolini. Philosophically he drew from Kant, Hegel and Marx—system builders. Among his works are *The Theory of Spirit as Pure Act* (1916), *Foundations of the Philosophy of Law* (1916) and the *Logic* (1917).

from neopopulists to neo-fascists, crossing mainstream conservative or right-wing forces such as the Forza Italia party created by Silvio Berlusconi. However, gradually the battle against the EU and the euro is definitely replacing the battle against immigration in the name of national sovereignty. It is no coincidence that in recent years, Casa Pound has intensified its 'blitz' on EU sites. The vice-president of Casa Pound in Rome, Simone De Stefano, was even prosecuted for stealing an EU flag in December 2013.

We can certainly wonder how, 70 years after the end of World War II, fascism can still be an ideology that attracts young people and even achieves some electoral success (in the last municipal elections Casa Pound won 7 per cent of the vote in the town of Trento). Where did liberal democracy fail? There is no easy answer to this question. In any case the economic crisis, austerity policies and disagreement among EU member states apparently incapable of solidarity and future vision have discredited the liberal democratic system. A liberal democracy cannot last long in the face of constant social tensions that are changing the common feeling and generating endemic waves of fear and panic in the midst of social suffering.

References

Bartolini, S. (2010). *I 'nipoti del Duce' tra eredità, novità, persistenze e sviluppi all'alba del nuovo secolo*, in Quaderni di Farestoria dell'Istituto Storico della Resistenza e della Società Contemporanea di Pistoia, Anno X, N° 3, pp. 4–23.

Bulli, G., Albanese, M., & Castelli Gatinara, P. (2015). *Fascisti di un altro millennio? Crisi e partecipazione in CasaPound Italia*. Roma: Bonanno.

Cadalanu, G. (1994). *Skinheads: dalla musica giamaicana al saluto romano*. Lecce, Italy: Argo.

Caldiron, G. (2013). *Estrema destra. Chi sono oggi i nuovi fascisti? Un'inchiesta esclusiva e sicoccante sulle organizzazioni nere in Italia e nel mondo*. Milano: Newton Compton.

De Felice, R. (1996). *Fascismo, antifascismo, nazione. Note e ricerche*. Roma: Bonacci.

De Felice, R. (1997). *Mussolini l'alleato, Vol II, La guerra civile (1943–1945)*. Torino, Italy: Einaudi.

De Felice, R. (2002). *Breve storia del Fascismo*. Milano: Mondadori.

Di Nunzio, D., & Toscano, E. (2011). *Dentro e fuori Casapound. Capire il fascismo del Terzo Millennio*. Roma: Armando.

Di Tullio, D. (2010). *Nessun dolore. Una storia di CasaPound*. Milano: Rizzoli.

Diamanti, I. (1993). *La Lega. Geografia, storia e sociologia di un nuovo soggetto politico*. Roma: Donzelli.

Diamanti, I. (1996). *Il male del Nord. Lega, localismo, secessione*. Roma: Donzelli.

Diamanti, I. (2010). *Populismo: una definizione indefinita per eccesso di definizioni*, in Italianieuropei, 4. Retrieved October 14, 2010, from http://www.italianieuropei.it/it/la-rivista/ultimo-numero/item/1793-populismo-una-definizione-indefinita-per-eccesso-di-definizioni.html

Dondi, M. (1999). *La lunga liberazione. Giustizia e violenza nel dopoguerra italiano*. Roma: Editori Riuniti.

Evola, J. (1963). *Il Fascismo. Saggio di una analisi critica dal punto di vista della destra*. Roma: Volpe.

Fasanella, G., & Grippo, A. (2009). *L'orda nera*. Milano: BUR, Rizzoli.

Germani, G. (1975). *Autoritarismo, fascismo e classi sociali*. Bologna, Italy: il Mulino.

Germinario, F. (2002). Destre radicali e nuove destre. Neofascismo, neonazismo e movimenti populisti. In P. Milza, S. Berstein, N. Tranfaglia, & B. Mantelli (Eds.), *Dizionario dei fascismi* (p. 691). Milano: Bompiani.

Haddock, B., & Wakefield, J. (2014). Thought thinking: The philosophy of Giovanni Gentile. *Collingwood and British Idealism Studies, 20*, 1–2.

Ignazi, P. (1994). *Postfascisti?* Bologna, Italy: Il Mulino.

Ignazi, P. (2000). *Extreme right parties in Western Europe*. Oxford, England: Oxford University Press (English translation of thein Italian: L'estrema destra in Europa, Bologna, Il Mulino, 1994).

Sabatini, D. (2010). *Il Movimento Politico Occidentale*. Roma: Settimo Sigillo.

Tarchi, M. (2002). Dal neofascismo al nazionalpopulismo. La parabola dell'estrema destra europea, Italianieuropei, September 2002. http://www.italianieuropei.it/it/la-rivista/archivio-della-rivista/item/1045-dal-neofascismo-al-nazionalpopulismo-la-parabola-dellestrema-destra-europea.html

Tarchi, M. (2003). *L'Italia populista. Dal qualunquismo ai girotondi*. Bologna, Italy: Il Mulino.

Tarchi, M. (2010). *La rivoluzione impossibile, dai Campi Hobbit alla Nuova Destra*. Firenze, Italy: Vallecchi.

Tarchi, M. (2013). L'INTERVISTA (Marco Tarchi) Le crisi, le destre, il populismo (a Spinning Politics), *Diorama Letterario, 312*. http://www.diorama.it/index.php?option=com_content&task=view&id=233&Itemid=48

Telese, L. (2006). *Cuori Neri*. Milano: Sperling & Kupfer.

Wiarda, H. J. (1977). *Corporatism and development: The Portuguese experience.* Boston: University of Massachusetts Press.

3

Far-Right Movements in France: The Principal Role of Front National and the Rise of Islamophobia

Annie Benveniste and Etienne Pingaud

Introduction

This chapter presents the current landscape on the French far right through an ethnographic study we led of two significant protagonists, the Front National and the network of activists fighting the phenomenon they call 'Islamisation'. We decided to explore them because of the specific innovations they have introduced to French politics. The Front National, known for a long time for its charismatic leader, Jean-Marie Le Pen, was the first 'modern' far-right party to achieve significant electoral success at the national level in the European Union, becoming a model for many parties in the years that followed. While the modern concept

We would like to thank Ari Rable for assisting us with editing and proofreading this chapter.

A. Benveniste (✉)
Department of Educational Science, University of Paris VIII, Saint-Denis, France

E. Pingaud
University of Paris VIII, Saint-Denis, France

© The Editor(s) (if applicable) and The Author(s) 2016   **55**
G. Lazaridis et al. (eds.), *The Rise of the Far Right in Europe*,
DOI 10.1057/978-1-137-55679-0_3

of 'populism' appeared in academic works around the electoral rise of Jean-Marie Le Pen, it was regarded with suspicion. Far-right[1] specialists felt the notion was not useful to describe Front National ideas (Collovald 2005; Dezé 2004). Its recent success owes much to the emergence abroad of a new generation of ideologically indeterminate leaders who challenge the classical typologies of political parties (Lipset and Rokkan 1967), and to the development of 'comparative politics' in French political science which has led to a proliferation of international comparisons.

In recent years 'Islamisation' has become a rallying cry for many activists across Europe that has given birth to transnational networks opposed to the 'Islamic invasion' they denounce. In the specific case of France, the issue has attracted people from various organisations and ideological trends, from leftist trade unions to far-right traditionalists, disturbing classical political cleavages.

France occupies a special place in the history of far-right movements and is regarded by several authors as the birthplace of the ideas, values and trends that led to the rise of fascism and Nazism in the surrounding countries (Nolte 1966; Sternell 1978). This particular history explains why labels such as 'fascist' continue to be used to characterise current far-right organisations. To make this point intelligible, this chapter first returns to the roots of the French far right. It describes the historical periods when the far right has gained success: World War II, the Algerian War, May 1968 and the years that followed. It shows the progressive building of strong organisations, as well as the conflicts, differences and ideological opposition that contributed to the current state of the far right. It explains the succession of central new issues, such as immigration in the 1980s, the European Union in the 1990s, the euro, and more recently, Islam.

The chapter continues by developing the main results of various fieldwork studies. First it explores the Front National, a party that has changed profoundly reinvented. At the centre of the far right since the

---

[1] We are using this topographic notion rather than the more ideological 'populism'. Far right is topographic in the sense that it describes a liminal position in the political landscape. Populism presupposes a special link between the leaders and 'the people', a questionable notion. Whether or not classical sociological studies have demonstrated the presence and the wide influence of a real intellectual 'populism', in the sense of a propensity to exalt 'the people' and popular culture, the concept cannot automatically be applied to political leaders.

early 1980s, the party continues to exercise strong leadership over radical groups whose positions differ from those of the Le Pen family. But the strategy has changed in recent years, because of the gradual withdrawal of the historical leader and Marine Le Pen's firm control over the party. In order to transform the party into a 'respectable' one, she decided to emphasise a social trend and to avoid public scandals.. She appointed her supporters to all the key positions of the Front National with a view to ensuring the diffusion of her strategic views. All the interviewees we met belong to this current orientation, which enabled us to study the new style and the principal new issues of Front National activists. The chapter goes on to focus on the development of mobilisation against the visibility of Islam in public spaces. This shift in far-right priorities is interesting to analyse. Activists who are involved regard Islam as the main threat, presenting themselves as the *Résistance* against a new form of occupation of the country (a reference to the resistance against Nazi occupation).

Finally the chapter describes some ways of combating far-right ideologies and hate speech. It looks at the everyday fight by several associations in France against what they all see as a dangerous increase in public hate speeches. Some of them focus on racial discrimination, others on homophobia, and several cover all forms of hatred. Their activities illustrate different aspects of 'hate speech' and responses to it, including legal action, practical help for victims and political activit.

The Historical Roots and Political Context of the French Far Right

The aims, narratives and thought of far-right activists and organisations are products of a specific history. The many authors who have tried to write this history date its beginnings from various different points. Is the French far right a legacy of the opponents of the French Revolution? Is it the continuation of the nationalist and anti-Semitic struggle against Captain Dreyfus? If we concentrate on the current leaders of the field, it is easy to identify three main decisive shifts in the field: the government of Maréchal Pétain, the Algerian War, and the events of May 1968, all of which were sources of political socialisation, times of intense activism and occasions of ideological shifts, because of the high levels of conflict and opposition. Nowadays they remain general schemes of reference for studying these far-right organisations.

The Pétain government during World War II is obviously a decisive issue for understanding modern-day French radicalism. The disqualification after the war of every person involved in affairs of state during the last years of the German occupation of the country (1940–1944) can be regarded as a real act of birth of modern far-right activism. A few organisations, some of them still active today, have drawn together the supporters of Maréchal Pétain and sometimes pro-Nazi activists. The best known, owing to the character of its leaders and its impact on activism, is Jeune Nation. Led by Pierre Sidos, the son of a leader[2] of the French pro-German militia during the war, it was the first movement to endorse the Celtic cross as an official symbol of the organisation. Jeune Nation was a place that could host people whose ideological opinions had been marginalised by years of conflict. Even though it remained a very small group, its influence was widespread. Following several prosecutions and bans, the Sidos group has been known for a long time as Oeuvre Française.[3]

The second major breakdown is the Algerian War, which made radical speech acceptable, popular and present in French political institutions. The conflict was in itself a focal point that concentrated many important issues: the French Empire and colonialism, the French army and De Gaulle's politics of independence. This war initiated the principal modern legacy of the French radical right: the first political party to enter Parliament on a platform of radical ideas prohibited since the end of World War II., A group of 52 MPs led by Pierre Poujade was elected in 1956. One of them was Jean-Marie Le Pen. It was also during the Algerian War that new activist movements were born on the far right, drawing particularly from the Sidos environment. These included the Nationalist Students' Federation,[4] a powerful force among right-wing

---

[2] François Sidos, who was sentenced to death at the end of the war.

[3] Œuvre Française was banned in June 2013, after the death of an anti-racist activist during a fight with skinheads in Paris.

[4] Fédération des Étudiants Nationalistes (FEN).

Parisian students. The Algerian issue was a key point legitimating far right-ideas, because it appealed to values of nationalism and French historical prestige. It initiated a time of political learning and profoundly altered political alliances and opposition.

The third decisive shift, which involved many actors in the Algerian struggles, was the May 1968 events and the changes that followed. The rise of far-left activism and the development of a counter-culture in France led to a new political and ideological shift among its opponents. Several thinkers started to revise current ideological concepts. They belonged to different schools such as the far right (Monnerot 1970a, b), conservative Catholicism (Molnar 1969) or conservative liberalism, for example Raymond Aron (1970), the founder of the review *Commentaire*. They came up with varying analyses of Marxism, third-world issues and strategic conflicts around the world. In this period, anti-communism and anti-leftism ideas also developed as new highly influential far-right ideologies for example *nationalisme révolutionnaire* or the ideas of Alain de Benoist[5] around the GRECE institute (Groupement de Recherche et d'Études pour la Civilisation). The far right grew in this singular era, becoming a field of many different associations and organisations, and a variety of leaders and ideologies (see below). Effective social evolution of the family and women, and youth emancipation became controversial. During the Second Vatican Council (1962–1965) and in reaction to it, a fundamentalist Catholic movement developed around Bishop Lefebvre, planting the question of conservatism and religion in the far-right movement, alongside nationalism and anti-leftism.

The far right is a space of wide divergences between actors and protagonists, leaders and followers. Most of the people involved in these movements belong to small groups of no more than 100 members. It is difficult to provide a strict classification of active groups, because as is the case across the political landscape, most visible activity is based on topics that appear to be central in the news at any specific moment. By mixing classifications produced within the social group (from the subjects'

---

[5] Alain de Benoist, who created the GRECE in 1969, was a New Right thinker who defended European culture against Judeo-Christian values,and individual liberalism against Marxism, socialism and equality. He was also opposed to the productivist society. Cf. Camus (2009).

perspective) and outside (from the social scientists' perspective), we can try to establish categories within the field:

1. The 'political' forces. Among far-right organisations, Front National has had the highest number of activists, sympathisers and voters since 1983. It is supported by foreign far-right groups. There have been other far-right groups at each election, but most of them were established by former Front National leaders expelled from the party because of rivalries with the leader, for example, Bruno Mégret's Mouvement National Républicain (MNR) in the late 1990s, or more recently Carl Lang's Union de la Droite Nationale.

2. Around those main political organisations, many small groups maintain links with them. They are currently active inside the Front National and around websites such as VOXNR. An example is the National Revolutionary trend that mixes strong nationalism with anti-capitalist views.

3. There are still a few groups promoting skinhead ideology, especially around some music bands, sometimes in association with foreign groups. They have had the same leader in Paris since the 1980s, Serge Ayoub (known by his nickname, 'Batskin'), and may coalesce with small groups such as Jeunesses Nationalistes Révolutionnaires (National Revolutionary Youth) or Troisième Voie (Third Way). They are considered as extreme activists, who avoid publicity.

4. The new rising force of the 2000s is the Identitaires, which brings together ideologies inspired by Alain de Benoist's ideas (cf. note 5), and its think tank. *Identitaires* is a network of several small and local organisations and believes in the power of cultural identities. They played a decisive role in the 'cultural turn' of the French far right, by according 'cultural' issues a central place in their struggle. They apply the methods of leftist groups, such as the Gramsci-inspired 'cultural war', to diffuse their ideas by any possible means. They have taken part in several elections, especially in the south of France where they are well established. Some of them have been close to the skinhead movement in their early violent activities.

5. If these groups can easily claim to be in favour of revolution, there are more conservative groups that can be regarded as influential on the far

right. On the intellectual level there are groups such as Oeuvre Française around Pierre Sidos or its youth section, called Jeunesses Nationalistes. Nostalgic for Maréchal Pétain's views, they don't hesitate to use the same motto: 'Work, family and patria'. They have been the most radical active group in demonstrations against same-sex marriage, calling for the renewed criminalisation of homosexuality.

6. Jeunesses Nationalistes and Oeuvre Française were the only ones to participate in the specific events and street demonstrations organised by the Catholic conservative group Civitas. Catholic fundamentalists remain an important faction on the far right, their new visibility owing to the main issues of the moment: same-sex marriage, transformation of the family, new assisted reproductive technologies and gender topics. While Civitas' methods appears to be more radical (e.g., public prayers on the streets), the Catholic conservatives continue to disseminate their ideas through newspapers (such as *Présent*) and associations.

Far-Right Organisations

We decided in our fieldwork to focus on two different organisations—Front National and Activists Against Islamisation—illustrative of the history of the French far right. Front National is the most important far-right organisation and remains at the centre of the game, increasing its audience and electoral performance. Activists Against Islamisation is a network built around a specific issue that is becoming important, the supposed Islamisation of the country. In each case, we studied in depth the textual, ideological and intellectual production of the movements, observed a number of specific organised events, and conducted interviews with members and activists.

Front National

Front National (FN) was born in 1972 as an electoral coalition of most of the components of the radical and national right, meaning the 'true right wing' opposed to the centrist issues of Christian democracy and the leadership of De Gaulle's legacy on the French right wing. The early 1980s mark the real rise of the FN, whose performance in elections has been increasing for years.[6] The new status of the Front National attracted radical right-wing ideologies. Many activists joined the organisation, which became a real political force able to build and produce intellectual work.[7] Most of the activists from small French groups such as the Neo-fascists, Skinheads and National Révolutionnaire were at some point Front National members. At present the party embraces a wide spectrum of radical conceptions of otherness. The focus on immigration helped to define a consensual political line, pitting 'French' against 'immigrants', and placing nationality at the heart of the definition of identity ahead of religious or regional affinities.

In 2011, the retirement of Jean-Marie Le Pen generated an internal succession war often presented as a conflict between old-guard leaders (traditionalist Catholics, conservatives, new pagan racialists, etc.) and supporters of modernisation, united behind Le Pen's daughter. The victory of Marine Le Pen was the start of a process called *dédiabolisation* of the FN that sought to build a more respectable image for the party.

This transformation is seen as 'neopopulist', based on the model of the new radical right growing in northern Europe, exemplified by Geert Wilders in Netherlands or Pja Kjaeersagard in Denmark. FN embarked on an ideological turn inspired by *nationaux-révolutionnaires*, combining the struggle against capitalism with a strong nationalism, with a mix of social and conservative values to win a new electorate coming on one side from the working class and on the other from the classical right wing., and taking advantage of the weak demarcation between right and far-right positions. We will focus on this process because it profoundly changed the nature of public speeches and the face of 'the other' in FN

---

[6] Front National only got 0.18 per cent of the votes in the 1981 parliamentary election, and 0.2 per cent in the 1982 local elections. It increased its share of the vote to reach 10.95 per cent in the 1984 European Election, gaining 35 MEPs in 1986. Since then their share has increased to 15 per cent in the 1990s, rising to 25 per cent in the 2014 regional elections.

[7] Bruno Gollnish, *Une âme pour la France. Pour en finir avec le génocide culturel*, Albatros, 1985.
David Mascré, *De la France*, Éditions de l'Infini, 2010.
Christophe Guilluy, *La France périphérique. Comment on a sacrifié les classes populaires*, Flammarion, 2014.

rhetoric: immigrants are no longer seen as the source of the problems, but as the victims of a capitalist strategy led by big business to increase their profits. Marine Le Pen has sought to merge with some minority groups including Jewish or LGBT organisations. By contrast, Islam has become the main opponent, as a result of a 'cultural shift' in far-right ideology.

When it was founded, FN created a youth section, the Front National de la Jeunesse (FNJ), regarded as a key training ground. It created close links to other far-right student and youth organisations, such as the former Renouveau Etudiant or Groupement Union Défense (GUD) in several universities. They formed a strong element of the demonstrations against same-sex marriage. After Marine Le Pen's election to the leadership of the party, the leaders of the FNJ decided to 'cleanse' the organisation, expelling activists regarded as too radical, in accordance with Front National's modernisation strategy.

FN is now a big political enterprise, with a mainstream organisation style. Consequently, it has entered the online political scene and is very active on the web. The party's website is updated daily, its Facebook page is liked by 99,000 people, and it has accounts on Twitter, YouTube and Dailymotion. It has its own WebTV. Most of the leaders of the FN have their own website or blog. Online media are seen as key strategic places to take control of the organisation's image.

Activists Against Islamisation

Islam became a principal target for many radical right organisations in Europe, leading to the development of a 'modernised' far right that defends liberal values or European welfare states against 'Islamic invasion'. But in France it was only later to become a central political topic, partly because the Front National, the dominant far-right organisation, did not focus on Islam until 2011. In consequence, small and radical groups like Bloc Identitaire were the first to mobilise against Islam. This growing activist movement is explicitly concerned about what is seen as an excessive visibility of Islam in public space: mosques, women's headscarves, *halal* shops, Muslim associations, etc. A series of anti-Muslim events has been organised over the past ten years, bringing together people from very different political and ideological positions. Since 2003, 'charity soup kitchens' have been established in Paris and in other big towns, first launched by a few far-right organisations linked to the Identitaires. Soup with pork is given to homeless people, but practising Muslims are excluded.

These far-right activists were joined by a recently created structure called Riposte Laïque, an Islamophobic coalition of former Trotskyites, women's rights activists and secularisation partisans denouncing Islam as a new fascism. Initially an online magazine founded in 2007, Riposte Laïque were actively involved in organising a big event in association with Identitaires in 2010. The so-called *apéro saucisson-pinard* (aperitif with sausage and wine) was supposed to take place in a popular street of Paris where Muslims pray every Friday on the pavement, because of the small size of the mosque. The police eventually banned the demonstration, which then took place instead on the Champs-Elysées. A few months later, the same two networks organised a new event called Assises Contre l'Islamisation in the presence of the Swiss leader Oskar Freysinger, with a large audience and media coverage.

Studying these events is particularly useful for an understanding of the building of a new 'enemy' and its consequences: new alliances, new supports and ideological shifts that put cultural issues at the forefront and lead organisations to present themselves as spokesmen for a cultural identity threatened by the growth of Islam. A new kind of rhetoric is used that borrows all its symbols from the *Résistance* ('resistance', 'occupation', 'collaborationists', etc.), to promote the idea that fighting Islam is as important fighting the Nazi occupation. To justify this struggle, anti-Islam activists are developing ideological work around the necessity of defending French culture against Islamic attacks and gaining some support among intellectuals and columnists. Most of them are internet activists who communicate through social networks, updating websites and collecting on them all the facts that can be used to spread this idea of 'Islamisation'.

Front National Members

All the interviewees we met are members of the new modernised party. They have responsibilities within the organisation and illustrate the transformation brought about in the party by Marine Le Pen. The leadership of Le Pen's daughter has led to a strictly controlled public image for Front National, which has two aims: expelling all the extremists, and avoiding the formation of an internal opposition to Marine Le Pen. A lot of new recruitment and promotion has taken place since she became president, with many activists dismissed from the party. For example, a local candidate was expelled when she compared the black Minister of Justice to a monkey. This rise of internal control is part of the party's new strategy of acceptability. Marine Le Pen does not want to endorse the same labels as her father.

In this context, control of the youth organisation is obviously decisive. All our interviewees[8] belong to the Front National Jeunesse (FNJ), the recruitment of young people being key to the *dédiabolisation* strategy of Marine Le Pen. In the 1990s, the youth organisation played a decisive role in the modernisation and Marine Le Pen herself belonged to this faction. Its leader Samuel Maréchal, husband of Marine's sister,[9] instigated the new political and ideological orientation of the party between 1992 and 1999. Many of the activists who surrounded him are now at the top of the Front National around Marine Le Pen.

It is remarkable that, with one exception, all our interviewees are new members who became involved in the party around 2010–2011, when Marine Le Pen took the control of the organisation. They now have positions, partly because of their support of Marine during the internal succession war. It is very difficult to interview young activists privately unless they are spokespeople, i.e., secretaries of local sections, or members of the national executive committee. Most of them have been or will be candidates in several local elections, and they are all responsible for training new recruits. Our panel is thus of great interest when it comes to understanding the how new strategic goals are disseminated from the top to the bottom of the whole organisation.

If we focus on routes to membership, another generation-related issue is the fact than half of our interviewees have parents who had been members or sympathisers of Front National since its first electoral successes in

---

[8] Interview 1 and 2: leaders of FNJ Parisian sections; interviews 4 and 5: leaders of FNJ Alsacian section; interview 6: leader of FNJ section in Nantes; interview 3: Vice president of FNJ.
[9] He is also the father of MP Marion Maréchal-Le Pen, granddaughter of Jean-Marie Le Pen, elected in south-east France.

the 1980s. One of them (interview 6) is the son of Christian Bouchet, one of the main intellectuals of the *national-révolutionnaire* trend.

Another (interview 4), responsible for an Alsace section, is herself the daughter of a couple of Front National candidates of the 1980s. And the member of the national committee whom we met (interview 3), a graduate of the prestigious Sciences Po Paris, is the daughter of a former FN sympathiser of the FN. This familial configuration is a real new deal in Front National's history. The first electors, activists and sympathisers were all people who had sometimes voted for mainstream parties before Le Pen's rise. For these new supporters, the attraction was partly established inside the family, with a domestic predilection for Le Pen's ideas.

> My entire education came from mealtimes, because we used to sit for a while, talk about the news, analyse, particularly history, …how the world was changing around us, the rise of unemployment, increasing social inequality … All of this needs talking about, especially in a united family where we talk a lot. (Interview 3)

Before the rise of the FN, it was not possible to stress the role of transmission in a far-right institution. The party is changing in a way to become comparable to big political organisations in France. FN has managed to generate the conditions for its own reproduction. This phenomenon is partly due to the successful transition in the leadership of the party, with Jean-Marie Le Pen passing the direction to his own daughter Marine.

For other interviewees, the family influence operated in other ways. It is difficult to estimate precisely how education influenced their way of constructing the social world. They know how their parents voted during the main elections, socialist left-wing (interview 1) or Nicolas Sarkozy (interview 5). But they do not link their political involvement to their family. They even explain their lack of political and ideological background by a rejection of that influence. They usually emphasise their efforts and the work they had to do themselves to learn about political issues and topics. To explain their attraction to Front National values, they often cite the difficult situation in French schools: fights, lack of respect for teachers, bad education … supposed to illustrate the main party orientations: "My mother is a suburban teacher, she can see in her classrooms: French language not acquired, codes, social codes that are not respected" (interview 1).

These personal experiences happen around high school or university years mostly through the organisation's internet networks. They all emphasise the contribution of social media to their knowledge of the party. The youngest member of the panel, became a Facebook friend of the local chief of the section in Alsace (Patrick Binder). At some level, the internet compensates for the relatively small number of activists present in the field.

The universities play a role by getting them away from supporters of left-wing organisations: 'they make interventions in classrooms; every week or two you have someone talking, not necessarily from a student union, but someone coming to give a talk … There was never Front National in all this' (interview x) . 'In the University there was a monopoly led by all the student unions, and it create a bad climate' (interview 2). The final stage of becoming a member, contact with the institution, is completed online, a facility that did not exist for earlier generations, which reduces the both decision-making time and involvement. All interviewees began their activism early, often being appointed candidates just after their first meetings.

> Then, 2 or 3 months after I joined, I was already very involved, she (Marine Le Pen) told me: 'for the Regional department elections, wouldn't you like Guebwiller? we need someone.' (Interview 4)

Marine Le Pen's supervision has consequences for activism inside the organisation. It illustrates the strength of the top-down approach to transmission, which is regarded as the most effective way of becoming the respectable government party Marine is seeking to build, avoiding the free expression of racism, extreme or inappropriate unmonitored pronouncements. In the case of our interviewees, the dual function of activist and trainer is not a succession through promotion, but a parallel involvement linked to the particular skills and properties the party associates with them as well as the support of Marine Le Pen in the internal debates.

The Construction of Otherness

New Trends

Immigration, which has been regarded as the central problem in France since the rise of FN, is less often named as the source of other problems such as security, theft and other types of crime, loss of national cultural identity, the rise of Islam, multiculturalism and communautarism. This view of immigration as the cause of national decline is slightly associated with right-wing and conservative views. It does not fit with the *dédiabolisation* campaign which uses the more acceptable rhetoric of positioning capitalism at the heart of national 'problems'. Immigration is no longer the cause, but merely the effect of a bigger issue, the omnipotence of big business, which needs low wages, and flexible and docile workers at a time when trade unions are week.

'Immigrants are the *dindons de la farce* [victims] of a system that exploits them and make their countries of origin more and more poor because these people, if they are in Europe, they don't make Africa richer anymore (interview 6).' Job thieves and cultural enemies in the 1980s, immigrants are now seen as victims in Front National speeches—a profound inversion of classical internal values. The different governments are denounced as immigration producers, lying to immigrants and welcoming them to France without any guarantees for the future.

Old lines about the topic are now avoided, especially those that emphasised ethnic or cultural differences to explain the problem of immigration. Only once in all of our interviews was the term 'Arab' used, while it is the basis of ordinary racism in France. This huge shift is an effective way of distinguishing FN from other movements, such as the Identitaires networks, who propagate 'culture-oriented' ideologies. Avoiding these ideologies had led to the recruitment of some second-generation immigrants by emphasising an anti-Israel position. All these new conceptions do not mean that there is no longer any racism in the Front National. At the local level, especially among older party members, there is still a lot of talk about Arabs, Blacks, Roma or Muslims (Checcaglini 2012). But despite these internal debates, all the public speeches are under control, and every word that can provoke controversy leads to sanctions, mostly expulsion from the party. Front National is no longer allowed to appear a real racist party, except as far as historical leaders of the organisation, , principally Jean-Marie Le Pen, are concerned.

The Front National's positions demonstrate continuity as far as 'Nation' is concerned. French Nation remains a central value defended by the party. But the enemies of the Nation have changed during recent decades. Supporters of the independence of the colonies in the 1960s were replaced by the communists in the 1970s. At that time the immigrants were seen as the main threat. But in Marine's configuration other forces are regarded as more dangerous: big business and its vassals, especially the European Union. All our interviewees emphasise the historical role of the EU in the loss of France's influence on the international scene ('A lot of people feel betrayed by the current European Union'). The sovereignty of the country is felt to be completely eliminated by the whole process of 'Europe-building'. One of the interviewees explains very precisely:

> The bigger problem at the moment is that we are dependent on the European Union, on a globalised system, and everything is linked: ultra-liberalism and the European Union, their logic is related. And we lose all our sovereignty ... Nowadays the European Union controls our budget, we don't have our own borders anymore. (Interview 1)

Since taking centre stage in the political debate, following the French referendum which rejected the Maastricht Treaty, the EU has been perceived as an affront to the principle of nation itself and as the source of many current problems. . Economic crisis, unemployment, immigration, liberalism, government inefficiency, everything can be seen as an example of the powerful and bad influence of Brussels on the France's political exercise of concrete power.None of our interviewees talked to us about the minorities who are usually the victims of hate speeches: Blacks, Jews, Roma or even Arabs. We were not able to observe Marine Le Pen's initiatives to create a 'French Islam' or to increase links with French Jewish organisations. But the context of strong opposition to the law in favour of same-sex marriage provided opportunities for participationin many demonstrations. The LGBT issue is not such an obvious topic for the Front National. The party's two MPs took part in the demonstrations, as did the FNJ national leader. But Marine Le Pen herself did not take part, claiming that the debate on same-sex marriage is hiding the real central issues, such as economics and immigration. Many observers believe she would have liked to show support for LGBT rights, and to endorse a modern far-right label, as Pim Fortuyn did in the Netherlands. Opponents are even denouncing the existence of a 'gay lobby' around her, since many homosexuals fill leading positions in the organisation. The opinions of our interviewees on same-sex marriage show that they are not comfortable with it ('the topic is a trap, we should not have given importance to that'). They defend, in accordance with the party line, the Civil Union against which the party was fighting 10 years earlier. Nevertheless, they all denounce the negative consequences that would follow the introduction of same-sex marriage, particularly adoption and surrogacy which they oppose. And once again, anti-capitalist arguments are used to defend the party's positions: the building of a motherhood market, transforming children into consumer products.

> "We are against homosexual marriage but we agree to enforce the PACS [civil union legislation], to let them have the rights they say they don't get with the current system" "I am not in favour because I think marriage is a really old institution that means the union of a man and a woman" But consumer traffic will come; look at the example of Ukraine, where surrogate mothers are subjected to the rules of customer couples. (Interview 6)

The issue of same-sex marriage could be seen as decisive for the orientation strategy of the new Front National. Marine Le Pen faces a paradox: how to look like a modern government party for a conservative electorate? To gain power the FN will, implicitly, need to refresh its image and appeal to a new audience. But the mosty loyal section of the electorate is conservative and favours a Front National that would speak out for 'enduring' French values, cultural tradition against an aggressive modernity. This ongoing tension can be seen in any topic to do with family and sexuality. While most of the far right subscribe to the Catholic model of family and socialisation, Marine Le Pen has tries to introduce innovation. She has herself been divorced twice and claims to support abortion. But the party's position on gender issues and sexual roles is more conservative.

Some groups such as Antigones which are linked to the extremist movement against same-sex marriage are promoting a new form of 'femininity' as a better way to define women. Some interviewees defend women's right to be housewives, as a way of protecting women in a competitive labour market, as well as promoting a new nativist politics: 'We have a lot of women nowadays who are forced to work in jobs they don't like, whose children are guarded by other women. It is really frustrating for her. We realise that a "mother income" would be a solution, and it would encourage more births. Because today, what we hear is: "I can't have kids, I could not feed them". These issues are probably going to play a central role in the future. Modernisation will be increasingly evaluated using these kinds of criteria.

Building a New Enemy

Anti-Islam has been chosen by far-right fractions close to the group called Identitaires. This new trend on the far right has forced everyone to endorse a position either for or against the appeal to place Islam at the centre of the struggle. Forms of re-alignment and alliances between organisations could be seen, for example, in the 2014 annual Front National demonstration in Paris,[10] where a woman held up a sausage to 'keep Muslims away'. The 2010 event called Assises Against Islamisation (see p. x), saw the birth in France later than in many other Europeans countries of an anti-Islam activist sphere with its own references, authors, concepts and ideas, whose circulation across countries and continents has been facilitated by social media. One of the main concepts developed in recent years is 'Eurabia', invented by Bat Ye'Or (2006), an essayist who writes in English and French. In far-right semantics, Eurabia means the idea of an explicit alliance between European and Arab governments and leaders, to compete with the leadership of the United States and its alliance with Israel. This alliance is said to be based on the free trade of resources and people, mixing neoliberalism and immigration, and it is claimed that the dynamics of this process are the root cause of the current situation—a

---

[10] Held on 1 May in celebration of Joan of Arc.

Europe dependent on Arab interests and invaded by a population with higher birth rates. The fear of Eurabia became a rallying cry for many anti-Islam activists. In France, many authors and groups, such as Riposte Laïque, Résistance Républicaine and Identitaires, are now using this concept, as are some Catholic conservatives, for instance those belonging to the association known as Observatoire de l'Islamisation.

It should be noted that there is an ambiguity at the heart of these activists' arguments. In one way, Islam is seen as a threat to social progress because of its conservative elements. Among these elements, emphasised by opponents, are sexual and gender issues. The situation of Muslim women remains one of the main arguments opposed to the growth of this religion. The 'Muslim' is considered as misogynous and unable to accept the evolution of the condition of women:

> In Islam the woman is a slave. Sometimes the worst man in the country is still considered a better person than any woman. I mean all the rapes, the legal rapes, rapes never brought to trial, all the molested women, the forced marriages … and what about the excision? When will a brave politician in France say: I will jail everyone who practices excision?

Setting aside the interviews, publications by the anti-Islam network all focus on the issue of headscarves, symbols of their rhetoric. The whole history of women's rights and achievements is seen as swept aside by the 'Islamic invasion'. The male domination of Islam is seen as a paradigmatic illustration of the violent social relations believed to be the basis of this religion. Along similar lines, the question of homosexuality is a frequent topic of anti-Islam speeches, drawing attention to the backward-looking worldviews of Islam.

This reactionary character of the Muslim religion, in comparison to well-developed Western countries, could be associated with the forms of homo-nationalism denounced by influential authors such as Puar (2012) or Judith Butler (2010). It appeals to the same mechanics: Islam is the expression of an antiquated condition of societies. Reference to the Middle Ages is a recurrent topic, as is the obscurantist characterisation. This perspective allows the activists to present their fight as a struggle of the 'moderns' against the 'old guard'. It explains the war rhetoric always adopted to justify their involvement, a way of defending modern society against Islam's assault on Europe. Muslims are denounced for their supposed 'spirit of conquest'. It is relevant to note all the terms used associated with the rhetoric of religion wars: 'crusades', *'reconquista'*, 'inquisition'. Islam must be treated as it was in the years of its expulsion from Western Europe, after the golden age of Al-Andalus.[11] The Muslim man is not only a misogynist, he is a warrior and an invader. Modernity should remain the answer even if a new war is necessary to win.

The negative vision of Islam cannot be the sole explanation of the hatred and fear of French people and of the advantage that the far right tries to gain by playing on it. We have to consider its growing audience: number of mosques, Islamic associations, *halal* shops (Kepel 2012). This obvious increase of visibility has contributed to the spread of feelings of insecurity in the face of this new social area. It has been facilitated by the French prohibition on the publication of statistics about religion, preventing objective knowledge of the Muslim population in France. Unofficial statistics circulate among activists ('Sometimes you read 3 million Muslims, but everybody knows, all the researchers know it is really more, three or four times more'). This demographic argument is the basis of the new issue of Islamophobic activists spreading fear of a drastic change that will occur in the population of France, being replaced by a 'new one' with foreign cultures and religions: in effect, the 'white' natives are going to disappear under the influx of newcomers.

The fear of this growing number is tending to take the place, for those who use it, of the similar argument used about immigration and immigrant numbers in previous decades by Front National. The rhetoric of anti-Islam activism comes really close to this, with a progressive association with Islam of other social and political problems such as insecurity, delinquency and cultural conflicts. It is how anti-Islam is joining forces with the classical far right. If we consider that many aspects of the struggle took place in the name of modernity, there are similarities that explain this rapid appropriation by old far-right activists. Islam is also fought by emphasising conservative issues, sometimes in the name of the French Catholic past, sometimes in ethnic terms of cultural offence. But one

---

[11] 'Islam : out of Europe' is nowadays a regular slogan of far-right demonstrations.

of the main trends is to denounce the 'laxity' of the government, which is accused of having played an active role in this growth of Islam. The spirit of tolerance and anti-racism of the elites is rejected as vector of the diffusion of Islam. Most governments are usually considered complicit in this decisive turn. But this anti-state issue is also an opportunity for divisions, especially in terms of political strategy. In 2012, the new socialist government and its 'progressive' legislation, especially about same-sex marriage, has faced a very strong right-wing oriented social protest movement, uniting different kinds of contestation, anti-LGBT, Catholic, anti-taxes, which caused sharp divisions among anti-Islam activists. Far-right activists, Christians and a large fraction of Riposte Laïque decided to join the protests, even if it meant being associated with real extremists or Christian fundamentalists such as Civitas. Other leaders, including Christine Tasin, ex-leftist, refused to demonstrate with these excessively conservative groups. How far can a struggle focusing on Islam remain really active in the long term? Is the issue forceful enough to ensure sufficient activism to maintain these collective activities?

Good Practice

Anti-bodies Involved in Anti-Racist and Anti-Homophobic Activity[12]

How can civil society protest against this rising discrimination in public spaces? This section looks at action against sexism, racism and homophobia. There are multiple struggles concerning many domains of social activity. We decided to include in this analysis three issues that seem to be central because of the specific consequences they can imply: political, juridical and pedagogical action against discrimination. The first of them, political fight, is shared by most organisations actively involved in these

---

[12] We conducted interviews with four anti-racist organisations : Mouvement contre le Racisme et pour l'Amitié entre les Peuples (MRAP); Collectif contre la Xénophobie; Indigènes de la République; Collectif contre l'Islamophobie en France; two anti-homophobic organisations : Femmes solidaires; Le Refuge; two organisations combining the two issues of racism and homophobia : Perspectives Plurielles; Lesbians of Colour.

issues. The tools used are all those of classical demonstrations, lobbying and activism to show that racism or homophobia are not isolated views but products of a more general system of discrimination that leads to the normalisation of rejecting people. The juridical fight is a growing instrument, helped by developments in French law allowing any victim to sue in a specific court. We also chose to look at educational initiatives that try to spread good practice and show the social effects of discrimination.

Our field work was carried out with associations involved in two specific orientations, anti-racism and homophobia. In the first case, we interviewed people from MRAP (Mouvement contre le Racisme et pour l'Amitié entre les Peuples), one of the oldest organisations in the field. It was born from an active movement of the French Resistance during World War II, the National Movement against Racism, whose concrete goals were the protection and safeguarding of children at risk of deportation. After the war, it developed relationships with political organisations such as the French communist party. The MRAP has been a part of every historical step of the anti-racist struggle since then, and played a central role in the adoption in 1972 of the first law to ban racist language. It had to face the arrival of 'newcomers' in the 1980s, such as the SOS-Racisme movement linked to the Socialist Party. MRAP continued to occupy a strong left position, linked to social movements involved in the defence of minorities, Roma people or illegal immigrants claiming regularization. Apart from its singular historical background, the MRAP was an interesting organisation to investigate because of its position on Islamophobia.

We also decided to take an interest in Indigènes de la République, a controversial association that became a specific political party defending a 'postcolonial' approach to social and cultural problems related to immigration from previously colonised countries. Perspectives Plurielles and LOCS (Lesbians of Colour) are interested in the combined effects of three social relations: gender, class and origin, whether or not the notion of intersectionality is applied. They try to articulate individual, collective and official history. They analyse the different and unequal distribution of resources (time, economic and cultural capital, geography, mobility, etc.) along sex, nationality and social status lines. They integrate generational differences. LOCS's approach is defined as intersectional: members are all lesbians who have had experience of being racialised or dominated by mainstream feminism, which is white. They are French lesbians, of immigrant origin or refugees, all from former colonies, from a 'former slave background'. In their 'lesboprides' they promote debates on new populist right parties in Europe, seeking international ways of resistance and developing international solidarity.

LGBT Movements

To achieve broad coverage of the active LGBT organisations fighting discrimination, we selected organisations that differed in size and orientation. Inter-LGBT and Centre LGBT Paris are two large structures bringing together various smaller grassroots organisations. By organising events such as Gay Pride or providing refuges and support for LGBT victims, they fight homophobia. Fier-e-s strongly defends feminism within the LGBT action field. Association des Journalistes LGBT (AJL) tries to improve the treatment of these issues in the media. Finally, Acceptess-T defends transsexual rights.

One of the main priorities emphasised by LGBT activists is the need to build unity around the cause of LGBT rights. The feeling of loss after the huge 'anti-marriage-for-all' movement of 2012–2013 is closely linked to this inability to oppose a single strong voice. The scattering of organisations and the lack of involvement in all forms of political activity have left the 'community' without any big structure of representation, without channels to express an LGBT point of view that could be validated by a large proportion of members. The problem is reinforced by the fact that La Manif pour Tous has, on the contrary, managed to come up with a common set of values to defend in public spaces, thus giving an impression of unity.

The question of links with established political organisations has been discussed for a long time, as it is seen as a key explanation for the decline of LGBT activism. The claiming of the LGBT question inside the political sphere prevented the construction of a real strong independent political movement for LGBT communities. The government led the debates on the same-sex marriage bill in Parliament, particularly on all the issues concerning ways for gay and lesbian couples to have children, including assisted reproductive technology and surrogacy. To obtain rights it is impossible to avoid politics, but they represent the final step after the various grassroots activities central to the daily fight.

Many LGBT groups are willing to import the right to use new reproductive technologies that have been shown to be effective in other countries. Once again, it is from the United States that some ideas to be used in the French context have come to improve the spread of LGBT rights. The movement is being encouraged to make greater use of the courts, a key tactic in all the benefits won by same-sex couples in the USA. Even if France has a different legal tradition, there are French judicial tools not yet exploited by the activists. The judicial way has proved to be more effective than politics or many fieldwork activities. It is important in particular to consider the fact that the European Court of Human Rights has often ruled in favour of gay and lesbian couples; its Anglo-Saxon-inspired conception of judicial decisions is seen as a great opportunity by activists involved in minority rights.

Anti-racist and anti-homophobic organisations have been engaged in education and the transmission of good practices. Through scholarly activities and youth theatre, they try to make students think about clichés and change their attitude towards the 'other'. They organise group dynamics and role plays to increase students' awareness of the power of discrimination.

Conclusion

France occupies a special place in the history of far-right movements, as the birthplace, at the turn of the twentieth century, of the ideas, values and emerging trends that led to the building of fascism and Nazism in the surrounding countries. It also has a long history of racism and discrimination associated with its specific characteristic of an old country of immigration, already significant at the end of the nineteenth century. The country has recently seen the development of national far-right movements overtly supporting racist ideas. This development may be related to the so-called crisis of globalisation that is characterised by the growth of finance and decreased industrialisation in Europe. Although there have always been hate speeches against migrants, Jews, Muslims or any groups categorised as 'different', these were regarded as taboo subjects. Since the turn of the millennium common voices have been emerging. Several events, especially electoral ones, have facilitated the visibility and popular support of far-right forces. The presidential elections of 2002 when the leader of the National Front, Jean-Marie Le Pen, gained more votes than the Socialist candidate and was in the second round can be considered as the pick of the liberation of far-right ideas.

We decided to focus on Front National and the network of anti-Islam movements. We explained how the latter were inspired by dissident FN leaders when the party started its process of normalisation. Muslims became the target group for racist speeches and racist activity. Those undertaken by far-right fractions such as Identitaires are violent and they claim to be part of an international front against Islam.

Paradoxically, France is also the country of human rights where a strong panel of political and grassroots organisations have been active for a very long time. However, official investment against discrimination is fairly recent. The future of the issue seems to be really uncertain. On one side, Front National has achieved its best electoral scores in recent years and the influence of its ideas has been growing through the country. On the other side, opportunities to publicise discrimination and to 'fight it through the recognition of the victims have multiplied.

References

Aron, R. (1970). *Marxismes imaginaires. D'une Sainte famille à une autre.* Paris: Gallimard.

Butler, J. (2010). http://*nohomonationalism.blogspot*.com/2010/06/*judith-butler*

Camus, J.-Y. (2009). http://tempspresents.com/2009/08/31/jean-yves-camus-la-nouvelle-droite-francaise-et-son-rapport-avec-mai-68/

Checcaglini, C. (2012). *Bienvenue au Front.* Paris: Jacob-Duvernet.

Collovald, A. (2005). *Le populisme du FN. Un dangereux contre-sens.* Bellecombes-en-Beauge: Editions du Croquant.

Deze, A. (2004). Lectures critiques. *Revue française de science politique, 54*(1), 179–199.

Kepel, G. (2012). *Quatre-vingt-treize.* Paris: Gallimard.

Gollnish, B. (1985). *Une âme pour la France. Pour en finir avec le génocide culturel.* Paris: Albatros.

Guilluy, C. (2014). *La France périphérique. Comment on a sacrifié les classes populaires.* Paris: Flammarion.

Lipset, S., & Rokkan, S. (1967). *Party systems and voter alignments: Cross-national perspectives.* New York: Free Press.

Mascré, D. (2010). *De la France.* Éditions de l'Infini. Reims, Editions de l'infini.

Molnar, T. (1969). *The counter revolution.*

Monnerot, J. (1970a). *Démarxiser l'université.* Paris: La Table ronde.

Monnerot, J. (1970b). *La France intellectuelle.* Paris: R. Bourgine.

Nolte, E. (1966). *Three faces of fascism: Action française, Italian fascism, national socialism.* New York: Holt, Rinehart and Winsto.

Puar, J. (2012). *Homonationalisme. Politiques queers après le 11 septembre.* Paris: Amsterdam.

Ye'or, B. (2006). *Eurabia, l'axe euro-arabe.* Paris: Jean-Cyrille Godfroy. http://www.dreuz.info/2015/02/19/attentats-islamistes-contre-charlie-hebdo-lhypercacher-et-copenhague-lanalyse-geopolitique-de-bat-yeor/.

Sternell, Z. (1978). *La droite révolutionnaire: 1885–1914: les origines française du fascisme.* Paris, Éditions du Seuil.

4

Hegemonic Discourses of Difference and Inequality: Right-Wing Organisations in Austria

Birgit Sauer and Edma Ajanovic

Introducing Right-Wing Discourses on Difference and Inequality: From Margin to Mainstream

A discussion on right-wing discourses in Austria inevitably has to start by referring to the Austrian Freedom Party (Freiheitliche Partei Österreich, FPÖ). The FPÖ is not only the major right-wing player in Austria's political landscape and a competitor to the two established parties, the Social Democrats (Sozialdemokratische Partei Österreich, SPÖ) and the Christian-conservative Austrian People's Party (Österreichische Volkspartei, ÖVP) (Pelinka 2002) but also one of the pioneers of right-wing populism in Europe. In the 1999 national elections the FPÖ won 26.91 per cent of the vote, the same percentage as the ÖVP (BMI 1999). As a result the ÖVP formed a coalition government with the FPÖ in 2000

B. Sauer (✉) • E. Ajanovic
Department of Political Science, University of Vienna, Vienna, Austria

© The Editor(s) (if applicable) and The Author(s) 2016
G. Lazaridis et al. (eds.), *The Rise of the Far Right in Europe*,
DOI 10.1057/978-1-137-55679-0_4

(Pelinka 2001; BMI 2002). While in the following elections (2002) the FPÖ lost about 16 per cent of its votes the party has recovered since then. In the most recent national elections the FPÖ was third with 20.5 per cent of the vote (2013) and 19.7 per cent at the European Parliament elections in 2014 (BMI 2013, 2014).

Although it seems that FPÖ is occupying the right-wing political space in Austria, in recent years smaller groups and organisations, like the Austrian version of PEGIDA (Patriotic Europeans against the Islamisation of the Occident), Die Identitären (Identitarian Movement) and smaller Citizens' Initiatives have gained importance and public visibility with single-issue strategies focusing on immigration and religion. The ongoing debate on the building of mosques and Islamic cultural centres, for instance, has been addressed by Citizens' Initiatives, which protested against the construction of these buildings. Most of these initiatives are no longer active, but in 2007 and 2008 they mobilised thousands of people with their concerns and in 2011 they formed the network Movement pro Austria (Bewegung Pro Österreich, BPÖ). Although FPÖ and Citizens' Initiatives differ—one being a party while the initiatives can be perceived as civil society organisations—they have a lot in common and seem to complement each other. Together they construct and promote a hegemonic discourse of difference and inequality especially regarding the issues of migration, 'Muslims' and 'the' Islam. Both FPÖ and Citizens' Initiatives not only construct similar images of the immigrant and Muslim 'other' but they cooperate on local and community levels, for instance in Vienna.

There has been much literature in recent years seeking to explain the emergence and growth of the political right in Austria. Some of this literature refers to Austria's fascist past, others to the tradition of the country's political culture of consensus and the closed two-party system up to the 1990s; others refer to the neoliberal restructuring of the formerly strong Austrian welfare state (Heinisch 2012; Wiegel 2013; Poglia Mileti et al. 2002). This chapter intends to add two new aspects to this literature. It first aims at contributing to the explanation of the success of right-wing populist and extremist groups in Austria by analysing how they organise consent around issues of migration and thus create hegemony by mobilising racist, sexist and homophobic arguments of (natural or cultural) difference, inequality and hence exclusion. This struggle for consent based on shared understanding, moreover, evokes images of a natural binary constellation between 'them' and 'us', partly referring to an existing discourse of difference in Austria. The antagonistic chain of equivalence between 'them' and 'us' (Laclau 2005) not only turns migrants, Muslims, LGBT people, feminists and 'the' elite into 'others' but forges these narratives in a perspective of difference and inequality, of belonging and non-belonging. Second, we want to better understand counter-strategies of anti-discrimination and anti-racist civil society groups and assess their success or failure. While the Austrian political right has gained electoral success and has been able to influence public debates on immigration, several organisations and initiatives exist that try to fight discrimination, hate speech and racism. Some of their public activities, for example the Festival of Joy (Fest der Freude)[1] enjoy widespread popularity. Nevertheless, these anti-racist groups seem to be unable to stop the wave of successes of right-wing groups or to create a counter-hegemonic compromise against practices of inequality and exclusion. We contend that right-wing hegemony on exclusionary racism explains how difficult it is for anti-discrimination groups to establish a counter-strategy to the right-wing discourse of difference and inequality.

This chapter focuses on one hand on the FPÖ and Viennese Citizens' Initiatives against mosques and Islamic cultural centres, and on the other hand on seven NGOs fighting racism and discrimination. The chapter draws on interviews with four members of the FPÖ and three members of the Citizens' Initiatives conducted in 2013. In the pre-election atmosphere of 2013 top FPÖ functionaries were not available for interview. Therefore, our FPÖ interviewees came from the lower ranks of federal, municipal and district level. The sample was composed of one female member of FPÖ's Federal Council, two male members of municipal councils, one male member of a district council, and the spokespersons of three Viennese initiatives against mosques. We also attended one of the

---

[1] This event was first held at the Viennese *Heldenplatz* on 8 May 2013 by several organisations working in the field of anti-fascism. It now takes place annually on 8 May to celebrate the liberation of Austria from National Socialism. Until 2013 the right-wing fraternities had gathered at this historic place in the city centre and 'occupied' it for their annual remembrance march in memory of the fallen Austrian 'Wehrmacht comrades'. The Fest der Freude put an end to this controversial gathering.

Citizens' Initiatives 'regulars' tables' and did ethnographic research. During our participation and observation we listened without intervening to the agenda of meetings with questions—bearing in mind, however, that our mere presence as researchers was an intervention. We made field notes during and after the observations. The aim of our observation was to grasp the agenda of the meeting and to identify the roles of the participants in the organisation and their interactions. To interpret this material we conducted a content analysis and identified how—by applying which images, metaphors and symbols—right-wing populist groups use, produce and reproduce racist and sexist narratives in a discourse of difference and inequality. Furthermore, we interviewed seven representatives of Vienna-based organisations engaging in anti-racism, anti-fascism and anti-discrimination work. The organisations we interviewed can be divided into two groups: the first engages in legal, psychological and social counselling, the second focuses on advocacy work by campaigning against racism, right-wing populist discourse and practices of exclusion and 'othering'. Unfortunately we were not able to recruit self-organisations of migrants or asylum seekers for interview.

The chapter argues as follows. We begin our discussion with a contextualisation of the political situation of right-wing populist parties and organisations as well as NGOs fighting right-wing extremism and racism. To understanding both the rise of right-wing populism and the struggles of anti-racist and anti-discrimination forces requires a contextualisation in terms of both the transformation of party politics since World War II and the neoliberalisation of Austrian society and politics since the mid-1990s. Then we elaborate on our concepts of cultural hegemony and structural racism, i.e., on racism as a shared value and social practices of building consensus (Omi and Winant 2002: 29; Hall 2000). Racism, we argue, is not located at the margins but in the centre of modern Western societies. Also, we conceptualise racism as an ongoing process, as a struggle over meaning; racist structures and activities correspond, hence, to racist narrations, i.e., narrations of (natural) inequality. To be successful racism needs to become 'a shared attitude'. Therefore, our analysis concentrates on the assessment of metaphors, symbols and narratives of right-wing populist groups and their way of creating racist chains of equivalence by mobilising antagonism in the fields of migration, Islam, gender relations and sexual orientation. Thereafter, we scrutinise possible factors in the Austrian right wing's success by analysing the discourses of difference and inequality promoted by the FPÖ as well as the Citizens' Initiatives. Right-wing actors not only claim freedom of speech and the right to tell the 'truth' about 'the' Islam and migration problems (Bojadžijev and Demirović 2002: 10) but, as we shall see, they mainstream their perspectives on 'others', presenting their worldview as a common, shared one by referring to conflicts and antagonistic structures in Austrian society. Finally, we present counter-hegemonic strategies and the struggle against right-wing hegemony by anti-racist and anti-discrimination groups. We elaborate the strategies undertaken by these organisations to oppose right-wing discourse and hegemony.

Right-Wing Populism in Austria: Contextualisation

Right-wing populism today has to be contextualised first in the country's political landscape after World War II and second in the neoliberal social and political transformations that have occurred since the mid-1990s. Furthermore, contextualising Austrian right-wing populism is ultimately linked to the emergence of the Freedom Party Austria, which has dominated right-wing populist discourse since the late 1980s. As we argue elsewhere (Ajanovic et al. 2016) most currently emerging right-wing populist movements and initiatives in Austria do not seem to compete with the FPÖ but rather complement their claims. The Austrian FPÖ—different from other right-wing parties in Europe—has a long tradition in the legacy of National Socialism. After World War II members of the former National Socialist Party (NSDAP) in Austria were given the opportunity to form a new party, the 'Union of Independents' (Verband der Unabhängigen/VdU). In 1955, the year of Austria's independence from the occupying powers the USA, UK, France and Soviet Union, the party was renamed as FPÖ, but remained embedded in a German-national ideology and anti-Semitist frames. While in the following decades, the FPÖ 'modernised' its ideology and organisational structures the German-national tradition shapes the ideology of the FPÖ to this day

(Pelinka 2002: 286ff). The party's notion of the 'folk' and the 'homeland', for instance, can be traced back to German-national ideology:

> The high-value term of '*Heimat*' (fatherland/home) triggers many emotional connotations and addresses more evocative and solidarity-promoting meanings than 'state' or 'nation'. It is therefore mainly used by German nationalists who endorse an ethnically defined nation alluding to a kind of greater 'German nation'. (Richardson and Wodak 2009: 254, emphasis in original)

Due to its fascist past and tradition, the party was for a long time excluded from the wider political landscape (Pelinka 2002: 286). Austrian postwar democracy from the 1950s was organised as social partnership (*Sozialpartnerschaft*) in a consociational democracy. After World War II and the experience of the civil war at the beginning of the 1930s the two major parties, the Social Democrats and the Christian-conservative ÖVP, the trades unions, the chamber of labour (*Arbeiterkammer*) and the Austrian chambers of trade engaged in a rather closed system of consensual decision making mainly, but not only in the field of economic and labour-market policies. In effect, this system divided social and political power between the two established parties (Tálos 2006). This 'division of power', often institutionalised as 'great coalitions' in government between the two parties, worked until the end of the 1980s, leaving hardly any room for other parties or movements (Sauer and Ajanovic 2014).

However, Austrian 'modernisation from above' from the 1970s (Penz 2010) slowly opened the political system up to social movements and new parties. In 1986, Jörg Haider launched a '*coup d'état*' within the FPÖ and systematically reorganised the party in the direction of a 'new' right-wing populist or 'anti-establishment party' (Schedler 1996). Since the late 1980s, therefore, the FPÖ has been able to position itself as one of the three major parties—however not fully abandoning its traditional anti-Semitism (Pelinka 2002: 287).

The era of economic globalisation since the 1990s and Austria's accession to the European Union in 1995 resulted in fundamental social changes. Austerity policies, cuts in social welfare provision, the creation of low-wage sectors and the consolidation of precarious working conditions have led to rising unemployment, the precarisation of working conditions, growing social disintegration and rising poverty (Penz 2010). This neoliberal restructuring has nurtured fears of social degradation, marginalisation and the insecurity of both the working and lower-middle classes (Sauer and Ajanovic 2014; Poglia Mileti et al. 2002: 5). As a result of these transformations both the Austrian two-party system and the social partnership model lost their legitimacy. This situation created a window of opportunity for the participation of civil society groups, for the establishment of new parties, such as the Greens, but also for the FPÖ to enter the political stage (Heinisch 2012: 372). The FPÖ campaigned particularly on opposing the consensus-oriented system of social partnership as a corrupt system. Hence, it was able to criticise the neoliberal project, which in its view stood for a 'politics of deterioriation' in need of a new legitimation strategy (Bojadžijev and Demirović 2002: 12, own translation). While the neoliberal project tried to disempower workers' organisations, the FPÖ shifted the antagonism of workers versus employers to new antagonisms such as anti-establishment, 'lazy unemployed' and migrants, who were now portrayed as a burden. This strategy was successful in winning support at least from the group which seemed and feared to be affected by the restructurings of the neoliberal project—namely the Austrian workers (ibid.: 13).

It is hence not surprising that the conservative Wolfgang Schüssel of the Austrian People's Party (ÖVP) found a partner in the FPÖ for the government coalition after the 1999 national elections (ibid.: 12). This coalition of 2000 was subjected to fierce national and EU criticism. Nevertheless, FPÖ and later BZÖ[2] remained in government until 2006 and pushed through a neoliberal agenda by weakening the unions and the Chamber of Labour (*Arbeiterkammer*). After Haider's death in 2008 Heinz-Christian Strache re-oriented the FPÖ on an anti-immigration and anti-Muslim course. However, migration had already become an important topic for the FPÖ with the introduction of the 'Austria First' referendum in 1993 by the FPÖ, calling for a curb on immigration and restrictive immigration laws. Since then the FPÖ has systematically established a discourse of difference and exclusion, especially with regard to immigration and,

---

[2] In a move to reorganise the FPÖ Haider split the party and founded the BZÖ (Bewegung Zukunft Österreich/Movement for the Future of Austria) and gathered liberal-conservatives while trying to exclude the extreme right (Wiegel 2013: 115).

since the turn of the century, 'the Muslims'. As the established parties, and especially the Social Democrats, also moved away from the idea of equality, the FPÖ propagated antagonisms 'diligent' vs. 'lazy workers' or 'our people' vs. 'migrants' became increasingly common parlance (Flecker and Kirschenhofer 2007: 158; Zilian 2002; Albertazzi and McDonnell 2008: 220). In the following years FPÖ's demands were increasingly implemented into a restrictive immigration and asylum system.

> Looking at some of the claims [of the Austria first referendum, comm. by the authors] it is clear that Austria with respect to the discourse as well as the legislation was never closer to these—back then 'no-go' claims—than ever before in the history of the Second Republic. (Zerbes 2012, own translation)

A comprehensive shift in migration legislation, the Alien Law of 2005 (*Fremdenrechtspaket*) was pushed through by ÖVP, SPÖ and FPÖ/BZÖ votes (Schumacher 2008: 1; Zerbes 2012). Hence, some of the initially 'no-go claims' of the 1990s became exclusionary laws in the frame of the shift towards more 'inequality' among the established parties and in general.

This backdrop of restrictive migration policy and communal racism towards migrants and Muslims—introduced on a global level, especially after 9/11—further paved the way for anti-Muslim civil initiatives such as those opposing the building of mosques—to jump on this hegemonic bandwagon of difference, inequality and exclusion. The anti-mosque movements did not necessarily introduce 'new' topics, but rather intensified the already existing discourse against immigrants and Muslims which was strongly shaped by the FPÖ. Nevertheless, as we will argue below, Citizens' Initiatives mainly focus on anti-Muslim racism, while the FPÖ's claims are more diverse—also focusing on the antagonism between 'us'—the Austrians—and 'them'—the migrants in general.

Fighting for Hegemony: Racism as a Social Practice

Once and for all I will state this principle: a given society is racist or it is not. (Fanon 2008: 63)

In this section we elaborate our concept of racism and hegemony by discussing particular characteristics, forms and functions of racism. Understanding racism as a social practice gives an indication of why right-wing populist and extremist groups are successful and why—although present in a great number—anti-racist, anti-fascist and anti-discrimination movements and parties that follow inclusionary politics are marginalised and in a 'weak' position (Pühretmayer 2002: 304). In the context of right-wing extremist and populist groups, racism, as one of their major ideological pillars, is often discussed as an 'extreme' practice (Schiedel 2007: 24). We argue following Terkessidis (2004: 68) that racism is not a phenomenon located on the fringes of society but has to be understood as a social practice functional for European societies (also Hall 2000: 10, 12). In Colette Guillaumin's (1995) understanding, racism is an everyday behaviour as well as being embedded in state and institutional structures. Its 'banality', the fact that it is deeply embedded in everyday practices and that it has become a form of societal knowledge explains its persistence (Terkessidis 2004: 109). Moreover, racist thought patterns and undisputed practices build a solid foundation for right-wing populists to create a 'shared purpose' and a hegemonic discourse based on (natural) inequality and, hence, exclusion.

As we shall see, racism as a social practice is used in Austria for the political project of right-wing parties and groups. Both focus their strategy to at the same time reach and construct 'the people' by creating antagonistic chains of equivalence between an 'us' versus 'the other', be it migrants, the elites, the establishment, feminists or homosexuals. At the same time they appeal to society as a family, to 'national purity' and to 'order' (Guillaumin 1995: 168). The construction and legitimation of difference and inequality—based on biological or cultural arguments—is central to racist practices. This struggle for hegemony therefore includes gender as well as sexuality to stress the argument of biology. It includes first, the production of knowledge with regard to allegedly 'distinct' groups of humans, also known as 'processes of racialization' (Miles and Brown 2003: 90, 99). This form of knowledge gives meaning to certain characteristics in order to classify and divide human beings. Second, racist hegemony encompasses practices of exclusion of particular 'groups' from material, cultural and symbolic resources (Hall 2000; Terkessidis 2004). Hence, right-wing discourse and strategies include 'inequality' and 'difference' as characteristics (Holzer after Schiedel 2007; Goetz 2014).

In the following we discuss the characteristics and functions of racism on which our analysis of the discursive strategies of two right-wing groups and counter-strategies rests. Racism as social practice and as struggle for hegemony includes processes of racialisation, i.e. social processes 'by which meanings are attributed to real or imagined human characteristics' (Miles and Brown 2003: 87). Moreover, practices of exclusion based on racialisation contribute to a right-wing racist project, however with important contextual differences (Bojadžijev and Demirović 2002; Guillaumin 1995: 160). While biological racism has been to a certain extent replaced in the 'new' right's discourse and strategy, the construction of cultural differences, i.e. racialisation based on cultural characteristics and exclusionary practices, has become more evident (Hall 2000: 11; Balibar 1991). However, this does not mean that 'nature' is banned from right-wing discourse. On the contrary, an important characteristics of processes of racialisation is to give meaning to alleged phenotypical, to sociological, symbolic or imaginary differences while at the same time presenting these characteristics as natural differences (Hall 2000: 8; Guillaumin 1998: 166, 167). Classification on natural and cultural grounds not only serves to hierarchise groups (Miles and Brown 2003: 102) but also to exclude certain groups or to force these groups to assimilated. 'New' forms of racism, for instance ethno-pluralism, do not explicitly hierarchise but call for the preservation of different 'cultural units'—allegedly perceived as equally important—and for the 'right and [and duty] to be different' (see also Terkessidis 2004: 82). However, this also leads to separation into distinct groups. Furthermore the right and duty to be different naturalises the idea of 'our folk' and implies that the presence of 'others' in the 'own cultural unit' is already problematic (Balibar 1991: 21). Therefore, racialisation involves power, as it shifts power to the 'us' group and at the same time disempowers the 'others' (Terkessidis 2004: 99). Hence, the power to differentiate is linked to a particular practice of exclusion or the power of one group to exclude 'the other' from material, cultural and symbolic resources.[3] Symbolic exclusion, then, is the allocation of the constructed group of 'others' outside the 'family of nation', i.e. the 'us' group (Hall 2000: 13, 14). Against this backdrop symbolic exclusion is a process that not only intensifies the construction of 'the other', but also serves to consolidate the 'us' group as homogeneous and as sharing a common set of values (Terkessidis 2004: 105). To put it another way, the antagonistic relationship of 'us' and 'them' refers to the fear of not knowing who 'we' are (Hall 2000: 15). Therefore, the 'others' serve as the 'mirror-inverted opposite' of the 'own' values (Terkessidis 2004: 105). Racism as a social practice of racialisation and 'exclusion through inclusion' (ibid.: 101) not only legitimises the privileges of the 'us' group but aims at establishing a 'consensus' within the 'us' group (Hall 2000: 14) and, hence, cultural hegemony (Terkessidis 2004: 104).

We might conclude that right-wing populism establishes a political project of racism as a hegemonic practice. The fact that right-wing discourse appeals to existing racist knowledge and actively creates racist antagonism by evoking chains of equivalence of sexism, homophobia, anti-intellectualism and anti-elitism explains to a certain extent the success of the right wing in fostering discourses of difference and inequality as well as exclusionary practices in institutions. Our analysis of two Austrian right-wing organisations in the following section will discuss the discursive strategies which serve the construction of a particular 'other'—currently constructed as 'the Muslims' and 'the migrants',—the naturalisation of 'differences' between 'us' and 'them' and (the legitimation of) (symbolic) exclusion.

---

[3] For an analysis of the construction of 'foreigners' in Germany and their exclusion on different dimensions, see Terkessidis (2004).

Right-Wing Discourses in Austria: Constructing 'Others', Intensifying Difference, Inequality and Exclusion

> Back then a particular ethnic group was blamed. Today, it is a different one. (FPÖ Int. 1)

The FPÖ and the Citizens' Initiatives against the building of mosques feed into racist discourses by intensifying the idea of natural and irreconcilable 'difference' among human beings or 'groups'. In current right-wing discourses in Austria we have identified two forms of racism, one focusing on Muslims,[4] the other on migrants as the constructed 'other' (Krzyanowski 2013). The latter can be understood as xeno-racism, as Liz Fekete (2001) convincingly argued. In xeno-racist articulations it is the 'foreigner' (*Ausländer*) or 'migrant' who is constructed as 'the other'. An ideological grounding against the constructed 'others' is missing in such articulations and the antagonism is rather based on a naturalised logic of ethnicised competition. In the following we will describe right-wing discursive strategies that construct the (unequal) 'other', symbolically excluding this 'other' and legitimising the superiority and privileges of the 'us' group. This demonstrates how right-wing groups intensify 'discourses of difference' (Hall 2000) and in doing so appeal to the 'racist knowledge' that is embedded in society (Terkessidis 2004) and create a common sense of inequality and exclusion.

Migrants: A Conditional Inclusion

Since the FPÖ's 'Austria First' referendum in 1993, migration has become the key topic in Austrian right-wing populism. Since then, migration has acted as a catalyst for the party's transformation into a populist party. The FPÖ's major mobilisation strategy includes a shift towards an antagonistic understanding of the relationship of 'us' and 'them', represented by migrants. The referendum called for restrictions on immigration.

---

[4] For a theoretical discussion see Müller-Uri (2014).

Although the referendum was not successful, it was the starting point for a transformation of Austrian public discourse on migration. Its nativist rhetoric is still present in the current discursive strategies (Richardson and Wodak 2009: 261). Following the logic of racism, the FPÖ constructs an antagonism between migrants and the 'us' group while leaving open the question of who actually belongs to this group of 'us'. To make 'the people' an empty signifier feeds the idea that everybody 'knows' who belongs and who does not belong, who is Austrian and who is not. In other words, not defining 'the people' suggests a common understanding and consenting definition of this entity. The alleged 'contradiction' between 'us' and 'them', moreover, underlines that the symbolic inclusion of migrants in the 'us' group is conditional and this feeds into the racist construction of 'the migrant other'.

> Austria first. First we have to look after our people and those who have migrated here but are already Austrian, or who are not yet Austrian, but are well integrated, and who work, who are not criminal. Then I don't care whether or not they already have Austrian citizenship, whether or not they are neo-Austrians. Once he is an Austrian, than he is an Austrian, regardless where he came from. He just has to behave properly. (FPÖ Int. 2)

The statement 'Austria First', already used in 1993, points on the one hand to the importance of policies that serve the needs of 'our people'. On the other hand it constructs 'our people' as commonly understood. However, the FPÖ official above cited takes it upon himself to define and expand the notion of 'the people'. In his statement he includes migrants who have acquired Austrian citizenship but at the same time he defines important characteristics of 'our people': 'those who are well integrated, and who work, who are not criminal' and those 'who behave properly' (FPÖ Int. 2). It is thus citizenship on the one hand and a set of common values on the other hand, which seem to be the criteria for inclusion. However, this belonging and inclusion is only conditional. Migrants with Austrian citizenship are singled out as 'neo-Austrians' (ibid.) in contrast to a genuine 'us' group, probably based on the understanding of a homogeneous 'folk' of Austrians, essential to racist discourse of right-wing groups in Austria (Schiedel 2007: 25; Holzer 1993: 34, 35). This is also evident in another statement, which differentiates among allegedly homogeneous 'migrant groups', again demonstrating that 'Christianity' (FPÖ Int. 2) can serve as a criterion for inclusion and the construction of the rather different other, i.e. 'the Muslims' (ibid.). Christianity serves as a 'natural' common ground for understanding—in contrast to the alleged 'natural' difference of 'Muslims'. The following quote illustrates this division between migrants who fit and those who don't fit by referring to religion and to a sort of 'natural' 'national pride':

> [B]ecause we have cared a lot about the Serbs as a voter group, because they are Christians like us, we have more in common with them than with the Muslims, e.g. the Turks. ... They also do not speak German perfectly, but they work and integrate and do not stand out negatively. They often come to us because they are from countries where national pride is the norm. (FPÖ Int. 2)

The FPÖ party official frames 'the Serbs' as similar to 'us' by claiming that they 'work and integrate and do not stand out negatively'. At the same time he constructs this group of migrants in opposition to 'the Muslims' and to Turks (ibid.). While Serbs are included in a Christian 'us' Muslims and Turks are excluded from this 'us' group due to a lack of similarities, lack of language knowledge and lack of the shared value of 'national pride'. Hence, the antagonism between 'us' and 'Muslims' is presented as irreconcilable while other migrant groups such as refugees might be included if they 'behave properly' (ibid.) or do not 'exploit the asylum system' (FPÖ Int. 2). This differentiation among the constructed groups of migrants further demonstrates the mechanism of hierarchisation inherent in most forms of racism.

Muslims

Anti-Muslim racism is not only the most obvious form of racism applied by the FPÖ and the Viennese Citizens' Initiatives but has become the main form of racist articulation among Europe's right. Although both the FPÖ and the Citizens' Initiatives use anti-Muslim racism, we argue that this is the main issue for the Citizens' Initiative, while the FPÖ is constructing their 'enemy' in a more diverse way—as discussed above—in the form of xeno-racism.[5]

The inequality debate is apparent in the construction of Muslims' insurmountable difference serving as legitimation for their symbolic exclusion. They do not fit into Austria's culture because of their alleged different values (e.g., on gender equality, respect for LGBT, enlightenment, freedom), different habits and customs (food, Christian everyday religious rituals) and different appearance and behaviour (women's body covering) (FPÖ Int. 2, CI Int. 3).

> I don't accept that we have to make adjustments. Pork disappeared from kindergarten but not for health reasons, because it is no worse than beef or turkey …. The crucifix has also been disappearing in schools. And the Nikolo-celebration [performed in schools and kindergartens to honour saint Nikolaus of Myra, comm. by the authors] is also partially abandoned, because the children are afraid. But they were afraid also back then or simply they were not. That is a part of our tradition. (FPÖ Int. 2)

The FPÖ's anti-Muslim mobilisation since 2009 has focused on veiled Muslim women. They are presented both as victims of their patriarchal family and as perpetrators, as they are seen as unwilling to integrate. 'Free women instead of forced veiling', one of the party's election slogans of 2005, not only constructs the Muslim female 'other' but also the emancipated 'us' group. These constructions can be labelled elements of anti-Muslim racism as they tend to 'naturalise' differences and suggest—at least—symbolically excluding Muslims from Austrian society. This framing also shows how right-wing populist antagonism uses gender difference and the issue of sexual identity to construct and exclude the 'other' and to integrate the 'us'.

The FPÖ has successfully spread anti-Muslim racist sentiments. As one consequence Citizens' Initiatives against mosques in several Austrian cities have emerged and anti-Muslim racism has become the single cen-

---

[5] This could also be identified as one difference between the party and the Citizens' Initiative with regard to the analysed material.

tral issue for Citizens' Initiatives. They outline various reasons why the building of Islamic centres and mosques in Vienna is a problem. One argument, for instance, is 'noise pollution' (CI Int. 2), perceived as a problem due to the concentration of people and volume of traffic during prayers in the area where the centre was to be built. However, as the statements below show, the mere presence of 'foreign' people is also portrayed as a problem—again implying a natural difference between 'the people' who are 'scared' and the 'foreigners':

> The problem [with the Islamic Cultural Centre; comm. by the authors] is disturbance] Accordingly … partly aggressive behaviour, when the people are requested to be less loud. Then there is no peace, but it comes to offensive behaviour and therefore people feel threatened. (CI Int. 2)

One interviewee from the FPÖ made a similar argument:

> People are now afraid that many people will come together. They see many foreigners of whom they are afraid anyway…. It is more the symbolic character and the gathering of foreign-looking people that scares people. They are really frightened by it. (FPÖ Int. 1)

'Difference', we contend, is intensified by right-wing populist discourses. Muslims are constructed as a threat and disturbance, as they are 'innately louder, gesticulate more and stand together in groups more often', because 'they' come from 'Southern, Mediterranean countries' (CI Int. 3).

In the statements above, the FPÖ's and Civil Initiatives' officials both refer to a common sense of anxiety and perceived danger to the Austrian population: migrants and especially Muslims are perceived as offensive by 'the Austrians'; Austrians are therefore 'scared' by Muslims. The Muslim 'foreigner' (FPÖ Int. 1) is constructed on different levels, one being the alleged difference in values, as the following statement shows:

> They overrun us and make demands, but I don't want to live like that. We developed from the Middle Ages up, we fought to be able to vote, for social security, to live in peace and now I have to give it up because of a religious war? That's what will happen. (CI Int. 3)

The 'we' are perceived as enlightened, having 'developed since the Middle Ages' and established 'peace' and 'social security' (CI Int. 3). At the same time Muslims are seen as importing war to peaceful Austria, as uncivilised and barbaric and therefore as a threat to the 'own' values (see also Fredette 2015: 55). This statement shows the discourse of difference and inequality intensified to feed into anti-Muslim racism, which serves to consolidate the 'us' group. This consolidation often takes the road of 'femonationalism', as Sara Faris (2012) calls the creation of a gender-equal (Austrian) in-group by the framing of a patriarchal out-group.

Gender and Gender Equality Policies

The intersection of religion and gender creates another antagonism: the issue of traditional gender roles in Muslim communities vs. gender equality in Austrian society.

> [W]hen girls walk alone around the Reumannplatz to the subway, the bus, the foreign youth declares open season on them. Or not the youth but mostly the Turks. They whistle or talk to them stupidly. It's not comfortable and then they do not dare to go out in the evening alone. (FPÖ Int. 2)

In the above statement the 'foreign youth' or 'Turks' (FPÖ Int. 2) are portrayed as not following gender equality values, and contrasted to an imagined 'our youth'. 'Foreign' boys and young men are accused of harassing native girls and failing to value the integrity of women. Hence, migrant young men are perceived as aggressive perpetrators and a threat to Austrian girls and women. On the other hand Austrian girls are seen as victims disciplined through fear. However, our analysis shows rather contradictory strategies with regard to gender equality claims. Gender equality is by no means a political project of the right-wing groups. On the contrary, man and woman are perceived as different 'by nature' in right-wing ideology and discourse (Goetz 2014). The constructed 'others' are, for example, portrayed as family units 'where the woman is not allowed to leave the house without the man' (FPÖ Int. 2), while on the other hand the FPÖ in particular is trying to enforce a 'traditional' gender order. Again, the gender issue serves as an arena to create a common cause against gender equality policies by claiming that women in general are not interested in politics and that feminist demands for gender equality are against women's own will:

> Should we introduce 50:50 [refers to a potential gender quota in his party, meaning that half of the representatives should be women; comm. by the authors] then it is men who would be discriminated against, because interestingly it is men who are more interested in politics than women. You can see that in private life too, my girlfriend is not interested in it at all. (FPÖ Int. 4)

Our analysis also shows that the right-wing discourse relies on a 'natural' difference between men and women, as other authors have shown (Goetz 2014). For instance one representative criticises the 'social shift' that 'women' do not want to have children because they are 'forced' into wage labour (FPÖ Int. 2 and 3). While women's decision not to have children is seen as detrimental to the Austrian nation, the political elite and feminists are held responsible for this decline of the birth rate. The blaming of elites, here represented by the liberal Greens and Social Democrats, is illustrated by the following statement, in which an FPÖ representative explains why Austrian society is endangered by youth who are becoming increasingly 'irresponsible' (FPÖ Int. 3):

> This social change, with more and more women … having to work and day-care outside the home increasing, and I believe that you cannot learn social skills in day-care outside the home, as the Greens and the SPÖ argue. I still argue that it is the family, that can teach children how to behave. (FPÖ Int. 3)

The Struggles of Counter-Strategies: Civil Organisations Fighting Racism and Discrimination

> To live in a society without anti-racist politics means to be condemned to live in a racist society. (Hall 2000: 9)

In a reaction to the FPÖ's 'Austria First' referendum of 1993, 250,000 people gathered on the streets of Vienna to protest against this petition in a demonstration named 'sea of lights' (*Lichtermeer*). Civil society organisations mobilised against the FPÖ and were able to unite other parties against this exclusionary referendum. This was a starting point for the emergence of a great number of civil society organisations against racism and discrimination, which in the aftermath of the referendum created a constant counter-hegemonic project against racism, sexism and homophobia. In this section we elaborate on existing strategies and outline the possible successes and failures of civil society organisations fighting racism and right-wing extremism, and their potential to establish counter-hegemony. Counter-hegemony, we contend, needs first of all to deconstruct the chains of equivalence and hence, shared arguments against difference and inequality by stressing the right to difference and the necessity of equality and equal treatment. In general we found that in the context of everyday racism, of exclusionary hegemonic racism as embedded in everyday practices, including sexism and homophobia it is difficult to mobilise on a large scale and especially to permeate social and institutional practices. The following describes first, how representatives of anti-racist and anti-discriminatory civil society organisations perceive this context of racism as everyday institutionalised practice in the chilly climate of Austria and second, the variety of strategies they adopt.

Some representatives (Int. Law 1, Int. Law 2, Int. Lobby 4) working in asylum and migration legal counselling perceive institutional racism as one of the major problems in Austria. They identify 'racism as the exercise of power' applied especially by civil servants and judges. The same representatives are also critical of an institutional racism creating increasing restrictions in immigration law and—as it is framed—the 'criminalisation of asylum seekers' (Int. Law 1). Migrants and asylum seekers, they state, encounter 'systematic malignancy' from state institutions in legal proceedings (Int. Law 1). Increasingly discriminatory practice is, furthermore, identified in the context of citizenship laws and job opportunities for migrants (Int. Lobby 4). An organisation which mainly focuses on anti-racist work by monitoring racist incidents points out that state institutions and especially the police are crucial to the reproduction of racism (Int. Anti-Racism 3). The representative of another documentation and monitoring organisation stresses that they try to establish networks with the police in order to reach police officers and to make them aware of institutional racist practices (Int. Documentation 5).

Hence, in the perception of civil society organisations, racism is linked not only to individual behaviour but also to institutional practices. Most representatives of anti-racist and anti-discrimination organisations perceive this as a major problem. They state that it is difficult to fight institutionally and socially embedded racist images and behaviour. Nevertheless, the organisations engage in counter-strategies against racism and discrimination. What could be a strength might also be a weakness when it comes to forming a strong counter-hegemony to right-wing racist discourses (Pühretmayer 2002: 304). Another drawback in this struggle for counter-hegemony, which some representatives identified, is the lack of resources. Some civil society organisations receive state funding, however, most of them depend on donations (Int. Lobby 4, Int. Law 2). Their counter-strategies can be summarised as engagement in four fields: education/information, counselling, campaigning and monitoring.

Education, Information and Awareness Raising

Four of the organisations interviewed are active in the field of empowerment education and remembrance work. This includes the provision of training and workshops for pupils, students and companies in the field of anti-discrimination and anti-racism. One anti-racist organisation's emphasis is on the education of 13–19 year old pupils. The organisation stresses issues of empowerment as well as civil awareness of racism or conflict resolution (Int. Anti-racism 3). Their aim is to develop agency in situations when young people observe or experience racist incidents. Another organisation, focusing mainly on remembrance work and anti-fascist training, offers guided tours of memorial centres such as former concentration camps (Int. Remembrance 6). The organisation focusing on documentation also provides workshops for the prevention of right-wing extremism and racism, also mainly targeting pupils. Its representative emphasises the importance of a subject-oriented approach to anti-racism work. This strategy involves recognising how racialisation processes work by learning about oneself and not about 'the others' (Int. Documentation 5). Another organisation aims at raising awareness about institutional racism, which is manifest in everyday legal processes, especially in asylum-seeking proceedings (Int. Law 2).

Counselling

Counselling for migrants and asylum seekers or others who experience racism is the main field of engagement of another group of four organisations. Counselling includes legal advice for victims of racist attacks as well as general information on possible action against racism (Int. Anti-Racism 3). Another counselling organisation focuses on legal advice and psycho-social assistance for migrants including advice in cases of discrimination by state institutions or in the workplace (Int. Counselling 7). One major strategy is to empower their clients by informing them about their rights. This information about migrants' and refugees' rights seems to be the core of anti-discrimination work, as people who are not well informed about their rights are more often the target of discrimination by the authorities and institutional racism (Int. Law 1). While these organisations mainly focus on counselling people who are affected by racism and discrimination the organisation focusing on documentation is also a contact point for information about neo-Nazi groups and right-wing popular culture such as symbols, signs and music. They counsel parents and provide advice on exit strategies (Int. Law 2).

Campaigning, Communication and Events

Campaigning against racism and right-wing extremism is another pillar of most of the organisations we interviewed. One of the representatives emphasised that their aim is to weaken the right-wing-dominated anti-migration and anti-asylum discourse by promoting and lobbying for greater equality and human rights (Int. Lobby 4). One of their campaigns pointed out the difficulties of the new Citizenship Act or the 'Red-White-Red Card', which only permits highly skilled people—earning a certain amount of money—to migrate to Austria for work. The organisation is also involved in consultation on new legislation. Their lobbying activities have been successful to a certain extent in the past, when the authorities have made changes to parliamentary bills as a result of the organisation's lobbying and campaigning. Another successful strategy of awareness raising and prevention of right-wing extremist gathering is the *Fest der Freude* (Festival of Joy), which is organised by another organisation we interviewed (Int. Remembrance 6) (see also page. xx). It takes place every year on the 8th of May to celebrate the liberation of Austria from National Socialism. It is furthermore a way of countering explicitly right-wing public presence: The celebration prevents right-wing fraternities from gathering at the Viennese *Heldenplatz* in remembrance of the fallen Austrian "*Wehrmacht* comrades", which they did annually until the first *Festival of Joy* in 2013. Similarly, other organisations report that they also organise events and demonstrations or launch campaigns in response to actual racist or discriminatory events (Int. Law 2, Int. Lobby 4).

Monitoring

Monitoring of right-wing extremism, racism and hate speech is a major focus of two of the organisations we interviewed, one focusing on anti-racism and the other on documentation. It seems to be increasingly difficult to monitor the right-wing extremist scene, which is not easily accessible or highly visible in publicly available media. They seldom provide any publications or put information online (Int. Documentation 5).

A further difficulty with monitoring and documentation work is the risk of reproducing the discourses of difference when citing or illustrating their homepages or speeches (ibid.). Moreover, the prosecution for online racism is very difficult due to the 'transnationality' of online racism. Homepages are often anonymous and/or located on servers overseas. This is why the representative emphasises the importance of international cooperation to fight racism online. As a result this organisation joined the 'International Network against Cyber Hate', which shares information and works to counter cyber hate internationally.

The second organisation (Int. Anti-racism 3) provides a platform for people who witness racism and discrimination in the public sphere, be it on the street, in state institutions, on television or on the internet. It publishes reported cases in an annual *Racism report*. Although these reports do not provide a representative picture of racist or discriminatory incidents in the country, they serve as a way of capturing trends, such as the increasing importance of the internet as a medium for racist attacks (ibid.).

In Austria several important anti-racist and anti-discrimination organisations have developed various counter-strategies with regard to discrimination, racism and right-wing extremism/populism. They provide legal, social or psycho-social assistance, organise and launch anti-racism and anti-homophobic campaigns, fight anti-Semitism and promote equality, human rights and empowerment, in particular with regard to the young. The fact that racism is inherent in Austrian society, embedded in the midst of society and state institutions, renders it difficult to fight discourses of difference and inequality. Against this backdrop, Austrian civil society organisations need a clearer shift towards discourses of equality and inclusion in order to engage in this common purpose.

Conclusions

In this chapter we have tried to answer two questions. First, how can we explain the current success of right-wing populist groups in establishing a hegemonic discourse of difference and inequality in Austria? Second, what is the potential for anti-racist and anti-discrimination organisations to establish counter-hegemonic strategies to fight these exclusionary discourses? In order to analyse the current right wing's success we described how two organisations, the Austrian Freedom Party and the Vienna-based Citizens' Initiatives against the building of mosques, give meaning to difference and inequality in order to create hegemonic images of 'the other'. We were able to show that this, in turn, legitimises a 'conditional' inclusion, but more often the exclusion of this constructed 'other'. As we have shown, the right-wing discursive strategy in this regard is the creation of an antagonistic relationship between 'us' and 'them'. While the antagonism on a vertical level is always between 'us', the people, and 'them', the elites, the antagonism on a horizontal level very much relies on claiming a natural difference between Austrians and migrants, Christians and Muslims. While there is a tendency to symbolically include certain groups of migrants, for example, those who 'behave orderly' or those who belong to Christian communities (FPÖ Int. 2), the difference between Muslims and the 'us' group seems to be natural and insurmountable. We understand this classification as a racist practice. The re-naturalisation of difference and inequality enforces and intensifies existing images of 'the other' and presents racist images as a shared understanding. This creation of a (racist) consensus, we argue, has made the FPÖ in cooperation with other right-wing groups a major political player in the Austrian political landscape.

The rise of the right, however, has led to the involvement of counter-hegemonic groups fighting racism and exclusion in Austria. The seven organisations analysed pursue different strategies to counter racist right-wing discourse. They engage in educational work with a focus on youth, in legal and psychological counselling of migrants, asylum seekers and people who have experienced racism, in campaigning and lobbying, and in monitoring racism. We argue the difficulty of successfully introducing counter-strategies to racism and other social practices of exclusion is not only due to lack of resources. The intensification of the right-wing discourses of difference and inequality and the shared status of their arguments makes the work of civil society organisations more difficult. Also, we would contend that countering the shared right-wing sense of difference would need an explicit focus on the equality of people.

Interviews

Int. FPÖ 1, conducted on 14 May 2013
Int. FPÖ 2, conducted on 3 June 2013
Int. FPÖ 3, conducted on 7 May 2013
Int. FPÖ 4, conducted on 4 June 2013
Regular's Table, attended on 5 June 2013
Int. CI 1, conducted on 24 June 2013
Int. CI 2, conducted on 23 July 2013
Int. CI 3, conducted on 2 August 2013
Int. Law 1—Organisation giving legal advice, conducted on 21 June 2013
Int. Law 2—Organisation giving legal advice, conducted on 19 June 2013
Int. Lobby 4—Lobbying organisation, conducted on 4 July 2013
Int. Anti-Racism 3, conducted on 24 June 2013
Int. Documentation 5—Documentation and Monitoring, conducted on 29 May 2013
Int. Remembrance 6, conducted on 25 June 2013
Int. Counselling 7, conducted on 1 August 2013

References

Ajanovic, E., Mayer, S., & Sauer, B. (2016). Spaces of right-wing populism and anti-muslim racism in Austria. Identitarian movement, civil initiatives and the fight against 'Islamisation'. *Czech Journal of Political Science*.

Albertazzi, D., & McDonnell, D. (Eds.). (2008). *Twenty-first century populism: The spectre of western European democracy*. Houndmills, England: Palgrave Macmillan.

Balibar, E. (1991). Is there a 'Neo-racism'? In E. Balibar & I. Wallerstein (Eds.), *Race, nation, class: Ambigous identities* (pp. 17–28). London: Verso.

BMI. (1999). Wahl 1999. Retrieved May 28, 2015, from http://www.bmi.gv.at/cms/BMI_wahlen/nationalrat/1999/Ergebnis.aspx

BMI. (2002). Wahl 2002. Retrieved May 28, 2015, from http://www.bmi.gv.at/cms/BMI_wahlen/nationalrat/2002/Gesamtergebnis.aspx

BMI. (2013). Wahl 2013. Retrieved May 28, 2015, from http://wahl13.bmi. gv.at/

BMI. (2014). EU Wahl 2014. Retrieved May 28, 2015, from http://euwahl2014. bmi.gv.at/

Bojadžijev, M., & Demirović, A. (Eds.). (2002). *Konjunkturen des Rassismus.* Münster, Germany: Westfälisches Dampfboot.

Fanon, F. (2008). *Black skin, white masks.* London: Pluto-Press.

Faris, S. R. (2012). Femonationalism and the 'Regular' army of labor called migrant women. *History of the Present, 2*(2), 184–199.

Fekete, L. (2001). The emergence of xeno-racism. *Race and Class, 43*(2), 23–40.

Flecker, J., & Kirschenhofer, S. (2007). *Die populistische Lücke. Umbrüche in der Arbeitswelt und Aufstieg des Rechtspopulismus am Beispiel Österreichs.* Berlin, Germany: Edition Sigma.

Fredette, J. (2015). Examining the French Hijab and Burqa Bans through reflexive cultural judgement. *New Political Science, 31*(1), 48–70.

Goetz, J. (2014). (Re-)Naturalisierung der Geschlechterordnung. Anmerkungen zur Geschlechtsblindheit der (österreichischen) Rechtsextremismusforschung. In Forschungsgruppe Ideologien und Politiken der Ungleichheit (Ed.), *Rechtsextremismus. Entwicklungen und Analysen* (pp. 40–68). Wien, Austria: Mandelbaum.

Guillaumin, C. (1995). *Racism, sexism, power, and ideology.* London: Routledge.

Guillaumin, C. (1998). RASSE. Das Wort und die Vorstellung. In U. Bielefeld (Ed.), *Das Eigene und das Fremde. Neuer Rassismus in der Alten Welt?* (pp. 159–174). Hamburg, Germany: Hamburg Edition.

Hall, S. (2000). Rassismus als ideologischer Diskurs. In N. Räthzel (Ed.), *Theorien Über Rassismus* (pp. 7–16). Hamburg, Germany: Argument.

Heinisch, R. (2012). Demokratiekritik und (Rechts-)Populismus: Modellfall Österreich? In L. Helms & D. M. Wineroither (Eds.), *Die österreichische Demokratie im Vergleich* (pp. 361–382). Baden-Baden, Germany: Nomos.

Holzer, W. (1993). Rechtsextremismus—Konturen, Definitionsmerkmale und Erklärungsansätze. In DÖW (Ed.), *Handbuch des Österreichischen Rechtsextremismus* (pp. 11–96). Wien, Austria: Deuticke.

Krzyanowski, M. (2013). From Anti-Immigration and Nationalist Revisionism to Islamophobia: Continuities and Shifts in Recent Discourses and Patterns of Political Communication of the Freedom Party of Austria (FPÖ). In R. Wodak et al. (Eds.), *Right-Wing Populism in Europe. Politics and Discourse* (pp. 135–148). London: Bloomsbury.

Laclau, E. (2005). *On populist reason.* London: Verso.

Miles, R., & Brown, M. (2003). *Racism.* London: Routledge.

Müller-Uri, F. (2014). *Antimuslimischer Rassismus.* Wien, Austria: Mandelbaum.

Omi, M., & Winant, O. (2002). Racial formation. In P. Essed & D. T. Goldberg (Eds.), *Race critical theories: Text and context* (pp. 123–145). Malden, MA: Blackwell.

Pelinka, A. (2001). The Haider phenomenon in Austria: Examining the FPÖ in European context. *The Journal of the International Institute, 9*, 1.

Pelinka, A. (2002). Die FPÖ in der vergleichenden Parteienforschung. Zur typologischen Einordnung der Freiheitlichen Partei Österreichs. *ÖZP, 31*(3), 281–290.

Penz, O. (2010). Vom Sozial—zum Wettbewerbsstaat. Arbeitsbeziehungen und politische Regulation in Österreich. In A. Grisold, W. Maderthaner, & O. Penz (Eds.), *Neoliberalismus und die Krise des Sozialen. Das Beispiel Österreich* (pp. 139–178). Wien, Austria: Böhlau.

Poglia Mileti, F., Tondolo, R., Plomb, F., Schultheis, F., Meyer, M.-H., Hentges, G., et al. (2002). *Modern Sirens and their populist songs: A European literature review on changes in working life and the rise of right-wing populism*. Wien, Austria: FORBA. Literature Review (Deliverable 1, SIREN).

Pühretmayer, H. (2002). Antirassismus als emanzipatorisches Projekt und die Probleme antirassistischer Praktiken in Wien. In M. Bojadzijev & A. Demirović (Eds.), *Konjunkturen Des Rassismus* (pp. 290–311). Münster, Germany: Westfälisches Dampfboot.

Richardson, J. E., & Wodak, R. (2009). Recontextualising fascist ideologies of the past: Right-wing discourses on employment and nativism in Austria and the United Kingdom. *Critical Discourse Studies, 6*(4), 251–267.

Sauer, B., & Ajanovic, E. (2014). The rise of racism across Europe. In M. Sedmak, Z. Medaric, & S. Walker (Eds.), *Children's voices* (pp. 17–32). London: Routledge.

Schedler, A. (1996). Anti-political establishment parties. *Party Politics, 2*(3), 211–312.

Schiedel, H. (2007). *Der rechte Rand. Extremistische Gesinnungen in unserer Gesellschaft*. Wien, Austria: Edition Steinbauer.

Schumacher, S. (2008). Die Neuorganisation der Zuwanderung durch das Fremdenrechtspaket 2005. Retrieved May 25, 2015, from http://www.oeaw. ac.at/kmi/Bilder/kmi_WP12.pdf

Tálos, E. (2006). Sozialpartnerschaft. Austrokorporatismus am Ende? In H. Dachs et al. (Eds.), *Politik in Österreich. Das Handbuch* (pp. 425–442). Wien, Austria: Manz.

Terkessidis, M. (2004). *Die Banalität des Rassismus: Migranten zweiter Generation entwickeln eine neue Perspektive, Kultur und soziale Praxis*. Bielefeld, Germany: Transcript.

Wiegel, G. (2013). Rechtsverschiebung in Europa. In P. Bathke & A. Hoffstadt (Eds.), *Die neuen Rechten in Europa. Zwischen Neoliberalismus und Rassismus* (pp. 112–125). Köln, Germany: PapyRossa.

Zerbes, J. (2012). Österreich zuerst! Retrieved May 25, 2015, from http://www.univie.ac.at/unique/uniquecms/?p=1149

Zilian, H. G. (2002). Der 'Populismus' und das Ende der Gleichheit. In W. Eismann (Ed.), *Rechtspopulismus* (pp. 56–73). Wien, Austria: Czernin.

5

Right-wing Populism in Denmark: People, Nation and Welfare in the Construction of the 'Other'

Birte Siim and Susi Meret

Introduction

Scholars generally agree that Denmark and the other Scandinavian countries represent 'an exceptionalism' in Europe in terms of welfare state
and gender regimes (Esping-Andersen 1990; Borchorst and Siim 2002).
It has also been argued that this context influenced the rise, development
and consolidation of right-wing populism in the Scandinavian countries
with varying results (Rydgren 2012; Demker 2012; Jungar and Jupskås
2014). In particular, some of the literature focuses on the relationship
between nationalism and populism, suggesting that contemporary forms
of populism in Scandinavia have been shaped and influenced by the historical context and the construction and perception of 'the people', 'the

B. Siim (✉) • S. Meret
Department of Culture and Global Studies at Aalborg University (AAU),
Aalborg, Denmark

© The Editor(s) (if applicable) and The Author(s) 2016
G. Lazaridis et al. (eds.), *The Rise of the Far Right in Europe*,
DOI 10.1057/978-1-137-55679-0_5

nation' and 'the other' (cf. Brochmann and Hagelund 2012; Hellström et al. 2012; Hellström and Wennerhag 2013). This should also be the case for the Danish People's Party (Dansk Folkeparti, DPP) which discursively constructs party ideology and positions on exclusionary ideas of the nation and its native people. Within this nativist frame (see Betz and Meret 2009), the nation and those who belong to it are seen as threatened from outside by immigration and European integration and from within by Islam. This approach to the nation state is deemed to bear historical legacies which developed a particular type of 'welfare nationalism' (Brochmann and Hagelund 2012) which since the late 1960s has linked national issues with social equality issues, democracy and gender rights in the construction of national belonging and identity. This chapter suggests that these understandings of the nation and welfare state have in recent decades been effectively seized on by the populist right and re-interpreted by paradigms portraying increasing ethnic, religious and cultural diversity as irreconcilable, conflictual and threatening the integrity of the 'status quo' (defined in terms of social cohesion, national culture, identity, etc.). Thus, differences often take the form of dichotomised subjects, opposing natives vs. foreigners, deserving vs. undeserving, friends vs. foes, and so forth.

This chapter analyses two political organizations: the DPP (Dansk Folkeparti) and the Free Press Society (Trykkefrihedsselskabet, TS), the former being one of the electorally most successful and consolidated right-wing populist parties in Europe, the second a grassroots radical right-wing movement that focuses on the issue of Islam *vis-à-vis* freedom of speech and the free press. One set of issues deals with the relation between Danish populism and welfare nationalism/national politics of belonging, focusing on the intersections of the nation, the people and the welfare state from an historical perspective. This chapter asks to what extent we can identify a particular Danish or Scandinavian exceptionalism with legacies in both history and democracy that has influenced contemporary forms of right-wing populism and othering (see the Introduction to this book) in Danish politics and society. Another set of issues refers to the characteristics of contemporary Danish populism. The third set of issues address counter-forces combating hate speech and crime against the 'other', focusing on the strategies of civil society organisations and their relationships with public institutions. On the basis of the empirical analysis, we discuss how to understand the 'politics of fear' (Wodak 2015) permeating contemporary Europe from the Danish perspective. Here we propose that the articulation of fear of immigration, Islam and the Muslim 'other' is linked to the fear of losing a particular version of the welfare state.

Scholars have argued that in spite of, or perhaps because of, their historical legacies, the Nordic countries have serious problems accommodating ethno-cultural and religious diversity and integrating immigrant minorities as equal citizens on the labour market and in society (Brochmann and Hagelund 2012). Mainstream political parties have since the 1990s been engaged in re-thinking and reframing the relation between national, democratic and social questions. Arguably, it is within these cleavages that the influential Scandinavian right-wing populist DPP managed to appeal to Danish voters.

While the scholarly literature on populism has generally focused on political parties (Mudde 2007; Albertazzi and McDonnell 2008; Rydgren 2012) or on the concept and content of populism (cf. Arditi 2010; Mudde and Kaltwasser 2013), we suggest here that an important contribution to populist ideological development also comes from grassroots movements (see also Minkenberg 2008), often providing 'intellectual' content to populist right wing groups such as The Free Press Society. Both types of organisation mobilise public opinion and the electorate by means of a discourse and rhetoric that emphasize national and exclusionary sentiments of belonging and identity. Within this framing, liberal Western democracies play a central role in their fight for freedom, liberty and democracy against obscurantism, authoritarianism, religious fundamentalism and male chauvinism.

We suggest that Danish exceptionalism is embedded in a culturalist ideology that prioritises what are perceived as 'our' values, principles and rights against the threat represented by Islam and Muslim immigration. Our research findings suggest that a subtle 'intellectual labour' division exists between the two organisations: if the DF is characterized as the popular, or populist party fighting at parliamentary level the problems faced by the 'common Dane', in particularly when confronted by immigration and domestic and European political elites, the Free Press Society aims rather at addressing and debating aspects directly related to the danger of Islam and the future of free speech in the West, by attempting to keep the debate on a more intellectual level and outside the usual political arena.

The analysis thus poses interesting questions about the role of grassroots movements and radical right-wing intellectual elites vis-à-vis the political parties in the shaping of a 'Nordic-style populism'.

The Rise of Right-wing Populism in Denmark: Our Nation, Our People, Our Welfare

Danish society is built on a closed articulation between the nation, the people and the welfare state (Mouritsen 2006). This tradition goes back to the 1930s, when the governing Danish Social Democratic Party redefined the people of the nation, by linking the homeland they occupy to people's struggle for democracy and social welfare. As Danish historian Ove Korsgaard (2004) observes, this particular re-framing helped to create and consolidate consensus about the triple meaning of 'the people', which in the discursive national understanding refers at one and the same time to national, democratic and social questions. This section develops this point a little further in relation to contemporary Danish populism.

The formation of the modern democratic Danish nation state dates back to 1848. Like the making of other nation states (see Hobsbawn 1992; Smith 2001), the shift towards modern democracy raised controversial questions about the meaning of the nation and the notion of its 'people'. In particular: who should have the right to vote? Who belongs to the people? How should the people be constituted: by *ethnos* or *demos*? How should democracy be linked to the welfare state? Distinctively, in the case of Denmark, the loss of Southern Jutland in the 1864 war against Prussia and Austria had a strong impact on feelings of national identity and belonging in the light of the country's shrinking territorial power and jurisdiction.

During the first half of the twentieth century, the triad of nation, democracy, welfare was temporarily resolved by the growth of the Danish welfare state. The Social Democratic Party (*Social Demokratiet*, SD) played a key role in this political project, integrating the national question with the social one. One of the SD's objectives was to give shape to a model closely connecting socialism and democracy to the nation state, by encouraging national feelings of solidarity and belonging. The SD gained power in 1929 and formed a government with the Social Liberal

Party (Det Radikale Venstre, RV) which lasted until the end of the German occupation in April 1945. During the 1930s economic crisis, the SD under the leadership of Prime Minister Thorvald Stauning, ran a successful election campaign under the motto 'Stauning—or Chaos'. The SD-led government negotiated a national agreement with the Liberal Agrarian Party (Venstre, V), representing peasant organizations; the so-called Kanslergade Agreement (*Kanslergadeforliget*), which adopted reforms that helped establish the Danish welfare model.

In spite of historical differences between the various Nordic roads to statehood and parliamentary democracy, there were a number of similarities as regards political development (Hilson 2010). One example is the similar formulation of the national strategies of Scandinavian Social Democracy during the 1930s. The motto for the Danish SD was 'Denmark for the people' (*Danmark for folket*), which was also the name of the 1934 party manifesto in an echo of the ideological motto of the Swedish Social Democratic Party , 'the people's home' (*folkehemmat*). Scholars have attributed the relatively peaceful and consensual political development of the Scandinavian countries during the economic crisis and the consolidation of national socialism and fascism in the 1930s to the Red-Green coalition political compromise negotiated between the Social Democratic and Agrarian Parties that resolved potential class conflicts (Hilson 2010: 33).

The Nordic Social Democrats thus created a kind of social nationalism or 'welfare nationalism'. In 1934 the SD moved from a class to a 'peoples' party' and redefined the people as a social and political construct united by democracy. The democratic dimension made the concept of the people different from German National Socialism. The triple meaning of 'the people' made it possible to refer to the people as 'the working people', in whose interests the party acted, and at the same time to talk on behalf of democracy and the whole nation. The implications are that one is not only born into a national community, but also into a social community. The social and national can only be linked by understanding yourself as a part of the nation and the community (Korsgaard 2004: 422).

The discursive disagreements about the meanings of the nation and the people have implications for the understanding of the relationship between nationalism and populism. Reflecting on Danish political history, Korsgaard makes a crucial distinction between state nationalism and folk nationalism (*folkenationalisme*), i.e. between nationalism 'from above' and 'from below' (Korsgaard 2004: 342–347). This is connected with the fact that in some national movements the state has been the key driver, whereas in others it has been civil society (Smith 2001). This makes it possible to identify a decisive difference between Danish and German nationalism during the nineteenth century—German nationalism was based on the state, whereas Danish nationalism post-1864 was based on civil society movements. The Danish case illustrates how discursive struggles about understanding 'the people' may have conflicting implications for different historical periods and in diverse national contexts. During the 1930s the meaning of 'the people' was redefined by the Social Democrats in Denmark, Norway and Sweden to include almost everybody living (legally and preferably with citizenship status) within the national borders (Siim and Stoltz 2015).

Another peculiarity concerns the universal Scandinavian welfare state premised on a gender dimension, the dual-breadwinner model and state responsibility for care work (Borchorst and Siim 2002). Nordic scholarship has shown that the Scandinavian welfare states can be traced back to the reform of patriarchal family legislation in the mid-1920s (Melby et al. 2008), which reduced male privileges by establishing formal equality between the spouses in marriage. The universal welfare model, which was further developed by reforms of social and labour-market policies in the 1960s and 1970s, has been regarded as particularly 'women-friendly' (cf. Borchorst and Siim 2002), since state responsibility for care work enables women to combine paid work with care work.

Since the 1970s, Scandinavian welfare states have been relatively successful in economic terms and in the basic components of extended welfare policies and redistribution, a welfare model which is presently supported by virtually all mainstream parties. Social equality, democracy and gender equality have become crucial elements in the Nordic countries' sense or construction of national belonging. Yet, it has been argued that they face serious problems in accommodating ethno-cultural and religious diversity and integrating immigrant minorities as equal citizens (Togeby 2004; Mouritsen 2006). Recent scholarly analysis of the Scandinavian welfare model from a migration perspective suggests that there is a single model with three exceptions, all based on 'welfare nationalism that links welfare with access to national citizenship' (Brochmann and Hagelund 2012). Tensions also exist between gender-equality poli-cies and the recognition of immigrant minorities (Siim and Skjeie 2008).

Denmark's EU membership together with increased mobility and immigration have arguably re-activated conflicts about the meaning of 'the people' and reformulated the 'old' questions about who belongs to the people, how to define the borders of the nation and link national with social questions. In the 1970s and 1980s the Danish membership of the EU was a contentious question across the right/left divide. Since the 1990s immigration has raised new questions about belonging, borders (Hedetoft et al. 2006) and under what conditions the 'other', the 'alien', should gain access to Danish and European citizenship and welfare provision.

At present, all major political parties are engaged in re-thinking and re-framing the welfare state. One controversial issue is between an exclu-sive understanding of 'us', the people, and 'our welfare' tied mainly to the nation state, vis-à-vis inclusive and post-national notions of welfare and solidarity that include 'the migrant other'. Recent research suggests that Denmark has become highly and increasingly polarised (Minkenberg 2008) in relation to national identity and welfare questions. Within this framework, the populist DPP presents itself as the protector of an exclu-sive notion of welfare and solidarity, limited to 'our people', to those 'who have paid for [welfare] for generations and generations'. In the Danish context immigration and increased cultural and religious diversity have been followed by a 'culturalisation' process of the welfare issue and the integration discourse (Vad Jønsson and Petersen 2010: 204–209; Betz and Meret 2012) rooted in the particular understanding of national iden-tity, welfare and democracy. We argue that right-wing Danish populism has adopted a model influenced by Danish history and society. This model can be identified as: a welfare-nationalist approach with clear exclusionary drives; a strong anti-immigration/nativist agenda (Betz and Meret 2009) and an opportunistic gender equality agenda (see Meret and Siim 2013).

Contemporary Danish Populism

The term populism was first used by Danish scholars in the 1980s to describe and characterise the rise and development of the Danish Progress Party, (*Fremskridtspartiet*, FrP), predominantly characterised by tax protest and an anti-establishment stance. The first wave of neo-fascist parties was only marginally present in the country; the rise and development of the FrP belongs to the second populist wave (see Von Beyme 1988). The contemporary history of the DPP and the role of the party in Danish politics cannot be fully understood without considering the DPP legacies from the FrP. The DPP did not emerge from a political vacuum, but capitalised on the FrP political experience, agenda and developments. The FrP was born as a tax-protest, ultraliberal and anti-establishment party, a sign of the times of the populist tax-protest mobilisation in Denmark and in other Scandinavian countries (Norway in particular) that peaked in the 1970s and early 1980s. Later, the political agenda of these parties dwindled, but left a political window of opportunity open to a rising populist demand, yet this time driven by anti-immigration, strongly ethno-nationalist and anti-Islam.

Former uncontested and long-term DPP leader Pia Kjærsgaard joined first the FrP in 1978 and was elected an MP in 1984. She rose rapidly within the FrP, becoming a crucial actor in the political struggle for the leadership. In the early 1990s internal party divisions, disagreement and struggles for power led to a split in the party. Pia Kjærsgaard and four other FrP members left in protest in 1995 and launched the DPP. At the 1998 parliamentary election, the DPP won more than 7 per cent of the vote and from 2001 the party secured a decade of Liberal-Conservative government by supporting the minority cabinet at government.

In terms of voters' support, the DPP has until recently been a party of (male) manual workers with relatively low levels of education (see Meret 2010). This makes the DPP the most obviously working-class party in Danish politics (Meret 2010; Betz and Meret 2012), a characteristic that worries mainstream left-of-centre parties, in particular the SD. Populist right-wing voters—in this case the DPP voters—are intolerant of immigration, and ethnic and cultural difference, and the vast majority of them considers Islam a security threat, and a danger to national identity and social cohesion (Meret 2010). Low political and social trust among the DPP voters tends to corroborate the close relationship between anti-immigration, nationalist and ethno-centric positions, and anti-establishment feelings.

From 1995 the DPP gradually abandoned tax-protest and ultra-liberal approaches, incorporating pro-welfare attitudes in the party's manifestos and ideology (Meret 2010). The adoption of a welfare profile was in many ways pivotal to the transformation and consolidation of contemporary Danish right-wing populism and signalled a shift from its forerunner. Moreover the combination of welfare, nationalist positions, anti-immigration and European scepticism allowed the DPP to play on a different register when constructing and identifying 'the other' (Hervik 2011). The DPP's early days were difficult but the electoral breakthrough came relatively early at the 1998 general election, when they gained thirteen seats in the Danish parliament. This ensured fairly solid parliamentary representation for the party.

The pursuit of order and agreement within the party's own ranks was among the main imperatives in the process of 'normalisation' pursued by the DPP leadership to bring the party from the margins to the mainstream of Danish politics. This also implied a strongly centralised party organisation, intolerant of internal party conflicts and vertically centred on the party's central organ. The DPP was from the start characterised by rigid internal party discipline, which, contrary to what many believe, helped to make it one of the most modern, well organised and administered, and professionally marketed parties in Danish politics (Knudsen 2006: 140).

Between 2001 and 2011 the DPP played a key role as a support party for the Liberal-Conservative coalition government. The party exerted its influence on the political and public media discourse in the 'othering' of immigrants, especially Muslims. From November 2001 until 2011 the DPP was a party to virtually all major agreements on reforms of the labour market, welfare and public administration. Significantly, it also played a crucial role in drafting the new migration law; in foreign policy, the party's support was vital to endorse the Danish military participation in Afghanistan and in Iraq in 2001 and 2003. The only divergence was on European policy: the DPP has maintained a very sceptical stance, particularly towards further integration, which it believes would permanently undermine Danish national sovereignty.

When the Social Democrat-led coalition came to power after the November 2011 elections, the DPP lost its political role supporting the government, but in spite of the economic crisis and the general tiredness of the government coalition, the DPP lost relatively little electoral support (–1.6 per cent). In 2012, founder and leader Pia Kjærsgaard resigned and Kristian Thulesen Dahl became leader. The change of leadership did not have a negative effect on the party's popularity, as might have been assumed. In November 2013 the party won its first breakthrough at municipal level, winning around 10 per cent of the vote in the municipal elections and becoming the third-largest party after the Social Democrats and the Liberal Party. At the last European elections in May 2014 the party won a landslide victory, with 26.6 per cent of the Danish vote. This made the DPP the biggest party with all three mandates in the European Parliament (EP).[1] But the decisive sign that the DPP has today reached a solid position in Danish politics came at the June 2015 Danish general election, when the party came second with 21 per cent of the vote after the Social Democrats with 26.3 per cent. Despite this, the DPP did not want to be part of the government and is currently supporting the minority Liberal cabinet 'from the outside'.

Characteristics of Right-Wing Populist Organisations

This section analyses similarities and differences in the political communication, ideology and values of the two main organisations: the DPP and the TS. The DPP was an obvious choice as a case study, since virtually all studies within the field include the DPP as an example of the most influential populist right-wing parties in Europe (Rydgren and Widfeldt 2004; Mudde 2007). The selection of a radical right-wing movement[2] was a more difficult task, since there is still little empirical research on the extreme Danish radical right wing. Arguably the TS is a timely choice. Its founder and leader Lars Hedegaard is the society's

---

[1] After the election, the DPP left the Europe of Freedom and Democracy Group (EFD) at the EP to join the European Conservatives and Reformist Group (ECR), headed by British Conservative David Cameron. The EFD consists of Eurosceptic nationalist right-wing parties with no real influence in the EP. The DPP had tried to join the ECR in 2009 but was denied access due to its reputation as an extreme right-wing racist party.

[2] We conducted 20 interviews between 13 June and 10 September 2013: ten with members of political parties; four with members associated with the Free Press Society; and six with 'victim' organisations. All interviews by Jeppe Fuglsang Larsen (cf. Siim et al. 2013).

controversial public spokesman on 'free speech', particularly since the attack on his person, allegedly for his anti-Muslim rhetoric, in 2013. He was the co-editor of the TS newspaper *Sappho* and the co-founder (with Sweden's Ingrid Carlqvist) of the society's English-language periodical, *Dispatch International*. Another influential advocate for free speech, is lawyer Jacob Mchangama, who was also then a member of TS.

In contrast to the DPP, the TS remains a relatively unknown organisation. It has informal associations with the Free Press Society in other Western countries and it has close contacts with several international anti-Islam critics and bloggers, who argue that Islamisation in the West is threatening freedom of speech and society. Over the years TS has awarded its Sappho Award to Swedish cartoonist Lars Vilks, Danish cartoonist Kurt Westergaard, and Islam critics Thilo Sarrazin and Mark Steyn. In February 2015, the TS was on the mainstream media's front page, commenting on the *Charlie Hebdo* and Paris shootings and the Copenhagen killings,[3] which put the debate on 'free speech' at the top of the public agenda. Possibly these events contributed to 'normalising' the TS profile, along with mainstream media relatively uncritical approach to public discourses on 'free speech' and 'freedom of press'. A further factor could be that the DPP's efforts to normalise have created a window of opportunity for more radical right-wing attitudes to Islam and immigration, and the TS has endeavoured to fill this vacuum. The two organisations share an 'absolutist' defence of free speech in Western society and an intolerance of opposition and disagreement. Additionally, several individual members of the DPP were or are still members of the TS.

---

[3] The Paris shootings started with a massacre at the offices of the satirical magazine *Charlie Hebdo* on 7 January 2015, were followed by a shooting at the kosher market and ended with a huge police operation. At least twelve people were killed in the massacre: http://www.bbc.com/news/world-europe-30708237. In February 2015 two shootings occurred in Copenhagen, Denmark. The first on 14 February at a public event called 'Art, Blasphemy and Freedom of Expression' at the Krudttønden cultural centre, organized by the Lars Vicks committee, where a gunman killed one civilian and wounded three police officers. Swedish artist Lars Vilks was among the speakers and is thought to have been the main target because of his drawings of Muhammad. The second shooting took place later that night outside the city's Great Synagogue in Krystalgade. The same gunman killed a Jewish man on security duty during a *bat mitzvah* celebration, and wounded two police officers. Later that morning, the police tracked down and shot the man identified as Omar Abdel Hamid El-Hussein, whom police said was responsible for both attacks.

Populist Right-wing Political Communication, Leadership Style and Rhetoric

The DPP has over the past decade skilfully used simple and direct slogans and visual symbols in electoral campaign posters, in the media and on the web to get the party message across, such as: 'Your land—Your choice' (*Dit land, dit valg*),'We vote Danish for the Danish Kroner and the Fatherland' (*Vi stemmer dansk for kronen og fædrelandet*). Former leader Pia Kjærsgaard has taken on a central media role, promoting an image of herself over the years as a woman 'of the people and for the people' who is able to address matters of concern to the 'common Dane' (cf. Meret 2015). Kjærsgaard was the first female politician in Denmark to launch a new party, and was, for almost two decades, the only woman leading a populist radical right-wing party in Europe.[4] Arguably she symbolizes the charismatic populist leader able to attract followers and to achieve political success and leadership longevity (see Meret 2015).

The style of TS leader Lars Hedegaard is characterised by a provocative, contentious, often extremist and borderline rhetoric and style: his radical positions on Islam and Muslims, on hate speech and 'othering' are more outspoken than those of the DPP. In 2011, Hedegaard, was prosecuted for hate speech under the so-called 'racism paragraph' (§ 266b) of the Danish Penal Code[5] for his comments on 'girls in Muslim families [who] are raped by their uncles, cousins, or their fathers'. He was convicted by the Lower Court in 2011, but acquitted by the Higher Court in 2012 after claiming that his comments were made during a private meeting and were not intended to be made public. TS writings often deal with freedom of speech, targeting primarily—if not exclusively—Islam as a religion and Islamism, and featuring Muslim minorities as the inner enemies in Western society.

---

[4] This is no longer unusual: since 2006 Siv Jensen has been leader of the Norwegian Progress Party. Marine Le Pen took over the leadership of the French Front National from her father Jean-Marie in 2011.

[5] §266b, the so-called 'racism' paragraph of the penal code adopted in 1971 states: 'Everyone who publicly or with intent, expresses statements or distributes information in public, by which a group of persons is threatened, insulted or degraded because of their race, colour, national or ethnic origin, faith or sexual orientation shall be sentenced to a fine or up to two years' imprisonment'. *Stk.2. In determining the appropriate sentence, it is particularly serious if such statements take the form of public propaganda.'*

Our interviews show that both organisations are well aware of their role and of the role played by mainstream media in political communication. All our informants described themselves as strenuous defenders of free speech and in favour of the abolition of the 'racism paragraph', which would make racist and hate speech immune from criminal prosecution. This position correlates with the strong and uncompromising defense of *Jyllands-Posten*'s publication of the Muhammad cartoons in September 2005[6] and of the 'right' to 'offend' religious/Muslim minorities. Asked about the charges they faced for their outspoken racist and Islamophobic attitudes, informants had well-prepared replies, arguing in different ways but to similar effect that freedom of speech 'is a core value in Danish and Western societies' and needs to be safeguarded. This position is illustrated by a DPP MP's comments on hate speech:

The legal prohibition against hate speech or 'racism paragraph' is a big problem, because it prohibits freedom of speech; but apart from this there is no problem with free speech in Denmark. An open society [Karl Popper] and the open Danish debate have contributed to prevent extremism and neo-Nazism in contrast to what has happened in Sweden. … It is bullshit to talk about racism … it is not a question of racism, or race. I do not subscribe to racism as an ideology. The concept of Islamophobia is also bullshit. I relate to the religion Islam and to the things I see. And I see the big problems that Islam creates in Western societies. It is a pseudo-Freudian explanation that you criticise, is something you also must be afraid of. … the word racism becomes a form of crusade where everything is lumped together in relation to what racism can mean, apart from being about biological differences. If you are critical of Islam you are labelled a racist. This is an etymological perception of what the word means, and it is pure bullshit. (Interview by JFL 2013)

Here racism and Islamophobia are lumped together and both refuted with an argument that discards their 'actuality' or 'relevance' in contemporary societies and particularly in Denmark. Charges of racism and

---

[6] The 'Muhammad cartoons crisis' refers to the printing of twelve caricatures of the prophet Mohammed by the Danish newspaper *Jyllands-Posten* in September 2005, which caused the biggest Danish diplomatic crisis since WWII. http://www.faktalink.dk/titelliste/muha00/muhahele; http://www.huffingtonpost.com/peter-mcgraw-and-joel-warner/muhammad-cartoons_b_1907545.html.

Islamophobia are also believed to be detrimental to public discussion and thus automatically to freedom of speech, without reflecting on whether this really is the case. Several informants had a problem with the fact that the penal code prohibits free and open debate on controversial issues related to Islam, immigration and the integration of Muslims in Danish society. A good example of this is given by a well-known DPP MP: for her, the right to free speech is 'the right to offend/insult other people' (*krænkeretten*). Legal restrictions prevent people from starting controversial debates, because of the fear of being convicted for offending peoples' feelings. In her own words:

> I think that the racism paragraph §266b is wrong and restricts freedom of speech. It does not protect people against racism, but protects groups who feel offended. If you say something about a group you can be convicted, even if it is true. It is a paragraph about not offending people's feelings. If we keep this paragraph, you should only be convicted if what you say is not true. (Interview by JFL 2013)

Similar arguments were used to repudiate and dismiss accusations of populism. For example, another member of DPP denied all accusations that the party should be a populist party, asking:

> Does populism mean being in tune with public opinion (*folkestemningen*)? May be you could turn it around and say that we just share the same beliefs and attitudes as 'the people'? I could understand if we changed attitudes and opinions from case to case and had one meaning one day and another the next day. Then it could be true. All parties have a degree of populism because you say things when the timing is right. [But] our timing is better than the other parties', because we have people to help us determine when it is good to voice your beliefs. We do not change opinions but we address the issues directly and propose solutions when there has been a case of, for example rape, or a burglary at an elderly person's home. Popular opinion/ feelings is behind us when we say it, but it has always been our policy. (Interview by JFL 2013)

Populism as a concept is here re-formulated by referring to the proximity between the party and the voters, the party and the people, as well as the consistency and reliability of the party's policies over time, compared to the other parties. The TS primarily refers to the danger of Islam and Islamisation for the future of democratic Western societies. The interviewees are eloquent on the role of *Sappho*'s (the journal of the association) position on Islamophobia:

> *Sappho* debates Islam. It is about culture, freedom and about the future of Western societies. We are not racists; we are not interested in race. We are interested in freedom of expression, the fundamental right in a free democratic society. People can call me what they want. [But] it is ridiculous to call me a racist. Islamophobia is also ridiculous, but I will not accept the premise behind this concept. I believe the great Islamophobists, if you take the word seriously, are those who try to shut down the debate about Islam, because they are afraid of reprisals from hard-core Islamists. It is the people who closed down Lars Vicks' [Swedish author and cartoonist] exhibition because he is considered a problem. They are afraid of what will happen. There are publishers who do not dare to print the Mohammed drawings. They are the Islamophobes.

All TS interviewees are ardent defenders of freedom of speech, but have different attitudes towards Islam and Islamisation. The paragraphs above show that right-wing populist organisations consider free speech to be a goal in itself and not a means to create a democratic society; this explains why their official policy is limited to the removal of the 'racism paragraph'. For interviewees from these organisations, the defence of freedom of speech is an absolute value, which legitimizes the right to offend and insult 'the other', 'the enemy', constructed either as the immigrant, the asylum seeker or Islam. Freedom of speech is also used to repudiate accusations of populism, but also of racism and Islamophobia. There are debates about whether the 'anti-racism' paragraph is still useful,[7] but according to a 2010 poll the majority of Danes (about 69 per cent) want to retain it for the sake of individual and group rights and to keep public debate 'sober'.[8]

---

[7] http://www.cepos.dk/fileadmin/user_upload/billeder/JUNI_JULI_2011/Ugeskrift_for_Retsvaesen_26__juni_2011_Artikel_om_Racismeparagraffen.pdf; http://www.humanisme.dk/hate-speech/samlet.php#Lars Hedegaard/.

[8] http://politiken.dk/newsinenglish/ECE1081207/poll-danes-support-anti-racism-paragraph/.

It is worth noting that all interviewees are critical of the mainstream press and feel stigmatised by the media. The two organisations, DPP and TF, agree about abolishing the racism paragraph. There is, however, an important difference in the rhetoric of the two parties; interviewees from the DPP tend today to be more cautious about criticizing Islam than members of the TS. The quotes above demonstrate that TS perceives Islam as the major threat to freedom of expression.

Ideologies, Values, Policies and Target Groups

Interviewees from both the DF and the TS tend to construct 'the other' or 'the enemy' mainly on the basis of Islam, which they regard as opposed to most of what is thought Danish in terms of democratic values and principles, mainly epitomised by 'free speech', 'democracy', 'gender equality' and the like. Another strong divide is constructed on the opposition between 'us'—the democratic, tolerant, capitalist West—and 'them'— the authoritarian, male-chauvinist and intolerant Muslims.

Interviewees from TS (and International TS) also articulate radical anti-Islam attitudes together with the right to freedom of speech as an absolutist value. Both the editor of *Dispatch International* and the vice-chair of TF present their core value as freedom, broadly understood by quoting English writer George Orwell: 'if freedom means something, it is the freedom to say what people do not want to hear'.[9] Consequently, within this framing the right to free speech becomes the right to offend— and the Mohammed cartoon crisis is taken as an example to show that 'offended feelings are no argument against free speech'.

A division of tasks seems to characterise the roles of the DPP and of the TS when it comes to the way these organisations formulate their ideological views and rhetoric in the public sphere. The DPP prefers to feature populist positions addressing concerns arising from the meeting of the 'native Dane' and the immigrant and aiming to safeguard the interests and life of 'the Danish people'. The style and rhetoric of the TS is outspoken and its frequently discriminatory attitude towards Islam and Muslims

---

[9] See Orwell's Freedom of the Press, proposed preface to the novel *Animal Farm*. http://orwell.ru/library/novels/Animal_Farm/english/efp_go.

is justified by an appeal for the absolute need to safeguard freedom of speech. In addition the TS differs from the DPP in its aim of targeting radical right-wing intellectuals (though not to the exclusion of others), by exclusively debating the danger of Islam for the future of freedom of speech in the Western world, often inspired by anti-Islamism in the USA (e.g. Pamela Gellner, Robert Spencer, etc.). Despite the differences between the two organisations the TS still has close links with the DPP, although it stresses that there is no formal association. But the TS also includes in its membership individual members of several other parties, e.g., the Liberal Democrats, the Liberals, the Conservatives. An interviewee from *Dispatch International* explains how the journal explicitly targets intellectuals:

> I know that many of the people that read our paper are academics. Professors, doctors and you know ... intellectual people. The paper is written in a language that is not for the man on the street ... I would like to reach out to all the intellectuals, because the man on the street, the working class, they have already noticed what is going on. They were the ones that voted for Sweden Democrats. They are living in the same suburbs as these immigrants so they saw it coming many years ago, but the middle class, the intellectuals, they have the capacity to see that what we are writing about is really, really important; i.e. the question of free speech and free mind. The problem is that they are afraid to speak their mind, because they know it could cost them their career or even their job. (Interview by JFL 2013)

The two organisations also differ in relation to issues of gender equality and homosexual rights. The DPP generally believes that Danish women have achieved gender equality and have no reason to advance further, but the party does not call for the repeal of gender-equality legislation (cf. Meret and Siim 2013). The party primarily supports gender-equality policies directed towards ethnic minority women, as a key part of their 'integration', but its views do not normally diverge strongly from those of the mainstream. For TS, by contrast, issues related to gender equality and sexuality in general, including among ethnic minorities, are not part of their political agenda.

The interviews confirm that the DPP positions on gender equality and gay rights and homosexual marriage are not radically different from the mainstream (cf. Meret and Siim 2013). Interviewees tended to accept the status quo, which resonates with Danish legislation. However, the party is against proposals for earmarked paternity leave, the so-called 'father's quota', and is also sceptical towards gender quotas in companies and corporations. But the 'anti-quota' position is also in line with the three other parties in the Liberal-Conservative block, the Liberal Party, the Conservatives and the Liberal Alliance. Studies show that the DPP uses gender roles and family values strategically as 'populist' issues targeting Muslim minorities (Akkermann and Hagelund 2007; Meret and Siim 2013). Since forced marriages and the wearing of the veil or *niqab* are issues of less interest to the public agenda, the DPP has focused instead on *halal* meat in institutions and the building of local mosques. There are potential conflicts with mainstream attitudes to immigration/integration, but the party is aware these issues must be dealt with and discussed more carefully.

The above analysis of the various articulations of positions concerning Muslims and Islam shows both differences and overlaps as regards who is constructed as the 'us' and who is framed as 'the other'. In the case of the DPP, the 'us' is the native ethnic Dane, the 'common man', while 'the other' is Islam/the Muslim who threatens our future and our values. In the case of the TS, the 'us' is the universal us standing for free speech against the 'other' Islam. The TS targets Islamisation, including Islam as a culture, religion and everyday practice. Islam is perceived as an 'all-inclusive' threat to the survival of European/Western societies, culture, and democratic values and principles. Solutions are as various as approaches. For the DPP the solution is simple: to weaken the EU and give the Danish nation back its sovereignty by establishing efficient border controls, putting a stop to what is seen as migration for 'welfare tourism' and focusing instead on the 'assimilation' of immigrants already in the country. For the TS the solution is more complex: Muslim immigration not only to Denmark but to the rest of Europe must stop altogether, and natives must engage in a global intellectual 'war' against Islam/Muslims/Islamism. This can be interpreted as a strategic division of tasks between the two organisations and the overlap of membership is one indication of this, but it can equally be interpreted as an expression of real and opportunistic differences in positions and political ideology.

Counterstrategies to Hate Speech, Othering and Racism

This section gives a brief overview of diverse strategies to combat hate speech, othering and racism in the Danish context inspired by recent results from the RAGE project (Siim et al. 2014, 2015). Interviews with selected victims organisations and democratic anti-bodies targeting mainly immigrant, refugee and LGBT issues are reported. These studies help to illuminate the strengths and weaknesses of political culture, democratic traditions and present migration and anti-discrimination policies, in particular in relation to the challenges posed by the spread of right-wing populism and anti-immigration positions.

The role of democratic forces in opposing populism is explored by analysing two types of voluntary associations: victims organisations defending victims of hate crimes, discrimination and othering, and 'anti-bodies', defined as militants on the other side. The debate about how to combat hate speech, othering and racism raise questions about the understandings and practices of hate speech and racist behaviour directed towards diverse minority groups: Muslim immigrants, Jews, asylum seekers and refugees, and sexual minorities. In the Danish context all respondents from the selected organisations[10] pointed towards immigrants, refugees and asylum seekers, especially those of Muslim background, as one of the major target groups and the principal victims of racism and populist othering.

Extensive mapping identified a small number of voluntary organisations chosen for in-depth study through focus-group interviews.[11] The five

---

[10] Victims' organisations and anti-bodies were selected as active participants in public debate about discrimination against migrant and Muslim minorities (DRC & ENAR), including organisations of migrants and Muslim minorities (EMRK & NDU). Interviewees were from the following four victims' organisations: (1) The Documentation and Counselling Centre on Racism (*Dokumentations-og rådgivningscenteret om racediskrimination*, DRC); (2) Ethnic Minority Women's Council (*Etniske minoritetskvinders råd*, EMKR); (3) European Network Against Racism (ENAR); and (4) New/Now Danish Youth Council (*Nudansk Ungdomsråd*, NDU).

[11] All interviews were carried out by Jeppe Fuglsang Larsen. One interview was with SOS Against Racism; the other two with members of Sabaah and The Trampoline House. SOS against Racism is a Europe-wide organisation founded in 1984, with branches in many European countries and around 200 subscribing members in Denmark. Sabaah and the Trampoline House are new organ-

organisations addressed asylum seekers and refugees, racism, immigrants and LGBT minorities. SOS Against Racism—the Danish branch of an international organisation—targets racism; Sabaah targets immigrant youth inspired by the Danish LGBT movement; The Trampoline House, LGBT Asylum and Refugees Welcome all target asylum seekers and refugees in the Danish system. These associations and groups were mainly examined through focus-group interviews with activists.[12] The objectives were to discover how the organisations understand themselves,[13] whether as victims'organisations, 'anti-bodies' or counter-forces, and how they relate to other democratic forces fighting hate speech, racist behaviour and discrimination as well as to the mainstream political culture, institutions and right-wing political force in Denmark and Europe.

The Copenhagen area is still the main centre for anti-racists, LGBT and migrant rights' movements and activists, so most of the organisations are based in that city. The themes addressed central issues, such as representation and aims, strategies and alliances, and relationships with political institutions. In spite of the different 'target groups', we found that the interviewees generally did not see themselves as victims' organisations or 'anti-bodies' opposing political institutions, but rather as positive forces working to establish an 'us'. Organisations such as LGBT Asylum, Sabaah and SOS Against Racism all aim to combine the roles of activists and advocates, working both 'for and with' their target groups. LGBT Asylum, for example, mobilises LGBT asylum seekers and works together with them 'as activists', while at the same time acting as advocate for reform of the asylum system. This dual strategy, however, can lead to ideological tensions within the organisations.

Another example is the Trampoline House, which has created a participatory model aimed at encompassing all actors, or 'users' of the House.

---

isations based in Copenhagen. A focus-group interview with The Trampoline House, LGBT Asylum and Refugees Welcome was conducted in September 2014.

[12] See *Hadforbrydelser i Danmark—vejen til effektiv beskyttelse*, (Hate Crimes in Denmartk—the Way to Effective Protection), Udredning Nr. 8, Institut for Menneskerettigheder 2011;*Hadforbrydelser. En håndbog til politiet* (Hate Crimes: a Handbook for the Police), Institut for Menneskerettigheder, 2011.

[13] All the interviews were conducted using the common RAGE questionnaire guidelines, covering the following topics: (1) the goals, values and activities of the association/network/group; (2) demonstrations and campaigns; (3) collaboration with similar organizations; (4) political communication and members; and (5) the understanding of and strategies against racism (see Siim et al. 2015).

Their militant approach is articulated as a form of 'everyday activism', directed primarily towards the users of the Trampoline House and aimed at the empowerment of the 'users'. This practice does, however, reveal some tensions between forms of 'empowerment' and 'self-empowerment' of (immigrant and refugee) activists; for example, although the 'users of the House' are able to participate in the planning and decision making, there is no evidence of the extent to which these activities contribute in practice to their self-empowerment and agency. Ideological tensions may also exist between long-term strategies 'to change the whole system', e.g., closure of refugee camps, and 'everyday activism' aimed at improving the daily life of refugees 'here and now' (see also Fraternali 2015).

It is worth noting that our interviewees agree that in the Danish context public support for organisations targeting minorities who reside legally in the country, such as organised LGBT groups like Sabaah, is easier to attract than support for asylum seekers and refugees who have not achieved legal resident status, as in the case of LGBT Asylum and the Trampoline House. Thus organisations targeting issues of integration have a relatively good chance of receiving popular support, public recognition and funding compared to organisations targeting controversial issues related to immigration. This shows that the status and future prospects of the organisations depend to a great extent on the specific target group as well as on the political climate and opportunity structures.

The organisations selected had different target groups, histories, agendas and strategies towards racism, discrimination, hate speech and behaviour, and addressed the issues at local, national and international levels. Interviewees generally mentioned discrimination in society, especially in the labour market and the education system, as the main barriers to the integration of ethnic minorities in Denmark; others emphasised the increasingly restrictive immigration legislation adopted by the Danish authorities as the major political barrier. All respondents agreed about the importance of preserving the 'racism paragraph' to protect against hate speech. This contrasts with new voices from left-wing intellectuals, journalists and pundits, arguing that the racism paragraph is perhaps an admission of the failure of public debate and that the best way to combat racism is to remove it.[14]

---

[14] http://politiken.dk/indland/ECE2078167/kendt-debattoer-er-doemt-for-racisme/.

All organisations referred to 'new forms of racism', different from biological racism but nevertheless still racialising individuals and groups in
society, but their understandings of this and strategies to deal with it differed. Only interviewees from SOS Against Racism and The Trampoline
House referred explicitly to 'structural, cultural and institutional racism'
within the Danish asylum system, whereas Sabaah and LGBT Asylum
referred mainly to 'discrimination at the level of their own country of
origin, (mainly Muslim) community and families'. Some also mentioned
the importance of changing Danish political culture and the public
sphere through information and education. One strategy gave priority
to 'bottom-up everyday activism' as a way of changing the daily lives
of refugees with practices such as cooking and eating together in The
Trampoline House (see also Fraternali 2015). Other strategies gave priority to activism aimed at reform of the Danish legal system to bring it into
line with international human rights conventions.

One of the main strategies for combating hate speech, discrimination and racism adopted by Danish organisations was to integrate the
dual roles as advocates for and activists fighting with vulnerable groups.
Interviewees generally believed it was effective to combine diverse strategies, for example to aim at legal protection, reform of the court system
and immigration policies, 'everyday activism' and enlightening the public. Multiple strategies directed at both target groups and the political
and legal system can be seen as good for democracy, and the advocacy
role on behalf of vulnerable groups may help create frameworks where
self-empowering practices can emerge, although these do not yet seem to
be the principal goals of these groups.

The interviews raised general issues about the role of immigrants, asylum seekers, refugees and LGBT activism in the Danish context, and
especially about the danger of reproducing the gap between humanitarian ideas of 'passive' beings, 'victims' needing the support of local activists, and positions supporting and actively empowering the agency and
stimulating the political subjectivity of these people. A key question is: to
what extent do the approaches of different organisations help to empower
the agency of migrants and their own action-oriented capacity through
forms of self-empowerment?

Concluding Reflections: Counter-strategies to the Politics of Fear

This chapter has explored some of the key characteristics and features of present-day Denmark in terms of combating hate speech, racism and othering. The 'politics of fear' is a widespread and universal phenomenon influenced by particular historical and political contexts (Wodak 2015) which is articulated in various ways in different national contexts. Who is perceived as friend or foe, as well as how this perception is negotiated and influenced by politicians, institutions, authorities and 'the legal system' is among the issues central to an understanding of how 'othering' and discrimination occur and spread. This raises questions about what strategies are possible and desirable for advocates or/and activists within these contexts: to what extent are organisations able to combine different strategies? To create alliances also at transnational level and to cooperate with other groups? How can strategies be altered to take account of both obstacles and opportunities at national and transnational level? (see e.g. Monforte 2014).

The chapter has argued that right-wing populism is alive and well in Denmark in two slightly different versions. One is articulated by the DPP and has developed into a type of welfare national chauvinism closely linked to the defence of the welfare state for native and ethnic Danes only, targeting 'the immigrant other' and Islam. The other version of right-wing populism is articulated by the radical anti-Muslim position of the TS, which is informally linked to international Islamophobic movements in Europe and beyond, premised on an absolute defence of freedom of expression primarily targeting Islam and 'the Muslim other'.

In Denmark, the metropolitan area of Copenhagen is still the main centre for pro-migrant activities and activism and to some extent also for the struggle against racism, discrimination and hate crimes. It is worth noting that in the Danish context most groups are dependent on public funding and support from government institutions, which may influence their goals, strategies and activities. The groups working on similar issues, such as LGBT organisations, anti-racists or advocates of asylum seekers and refugees have diverse strategies, but usually collaborate and support rather than oppose each other.

In this chapter we also argue that the development of the populist right wing and the DPP's consolidation of its influence both within and beyond parliament has contributed to what we see as a division of tasks between the different right-wing populist organisations in the country, more specifically between the DPP and the TS: the same groups are framed as targets and victims in their political rhetoric, but they adopt different strategies and propose different solutions to the immigration question.

By focusing on conflicting values/culture and religion the TS has been able to target both Islam politically and Islam/Muslims in general—a rhetoric which in many ways capitalises on Huntington's 'clash of civilisations' approach.[15] The DPP also focuses on 'the threat of Islam' and on the importance of saving 'Danish values, principles and identity' by emphasising the perceived conflicts between Danish culture and cultural values and those of Islam/Muslims in Denmark. For the DPP the focus is not primarily on 'free speech' but rather on oppressive religion, patriarchal culture and lifestyle and the need to protect Danish democracy, welfare and gender equality. The recent DPP campaign for the May 2014 EP elections clearly shows that since the economic crisis, the DPP has also become increasingly concerned over mobility and 'welfare tourism' from EU member countries.

The 'victims' for TS and *Dispatch International* are native Danes and also more generally Western civilisation under threat from Islam. This is increasingly perceived as a security issue and the solution exacerbates the conflicts with Islam and Muslims in Denmark and outside. For DPP the victims are primarily Danish citizens who have built the welfare of the country by 'paying their taxes for generations' and should thus be the main beneficiaries of their ancestors' labour. The solution is stricter border controls, and less EU and more national control of welfare and migration policies.

---

[15] Samuel Huntington's 'clash of civilisations' thesis was first presented in *Foreign Affairs* in 1993: https://www.foreignaffairs.com/articles/united-states/1993-06-01/clash-civilizations.

The present study has raised a number of questions about hate speech, discrimination and othering in the Danish context that should be further explored. What are the most effective strategies for civil society organisations in the Danish context? To what extent do diverse civil society actors cooperate and negotiate with political institutions about hate speech, othering and racism? What needs to be done by mainstream institutions, for example adopting a National Action Plan against racism and hate speech? How has the political elite, including Social Democracy, helped to normalise and gain acceptance of the discourse and values of right-wing populism?

Within this framework, global mobility and European integration have put new issues on the political agenda that inspire a political and theoretical rethinking about, for example, the need to create more inclusive forms of democracy, citizenship, welfare and civil solidarity, i.e., new notions of European citizenship and belonging (Fraser 2007). This remains a highly contested terrain and the question is not merely what solutions are achievable, but which are especially desirable and practicable.

References

Akkermann, T., & Hagelund, A. (2007). 'Women and children first!' Anti-immigration parties and gender in Norway and the Netherlands'. *Patterns of Prejudice, 42*(2), 197–214.

Albertazzi, D., & McDonnell, D. (Eds.). (2008). *Twenty-first century populism. The spectre of western European democracy.* Basingstoke, England: Palgrave Macmillan.

Anderson, B. (1983). *Imagined communities.* London: Verso.

Arditi, B. (2010). *Politics on the edges of liberalism.* Edinburgh: Edinburgh University Press.

Betz, H.-G., & Meret, S. (2009). Revisiting Lepanto: The political mobilization against Islam in contemporary Western Europe. *Patterns of Prejudice, 14*(3–4), 313–334.

Betz, H.-G., & Meret, S. (2012). Right-wing populist parties and the working class vote: What have you done for us lately? In J. Rydgren (Ed.), *Class politics and the radical right* (pp. 107–121). London: Routledge.

Borchorst, A., & Siim, B. (2002). The women-friendly welfare state revisited. *NORA. The Nordic Journal of Women's Studies, 10*(2), 90–98.

Brochmann, G., & Hagelund, A. (Eds.). (2012). *Immigration policy and the Scandinavian welfare state 1945–2010.* Houndsmills, England: Palgrave Macmillan.

Demker, M. (2012). Scandinavian right-wing parties: Diversity more than convergence? In A. Mammone, E. Godin, & B. Jenkins (Eds.), *Mapping the extreme right in contemporary Europe. From local to transnational* (pp. 239–253). London: Routledge.

Esping-Andersen, G. (1990). *Three worlds of welfare capitalism.* Princeton, NJ: Princeton University Press.

Fraser, N. (2007). Transnationalizing the public sphere. On the legitimacy and efficacy of public opinion in a post-Westphalien world. *Theory & Society, 24*(4), 7–30.

Fraternali, M. (2015). *Everyday activism in pro-asylum movements. A qualitative study of the Trampoline House in Copenhagen.* MA Thesis, Department of Culture and Global Studies, Aalborg University.

Goul Andersen, J., & Bjørklund, T. (2000). Radical right-wing populism in Scandinavia: From tax revolt to neo-liberalism. In P. Hainsworth (Ed.), *The politics of the extreme right* (pp. 193–223). London: Pinter.

Hedetoft, U., Petersson, B., & Sturfelt, L. (2006). *Bortom Stereotyperne. Invandrere och integration i Danmark og Sverige* (Centrum för Danmarksstudier 12). Göteborg, Stockholm: Makadam.

Hellström, A., Nilsson, T., & Stoltz, P. (2012). Nationalism vs. Nationalism: The challenge of the Sweden Democrats in the Swedish Public debate. *Government and Opposition, 47*(2), 186–205.

Hellström, A., & Wennerhag, M. (2013). Nationalist Myth-Making and Populist mobilization in Scandinavia. *Partecipazione e conflitto, 6*(3), 30–53.

Hervik, P. (2011). *The annoying difference: The emergence of Danish neonationalism, neoracism, and populism in the post-1989 world.* New York: Bergham Books.

Hilson, M. (2010). *The Nordic model. Scandinavia since 1945.* London: Reaktion Books.

Hobsbawn, E. J. (1992). *Nations and nationalism since 1780.* Cambridge, England: Cambridge University Press.

Jungar, A.-C., & Jupskås, A. R. (2014). Populist radical right parties in the Nordic region: A new and distinct party family? *Scandinavian Political Studies, 37*(3), 215–238.

Knudsen, T. (2006). *Fra enevælde til folkestyre. Dansk demokratihistorie indtil 1973.* Copenhagen, Denmark: Akademisk Forlag.

Korsgaard, O. (2004). *Kampen om Folket. Et dannelsesperspektiv på folkets historie i 500 år [The struggle about the people]*. Copenhagen, Denmark: Gyldendal.

Melby, K., Ravn, A.-B., & Carlsson-Wetterberg, C. (Eds.). (2008). *Gender equality as a perspective on welfare: The limits of political ambition*. Bristol, England: Policy Press.

Meret, S. (2010). *The Danish People's Party, the Italian Northern League and the Austrian Freedom Party in a comparative perspective: Party ideology and electoral support*. SPIRIT Ph.D. series, Aalborg University, Aalborg, Denmark.

Meret, S. (2015). Charismatic female leadership and gender: Pia Kjærsgård and the Danish Peoples' Party. *Patterns of Prejudice, 49*(1–2), 81–102.

Meret, S., & Siim, B. (2013). Gender, populism and politics of belonging: Discourses of rightwing populist parties in Denmark, Norway and Austria. In B. Siim & M. Mokre (Eds.), *Negotiating gender and diversity in an emerging European public sphere* (pp. 78–96). Basingstoke, England: Palgrave Macmillan.

Minkenberg, M. (2008). *The radical right in Europe: An overview*. Gütersloh, Germany: Verlag Bertelsmann Stiftung.

Monforte, P. (2014). *Europeanizing Contention. The Protest against 'Fortress Europe' in France and Germany*. New York, Oxford: berghahn Books.

Mouritsen, P. (2006). The particular universalism of a Nordic civic nation. Common values, state religion and Islam in Danish political culture. In T. Modood, A. Triandafyllidou, & R. Zapata-Barrero (Eds.), *Multiculturalism, Muslims and citizenship* (pp. 70–93). London: Frank Cass Publishers.

Mudde, C. (2007). *Populist radical right parties in Europe*. Cambridge, England: Cambridge University Press.

Mudde, C., & Kaltwasser, C. R. (2013). *Populism in Europe and the Americas: Threat or corrective for democracy?* New York: Cambridge University Press.

Rydgren, J. (Ed.). (2012). *Right wing populism and the working class*. London: Routledge.

Rydgren, J., & Widfeldt, A. (2004). *Från Le Pen till Pim Fortuyn. Populism och paralmentarisj högerextremisk i dagens Europa*. Malmö, Sweden: Liber.

Siim B., Fulgsang Larsen, J., & Meret, S. (2013). *Danish populism: Hate speech and populist othering. Analysis of interviews*. Report from the Rage project (WS1).

Siim B., Fulgsang Larsen, J., & Meret, S. (2014). *State of the art. Militants from the other side. Anti-bodies to hate-speech and behavior in Denmark*. National Report from the RAGE project (WS3), May 2014.

Siim B., Fulgsang Larsen, J., & Meret, S. (2015). *Militants from the other side: Anti-bodies to hate-speech and behavior in Denmark: Analysis of Focus Group Interviews* (Work Stream 3).

Siim B., & Meret, S. (2013). *State of the art: Literature review: Danish populism.* National Report from the RAGE-project (Work Stream 1).

Siim, B., & Skjeie, H. (2008). Tracks, intersections and dead ends. Multicultural challenges to state feminism in Denmark and Norway. *Ethnicities, 8*(3), 322–344.

Siim, B., & Stoltz, P. (2015). Particularities of the Nordic gender—Challenges to equality politics in a globalized world. In S. Thidemann Faber & H. Pristed-Nielsen (Eds.), *Remapping, gender, place and mobility. Global confluences and local particularities in Nordic peripheries* (pp. 19–35). Farnham, England: Ashgate.

Smith, A. D. (2001). *Nationalism.* Cambridge, England: Polity Press.

Togeby, L. (2004). *Man har et standpunkt. Om stabilitet og forandring I befolkningens holdninger [Stability and change in peoples' attitudes].* Aarhus: Aarhus Universitetsforlag.

Vad Jønsson, H., & Petersen, K. (2010). Danmark: den nationale velfærdsstat møder verden. In G. Brochmann & A. Hagelund (Eds.), *Velferdens grense* (pp. 131–210). Oslo, Norway: Universitetsforlaget.

Von Beyme, K. (1988). Right-wing extremism in post-war Europe. *West European Politics, 11*(2), 1–17.

Wodak, R. (2015). *Politics of fear. What right wing populist discourses mean.* London: Sage.

6

Populism in the Slovenian Context: Between Ethno-Nationalism and Re-Traditionalisation

Mojca Pajnik, Roman Kuhar, and Iztok Šori

Introduction: Right-Wing Populism in Post-Socialist Slovenia

Populism in the context of Central and Eastern Europe is related to the shifts in the period 1989–1991 that saw the collapse of multinational political entities—the Soviet Union, Yugoslavia and Czechoslovakia— and the change in the political system from communist one-party rule to pluralist liberal democracies. The conflicts in the Balkans and the emerging new political systems were largely interpreted in the context

M. Pajnik (✉)
Peace Institute, Institute for Contemporary Social and Political Studies, Ljubljana, Slovenia

R. Kuhar
Faculty of Arts, Department of Sociology, University of Ljubljana, Ljubljana, Slovenia

I. Šori
Peace Institute, Institute for Contemporary Social and Political Studies, Ljubljana, Slovenia

© The Editor(s) (if applicable) and The Author(s) 2016   **137**
G. Lazaridis et al. (eds.), *The Rise of the Far Right in Europe*,
DOI 10.1057/978-1-137-55679-0_6

of (ethnic) nationalism, while at the same time populism entered the debate, mostly in relation to the rise of the extreme right in these societies (Mudde 2005; Ramet 1999a, b; Rizman 1999).

The populist extreme right, its 'racist extremism in Central-Eastern Europe' (Mudde 2005) relies on the will of 'the people' against the corrupt elites, where 'the people' means 'the natives', the ethnic majority, and is often organised around a strong authoritarian leader (Kuzmanić 2002; Mudde 2005). Analysing the extreme right in the post-1989 Central and Eastern European context, Ramet (1999a) relates its rise to intolerance, antidemocratic attitudes, hatred of reason and celebration of 'retro-invented traditional values'. This is acknowledged by Rizman (1999: 148–149) who points out that the rise of the right in Slovenia meant the emergence and rise of right-wing populism whose mixture of conservative ideology consists of authoritarianism, traditionalism, religion and nativism (cf. Mudde 2007). Back in the late 1990s Rizman (1999: 170) described the Slovenian Democratic Party (SDP) with its leader Janez Janša, and the ruling hierarchy of the Roman Catholic Church (RCC) as pertinent examples of populism in Slovenia. These two forces remain as examples today. This chapter's case studies focus on contemporary populism through the examples of the SDP, which has kept Janša, twice prime minister of Slovenia (2004–2008 and 2012–2013) as its leader since the establishment of the party in 1989, and the Civil Initiative for the Family and the Rights of Children (CIFRC), which has strong connections to the RCC. The strong connections between all three actors enable us to construct a triangular view.

Kuzmanić (2005) argues that in the context of former Yugoslavia, to which Slovenia is a successor state, we need to distinguish nationalist movements from 'Volkish populist movements'. Without implying that in the Yugoslav context there was no nationalism, Kuzmanić argues that it was more or less overshadowed by Volkish populist movements associated with a specific leadership, such as Janšism in Slovenia, Tuđmanism in Croatia and Miloševićism in Serbia, especially from the 1990s onwards. 'Populists of the Volkish kind do not want to establish either a nation or a state; they want people' (ibid. 11). Strong leaders appear as agitators mobilising 'the mob" at public meetings. In other words, populism as a neo-conservative revolution in the Balkan region connotes lack of state and of politics and it therefore comes as no surprise that populism activities discredit legal institutions (Bugarič 2008; Mikuž 2010) or, alternatively, suggest their own legal solutions that go no further than the protection of the leadership of strong populist agitators. Consequently, the region has seen an establishment of quasi-states, 'a radical Volkish populist version of a non-state or even of a *Volksgemeinschaft*', a kind of 'quasi-parliamentary democracy', which fails to function according to the principles of citizenship, legal equality and human rights. Rather, 'it consistently discriminates, harasses, segregates, excludes' (Kuzmanić 2002: 18–19).

Right-wing populism at the time, according to Rizman (1999), needed a fresh list of enemies when class/capitalism and the imperialist Western enemy faded away with the collapse of the regime. Populist re-traditionalisation of post-socialist Slovenia found the new enemies in migrants, former Yugoslavs, Roma, Muslims, LGBT people, also left-wing intellectuals, communists and politicians who did not prioritise national interests. The othering reproduced by right-wing populism in Slovenia, also referred to as 'extremist populism' (Dolar 1995), was closely related to the narratives about the emergence of Slovenia as an independent state. These narratives demonstrate anti-Balkan and anti-communist rhetoric that constructs the Slovenian nation as 'our people', while simultaneously excluding 'the others' using criteria of ethnicity, sexual orientation, religion, gender, political affiliation and so on.

The process of establishing independent statehood brought about two general frames within which the majority of 'othering' has occurred in the past two and a half decades. The first is linked with attempts to differentiate Slovenian national identity from anything regarded as Balkan (i.e., backward, primitive) and to place it within the context of Europe (i.e., progressive, democratic). An important platform for othering in Slovenia has hence been based on the creation and purification of the newly established Slovenian identity.

The second major context of populism was the re-traditionalisation of Slovenian society, with conservative and religious actors regaining power after years of repression under the previous political system. This gave voice to a number of attempts to take away rights already won (e.g. abortion), or to prevent their extension to groups not entitled to them (e.g. LGBT). Here, the extreme populist discourses and actions have been based on biological interpretations of culture and the common conceptualisations of what is normal and, consequently, what is not. This chapter analyses the two contexts of populism in the Slovenian example by unravelling the structures of ethno-nationalist and ethno-religious populism, focusing on narratives from interviews conducted with SDP members, CIFRC supporters and human rights activists.

Case Studies

The Slovenian Democratic Party and the Phenomenon of Janšism

It was in 1990 that new political parties emerged in Slovenia in preparation for the first post-World War II multiparty elections in April of that year. Certain opposition groups formed the Democratic Opposition (Demos) that based its pre-election strategy on anti-communism, while its avowed focus was on achieving a sovereign Slovenia with parliamentary democracy. Demos came out the big winner, defeating the former Communist Party by winning 54 per cent of the vote, and declaring the independence of Slovenia on 25 June 1991.

In the years that followed, several new political parties were formed. The parliamentary elections of 1992 showed steep gains for the Slovenian National Party (SNP) with its leader Zmago Jelinčič and his pervasive 'extreme nationalist', 'even fascistoid' rhetoric (Rizman 1999: 151) advocating the purification of the Slovenian nation (of Yugoslavs). The early 1990s also brought the rise of other populist parties, such as the SDP with its leader Janez Janša. The complex phenomenon of 'Janšism' exemplifies well the paradoxes of transition in the wider regional context. Janša, 'never a liberal, skeptical intellectual, but a familiar example of an East European dissident, an anticommunist authoritarian' (Rizman 1999: 161) was sentenced and imprisoned by a military court during the communist regime, and freed in 1988 after mass protests. A former Marxist, communist and pacifist who had aimed at the civilian control of the army under the previous regime, became, ironically, a defence minister in the new regime and a leading populist known for his demagogic rhetoric, anti-communism and othering of minorities. 'Yesterday's renegade' and 'today's authoritarian' (Rizman 1999: 156) represents a 'strange mixture of populism, egalitarianism, xenophobia, anti-intellectualism, and intolerance toward marginal groups with a political discourse and iconography which reminds one at the same time of Nazism and Stalinism, but who still tries to form his authoritarian posture inside the existing democratic order, and moreover demagogically swearing to it' (Miheljak in Rizman 1999: 160).

Janša's anti-politics organises 'rural folklore', a characteristic of Slovenian populism, around strong appeals to popular prejudice against 'the others', producing anti-equality-oriented discourses and policies about migrants, the erased, Muslims, Jews, Arabs, Southerners, gays and lesbians, Roma, punks, feminists, etc. (Kuzmanić 2003: 25, 31). The populist new right worships its untouchable leader, who uses a discourse of 'urgency': 'Slovenia has to take these measures or else' is a common justification in SDP rhetoric, as if the necessity is something genetically determined and unavoidable. Populism of the Janša type also reinforces gender hierarchies, producing and publicly spreading, more or less explicitly, sexist remarks, adopting policies that limit women's rights and reinforcing 'macho' culture. Tactics similar to othering are also used also to discredit state institutions, media and political opponents.

Janša, the undisputed SDP leader, represents himself as 'the real victim' both of former communism and of present democracy (Rizman 1999: 160). He garners support for his 'demagogic populism' from the populist intelligentsia previously grouped around the Cultural Forum (*Kulturni forum*) and The Assembly for a Republic (*Zbor za republiko*), who provide the ideological base for his populism. The RCC also reinforces Janšism and its populist provincialism.

Populism of the Civil Initiative for the Family and the Rights of Children

In 2008 the new government, with Social Democrats as the main party, introduced a new Family Code with new interpretations of family and civil marriage. The Code extended the definition of the family to all forms of biological as well as social parenting. The definition of civil marriage also changed to put heterosexual and homosexual partnerships and their civil marriage rights on an equal legal footing, including the right to single parent or joint adoptions (Rajgelj 2010; Kogovšek 2010; Švab 2010).

These changes had been a bone of contention for over three years. While the new Family Code was adopted in Parliament, it was later rejected at a public referendum in March 2012 with 55 per cent of voters against the new law. It was in the context of these processes that a new civil initiative—The Civil Initiative for the Family and the Rights of Children (CIFRC)—came into being. It was led by philosophy graduate Aleš Primc.

Primc, more or less the only publicly recognisable face of the CIFRC, is no stranger to conservative and exclusionary civil movements. In 2001 he was part of the campaign against the right of single women to artificial insemination. The issue was taken to a public referendum and the above mentioned right—which was in place from the mid-1970s on—was denied to all single women (i.e., only women in a heterosexual relationship were now entitled to artificial insemination for medical reasons). At the time, his populist discourse was framed with issues of what is natural and normal and—among others—a successful creation of moral panic that lesbians will give birth to children because they want to have children as toys to play with (Hrženjak 2001).

The CIFRC campaign in 2011 and 2012 was overtly directed against gays and lesbians, rejecting their civil rights, especially the right to adoption recognised by the new Family Code. Although the Code would bring many positive changes in terms of child protection and the work of, for example, social services and similar agencies, it was rejected as a whole only because it introduced marriage equality.

During the campaign against the adoption of the new Family Code, the CIFRC and other opponents (including the SDP) claimed—citing scientific research—that a child needs a father and a mother for a healthy growing up. The wider frame of the CIFRC's activities was the preservation of the Slovenian nation and culture, which can be best illustrated by Primc's speech in Parliament during the first public presentation of the Family Code. He said: 'I never thought that I would speak in Parliament for the first time with such an honourable task: to defend the family and the foundation of our culture.' His speech was a well-orchestrated show of hatred against a group of people in the society, hidden under the guise of caring for children and the future of the Slovenian nation (Kuhar 2010). The CIFRC's campaign was thus based on nationalistic and homophobic discourses, seeing LGBT people as a threat to the institution of Slovenian family. Furthermore, for the CIFRC 'others' consist of all who do not meet the standards of Catholic Church morality, particularly LGBT persons, same-sex families, single women, sex workers, and political opponents and NGOs engaged in protection of human rights.

Methodology and Sample

The analysis in this chapter is based on interviews that were conducted as part of two case studies, the SDP and the CIFRC. In each case study three groups of respondents were interviewed: visible members or supporters of the party or the organisation ('bodies'), representatives of various civil initiatives or organisations who act against racist policies and discourse or are opposed to the party's position on specific issues (victims' organisations, NGOs, the erased, migrants/workers, trade unions, women's organisations, LGBT groups) and victims of populist discourse and policies. For the SDP case study twelve interviews were conducted: five with members or former members of the party, six with NGO representatives and one with a victim. For the CIFRC case study nine interviews were conducted: three with opponents of the Family Code, who were also supporters of the CIFRC, five with the proponents of the Family Code and one with a victim of populist discourse.

While we did not face major obstacles in approaching respondents from the SDP, most actors from the CIFRC refused to participate in the interviews, probably because the research was conducted by the Peace Institute, which actively supported the Family Code and has been critical of the populist rhetoric and actions of the CIFRC. Field work experience suggests that some CIFRC protagonists were annoyed and did not want to comment further on an 'old story'—the field work took place in Spring and Autumn in 2013—giving the impression that they had been mobilised at some time, had achieved what they wanted to and then retreated from public life. It is also likely that their refusal to take part was jointly orchestrated. Eventually, we managed to conduct three interviews with opponents of the Family Code who often used the same arguments as the CIFRC. Bearing in mind that the CIFRC is strongly connected to the RCC, two of the interviewees were working in Church organisations, while one leads a Conservative family initiative. To enhance the analysis, materials produced by the SDP and the CIFRC (manifestos, news, media) and publications published in mainstream media were also included in the analysis.

Questionnaires for the 'bodies' (SDP members and CIFRC supporters), and victims' organisations as well as victims were different in content and scope. General questions on understanding of populism, othering and gender equality, and questions on the EU were included, while victims' organisations and victims were asked specific questions about their experience and anti-racism activity. All interviews for both case studies were complemented with field diaries, transcribed and analysed using a critical discourse analysis approach.

Ethno-Nationalist Populism: Claiming Slovenianhood Against the Balkans

As the research discussed above suggests, ethno-nationalist populism turns out to be the predominant frame within which othering has been enabled in Slovenia in the last 25 years, and the analysis of the interviews confirms this observation. It is linked with attempts to differentiate and purify Slovenian national identity from anything that is perceived as Balkan. Distancing from the Balkans is connected with the processes of othering within the nation (i.e., the separation of 'true Slovenians' from Southerners, Muslims and Roma), and in relation to distinguishing the (national) 'us' from 'them', the outsiders (e.g., migrants).

In parliamentary politics, ethno-nationalist othering is nowadays most represented by the SDP and Christian Conservative New Slovenia. Until recently the Slovenian People's Party, which is also responsible for othering, was represented in Parliament, while all three belong to the so-called Slovenian Spring parties, whose legacy is built on the nationalist-democratisation movement dating from the late 1980s. What connects them is their construction of groups of 'others' as endangering the Slovenian nation, and the discrimination they encourage through popular voting mechanisms such as referendums.

Populism, and in particular ethno-nationalist populism, is however not just a feature of right-wing party discourse and policy. Prime minister Miro Cerar of the liberal Modern Centre Party has repeatedly spoken of the currently pertinent issues of migration and refugee quotas, claiming that the 'integrational capabilities of our country and security factors have to be taken in account' before any decisions about quotas are made. This argument is strikingly close to populist extreme right discourse, which emphatically uses security arguments and refers to 'the tolerance threshold' of common people, reinforcing neo-racist ideas and policies (Baskar 2004: 146).

The idea of national purification was most starkly and poignantly illustrated by the secret removal of more than 25,000 names from the register of permanent residents of Slovenia in February 1992. This illegal and unconstitutional administrative measure later became known as the 'erasure'. Most of the erased, or at least one of their parents, were born in other republics of the former Yugoslavia, which suggests their erasure was based on their ethnic origin. The erased remained without legal status—without documents or access to health care and social security. With no entitlement to work, they were forced to resort to undeclared labour, so were in constant fear of persecution and subjected to exploitation. The erasure turned these once permanent residents into illegal immigrants. This was a systematic violation of human rights followed up with strategies of justification (Dedić et al. 2003; Kogovšek Šalamon 2012).

The erasure only became public knowledge because of the self-organisation of the erased and their appearances in the mass media. In 1999 the Constitutional Court declared the act of erasure illegal, but in practice the issue remained unresolved until 2012, when the European Court of Human Rights (ECHR) decided that the erased should be compensated for their suffering. The judgement stated that the reparations should ensure that all the erased should have their residence status regularised and were entitled to remedies and specific rights, i.e., extension of residence permits to all family members to avoid breaking up families abroad. A special Act was adopted to implement the judgement but the compensation was much lower and restoration of rights limited compared to the ruling of the ECHR. Fears of the high level of compensation the erased will apparently receive from 'us' is one of the main arguments of the parties that opposed the attempts to restore their rights, while the political will of the remaining parties to resolve this issue is not strong.

Most of the hostility towards the erased came from the Slovenian National Party. During a hunger strike by the erased in 2005 a sign appeared on the doors of its parliamentary group office stating: 'All erased invited to a dance, Jelinčič will play for you to the machine gun!' The main promotor of the othering of the erased was, however, the SDP which worked energetically to prevent the adoption of restorative legislation. In 2004 when the law that was to restore the rights was proposed in Parliament the SDP organised 30 MPs' signatures and submitted an appeal for a referendum on the law. The turnout was very low, at 31.5 per cent, but 94.7 per cent voted against the adoption of the law. This is a clear example of extreme right populist thinking with the state as a nativist concept where the 'voice of the people" takes precedence over the constitutional rights (of minorities) (Mudde 2005: 155).

The erased are constructed in SDP discourse as enemies who acted against the Slovenians and the independent Slovenian nation state. One of the populist tactics employed included challenging the self-assertive name with the term 'so-called erased', suggesting that the erasure never happened. While the SDP's activities are clearly attributable to populist othering and hate speech, in our interviews SDP representatives claimed that they 'never had anything against the so-called erased', but only wanted rights to be restored on a case-by-case basis. In practice this means separating 'good' members of the discriminated group from 'bad' ones. The quote below also shows how populism's consistency consists of its denial of populism.

> Now, regarding the erased, I have argued right from the beginning—and you can check on this wherever you want—just that there should be individual treatment from case to case and that it is unfair and offensive to everyone, also to the so-called erased, to lump everyone together. You have all kinds of people there, including those who were against the independence of Slovenia, but there are also unlucky cases who were caught by the flow of history and are indeed victims. And I have always said that injustices must be set right. But you cannot give credit to someone who attacked you. And this is no populism. (SDP member)

In addition to representing themselves as great patriots, members of the SDP have also used other, seemingly more rational grounds for the othering of migrants, categorically denying accusations of intolerance. One of the MPs spoke about apparently high criminality rates among migrants, expressing her regret that records of offenders' nationality are not kept. Her statements are speculations not based on any data: 'if we read about the misdemeanours, convicted, up and down, everything ends with an ić' (ić is a common suffix of surnames originating in some of the former Yugoslav republics). This interviewee also suggested that the whole system is structured in such a way as to privilege migrants who have contributed nothing, while 'our' hard working people are being punished. Another MP brought up migrants in connection with the abuse of the social security system:

> For example, now, I know that those who live in Slovenia have massive problems obtaining allowances—and this is happening on a massive scale. This has nothing to do with nationality. On the other hand there are many people who know how to cheat the system and claim benefits for their children, for families who are not here at all. I am sorry, but if we allow this in Slovenia then you have to ask yourself if we are out of our senses, put very diplomatically. (SDP member)

It is not only democracy, safety and welfare that are perceived as endangered by migrants in ethno-nationalist populism, but also Slovenian and European culture. While migration is understood as something inevitable, as part of humanity, the state is made responsible for defending local culture and Slovenian people (Slovenianhood), with the national identity in danger of extinction. Here is an example from a member of the RCC:

> I would say that Slovenia has to protect its culture. … Because if there is as much migration as we are having, national core values disappear. But there is a lot of life energy in our nation. Just take a look at how much migration there was at the time of the Yugoslav federation. And we survived and continue living. However, there are certain conditions. The state is required to preserve what makes our country Slovenian. (CIFRC supporter)

Importantly migrants are associated with the communist era and with left-wing parties. The ethno-nationalist argument is that communists imposed 'brotherhood and unity' as a way of destroying Slovenian national identity. Within Catholic and conservative parties and organisations the issue of migration is also associated with the 'demographic crisis', with the claim that in societies, such as ours, where there are not enough children born, migration is a 'natural process'. It is because of the lack of proper policies in support of the family that Slovenia has to face migration. This discourse, which reveals the centrality of family and gender in ethno-nationalist populism, is illustrated by with the activities of the CIFRC, which frequently uses the argument of the preservation of the Slovenian nation and culture in opposition to LGBT rights.

Another group targeted by ethno-nationalist populism are Muslims. The Muslim community has been seeking to build a mosque in Ljubljana for over 40 years, and it is only in recent years that the issue has begun to be resolved. Since most Muslims in Slovenia regard their ethnic affiliation as Bosnian, their minority status is not only as a religious group but also as an ethnic group. They are denied the status of a national minority, but the ethnic marker Bosnian comes with Eurocentric perceptions of 'the South' (i.e., the Balkans) and they experience socio-economic exclusion (Bajt 2011). It is not uncommon for SDP members to oppose the mosque that would 'surely upset the autochthonous population to such an extent that the positive attitude to Slovene Muslims that has existed till now would be ruined' as the president of the local SDP organisation stated.

One of the most widely reported racist incidents against Roma happened in October 2006 when the Roma family Strojan was evicted from their own land in the village of Ambrus by an enraged mob. The incident was directly supported by the government, with police minister Dragutin Mate of the SDP arriving at the scene and assuring the people that the Strojan family would never come back. In our interviews, SDP members felt that the most important area for improvement of the situation of Roma is education, with a view to 'integrating Roma' and assimilating them to the majority culture. Reference to essential differences between Roma and the Slovenian population are common and can be regarded as a discursive manifestation of cultural racism. The SDP's attempts to integrate 'the other' in society are understood as genuinely good intentions. This discourse is reminiscent of the Orientalist discourse of the civilising mission (*mission civilisatrice*) perpetuated by Europeans during colonial rule.

I think that the example of Prekmurje [a region in Slovenia] is a good one. These groups are integrated, they are told, these are the rules, and they get a certain amount of time to adjust to the rules. If they fail to adapt, we have to consider sanctions. The fact that a certain group from Žabjek [a small village in the region of Dolenjska] has more weapons than the whole Slovenian state, 'God help us'. (SDP member)

Our case studies also demonstrate the heterogeneity of populisms in Europe. European right-wing populist parties may be Eurosceptic or—as it is the case with the SDP and also New Slovenia—have mostly pro-EU attitudes. These parties not only support the EU as it is, but also receive support from 'Brussels' in the shape of the European People's Party. The SDP's views on the EU are, like many other issues, included in the anti-communist discourse, in which the ethno-nationalist arguments in favour of the EU are of particular interest. Membership of the EU is constructed as an escape and liberation from Yugoslavia—not just from communism, but especially from 'the Balkans', its customs and its people. By acceding to the EU Slovenia finally joined the family of 'culturally close' nations and, similarly, the party joined the 'culturally close' family of European parties. As a younger member of the party stated, the 'Balkan spirit' still prevents us from prospering, even now, in the EU. Consequently, even if criticism is expressed of, for example, the loss of sovereignty in relation to the EU, the argument always ends in favour of the EU, as everything is better than it was before. In this respect the political space in Slovenia is regarded as 'un-European', because most of the governments since inde-pendence have been led by left and liberal parties.

A layer of democratisation and human rights discourse is grafted onto Slovenian ethno-nationalist populism, which is usually presented as patriotism. According to the party's manifesto, the SDP stands for six core values: freedom, human dignity, justice, solidarity, patriotism and environmental awareness. While party members apply neoliberal eco-nomic discourse within everyday politics, one of the interviewees states that the SDP's self-proclaimed values are the 'values of ordinary people'. Reference to 'ordinary people' is commonly understood as a feature of populist politics, and often involves an anti-elite and anti-intellectual stance. Such is the case with the SDP. These values are, as we can read in their manifesto, the core values of 'our culture and civilisation', that of 'Europe and Western countries'. What is important in this message is what is unspoken: the party's positioning of itself against the South, the Balkans and Yugoslavia as an uncivilised world. As an SDP member said, the party strives to bring these values into the Slovenian political space, blaming 'old thinking patterns which are being carried on from the times before 1990' for all the problems the country is facing.

Ethno-Religious Populism: Defending the Nation's 'Right Family'

The starting point of the mobilisation of organisations and movements that can be defined with reference to ethno-religious populism is that political demands for equality that are deconstructing the patriarchal order of society are seen as not being in accordance with the laws of nature and normality. Minority groups, particularly sex workers, single women and LGBTs, do not fit into the hetero-normative notions of 'good citizens' and are directly opposed to the traditional patriarchal culture that is increasingly promoted by the RCC and related conservative organisations and political parties.

In the 1990s the RCC slowly but steadily regained its position as a 'collective intellectual', acquiring influence over numerous social and political issues (Kerševan 1996). Furthermore, the process of re-traditionalisation was often accompanied by a nationalistic quest for the 'true national self', which had been allegedly lost during the communist regime (Kuhar 2015). The major targets of ethno-religious populism are 'proper' gender roles, which to a great extent are perceived as biological givens, ahistorical and vital for the continuation of the nation. The populist debates are therefore concentrated around a 'heterosexual matrix' (Butler 1990) and the accepted essentialist conceptualisations of what is natural and normal and what is not. In the context of the 'heterosexual matrix', heterosexuality is seen as a 'natural' extension of both genders. For that reason heterosexuality is the only natural, normal and justifiable form of sexuality as it also contributes to reproduction of the nation. Other forms, primarily homosexuality, are at best tolerated, but are also persecuted—symbolically, culturally, politically and legally.

In the past few years ethno-religious populism in Slovenia has most often emerged in the context of a highly organised and structured 'anti-gender movement', a pan-European phenomenon. Its political agenda includes opposition to marriage equality, reproductive rights and abortion, sex education in schools and similar issues related to gender equality and sexual citizenship (Paternotte 2014). Over the past 25 years it is precisely around these issues that we find in Slovenia instances of an ethno-religious populism that today is part of a highly structured, organised, cross-border political movement.

In 2012 the CIFRC, using ethno-religious discourse and in close collaboration with the the RCC and right-wing political parties, successfully opposed the adoption of a new Family Code which would grant marriage equality and equal rights to same-sex partners. During the Family Code debate (2009–2012) the media insisted on debating this question in a for-and-against way, which they sought to justify as 'balanced reporting'. However there was also an implicit expectation of spectacle, which is guaranteed (and easily achieved) in such debates. This particular media format contributed to the endless reproduction and legitimisation of populism. Scientific arguments were rarely raised, and even in those few cases, they were often silenced by the loud and dramatic speeches of political and religious demagogues, whose interventions were often a well-orchestrated show of hatred against a group of people in society ('the other'), hidden under the guise of caring for children and family (to include proper gender roles) and the future of the Slovenian nation (Lešnik 2010; Kuhar 2010). It was a *déjà vu* from 2001 when the right of single women to artificial insemination was the subject of a referendum.

The RCC played an important role in the public debate on the Family Code. While in previous policy debates on the legal recognition of same-sex partnerships (the debate started in the early 1990s) representatives of the RCC often adduced God and the Bible in their opposition to the legal recognition of same-sex unions, such references were mostly absent from their public interventions during the Family Code debate. God and the Bible were replaced by the results of scientific research. However as these results do not support their arguments that same-sex families are a dangerous and an unhealthy environment for children to grow up in, they have falsified significant amounts of scientific evidence, presenting it in the form of catchy, populist results (Kuhar 2015). Simplistic, false, but effective messages created by the RCC, such as that a gay man can be a good father, but cannot replace a mother, worked. They worked especially when the Family Code was the subject of a public referendum where the majority (54.6 per cent) voted against it.

The common denominator of policy debates in the last 25 years in Slovenia around abortion, artificial insemination, prostitution and marriage equality is sexual citizenship, a concept that addresses how a political society, through (non-)recognition of citizenship rights, influences and controls sexual self-expression and choices related to bodies, feelings, identities, relationships, genders, eroticism, representations and so forth. According to Weeks (1998) it is the sexual citizen who enters the public sphere to reveal his/her intimate choices and turns them into political issues in order to be able to live his/her 'intimacy' both in private and, as a sexual citizen, in public. However in doing so the sexual citizen encounters resistance and anti-narratives. Both the SDP and the CIFRC (and other opponents of the Family Code, including the RCC) have been active conveyors for such resistance.

Populist discourse is generally based on simple, straightforward, goes-without-saying types of claims, which on the surface look rational and logic. However it is precisely this simplicity that conceals questions and issues that are not visible on the surface. In the context of gender and marriage equality, the potential for populism resides in the hetero-normative essentialist understanding of genders as simple biological categories. Consequently it is understood that male and female identity is biologically determined. Furthermore, biology is used as justification for unequal gender roles. On the other hand, feminist post-structural analyses of gender are understood as 'nonsense', 'a dangerous weapon', 'social engineering' used in schools against 'our children' and the natural binary system of male and female genders. One of our interviewees, a representative of the RCC, claimed:

'We believe that male and female sexes are biologically determined, and the idea that male and female sexes are the same and that it is even possible—on the level of gender—to exchange these roles and so forth ... and [that it is possible] on the basis of all these to establish even new social realities, such as redefinition of family or marriage ... these are things we do not agree with.' (CIFRC supporter)

Although all our SDP and CIFRC respondents support gender equality in terms of equal rights and opportunities, the latter should not in their view interfere with traditional gender roles and gender relations, which are seen as complementary. As the sexes are biologically different, they also play different social roles and any interference with such a binary system is seen as (unwanted) social experimentation. According to a CIFRC supporter, women's specific role is primarily due to the fact that they give birth and raise children. Men, he claims, should also participate in this—for example by taking care of social security for their families. However, according to him, a man should not participate in raising children 'at the expense of his male identity'.

The understanding of genders and their relations as natural is concretely reflected in the opponents' interpretation of marriage: our respondents believe that marriage is between one man and one woman. That is why they see no contradiction in terms when they simultaneously claim that there should be no discrimination against minorities in a society and that their human rights should be respected. As they do not see marriage as a human right also for same-sex couples, they do not see any contradiction in terms when claiming support for equal rights for everyone. 'We believe it is unacceptable to discriminate against anyone on the basis of sexual orientation', says a representative of the RCC. 'However, when we talk about marriage and family, our opinion is that this is not a human right' as such union is 'by its nature ... a union of a man and a woman'.

The opponents of the Family Code interpret the definition of marriage as a union of one man and one woman as non-discriminatory, as the same conditions apply to everyone. In other words, the institution of marriage is not discriminatory towards gays and lesbians as they also can get married 'under the same conditions'—that is if they choose an opposite-sex partner. Another CIFRC supporter adds that while he does not support gay marriage, he sees no reason why partners in same-sex partnerships should not enjoy the same 'interrelationship' rights and obligations as married couples. However, a union of a man and a woman should not be called the same as a union of two persons of the same sex. It should also not have the same 'social value' as homosexuals cannot reproduce. Accordingly, same-sex couples should not be allowed to adopt children as that is simply not natural. Family, says the chief editor of Catholic newspaper *Družina*, provides a natural environment in which children grow up with male and female elements. 'Both are needed. A man is different by nature and a wife is different. … Yes, equal rights (for same-sex couples) as far as joint life is concerned, but not children, children not at all.'

The same argument against marriage equality and same-sex families was put forward by the representatives of the SDP. The main speaker on the issue within the party was a former MP, a former Jesuit and physician by education, who described homosexuality as 'a psychological disease which should be treated". On other occasions he has said: 'The Family Code does not give anything to anyone, while it takes away special social importance from the natural union of a man and a woman'.[1] During the parliamentary debate he also argued: 'Proclaiming homosexuality, but also paedophilia and zoophilia for natural sexual orientations, does more harm than good to those who are in distress and would like to free themselves from unnatural sexual orientations' (14th regular session of the National Assembly, 2 March 2010). The argument of nature was also used by our interviewee from the SDP, who wondered: 'I do not know, maybe we are not mature enough for this question, but I can hardly imagine a child going to school and saying: "That is my daddy. And this is another daddy. Mum and another mum." Simply … that is not natural. This part is not natural.' Furthermore one of the CIFRC supporters believes that same-sex families are 'a social experiment, where children are the victims. Children are deprived of one right element—the right to know a father and a mother'.

Interestingly enough the SDP, when in power (2004–2008) was the first political party in Slovenia to adopt legislation on same-sex partnership and in 2005 Slovenia became the first country in the world where legal regulation of same-sex partnerships at national level was adopted by a conservative, right-wing coalition government. Even so the party does not enjoy a reputation as a proponent of the rights of gays and lesbians and particularly same-sex families, as they have actively opposed the adoption of the new Family Code. It is believed that the Registered

---

[1] Source: http://www.sds.si/news/10603 (accessed 15 January 2015).

Same-sex Partnership Act as a special institution for same-sex couples with only limited rights was adopted primarily in order to preserve marriage as a hetero-normative institution, which has legal and symbolic priority in Slovenian society (Kuhar 2006, 2010).

What seems to be at stake is primarily the symbolism of marriage. The opponents of the Family Code do not oppose legal rights for same-sex couples as long as this institution or their relationship is not called 'a marriage' and their relations with children are not called 'a family'. Furthermore, same-sex couples should not raise children as that is unnatural. It is precisely in this context that discrimination against same-sex couples and families occurs, despite their declared opposition to discrimination based on sexual orientation.

This problem is driven by what Bosia and Weiss (2013) call 'political homophobia'. It is a conscious political strategy by the state or a political movement through which they structure the experiences of sexual minorities. Homophobia as a political strategy takes different shapes and forms—from the processes of marginalisation, when the human rights of LGBT people are constructed as special or 'additional' rights, to interpretations that addressing such issues represent a threat to the nation or humanity as a whole as regards what is natural and what is not. Political homophobia is closely related to nationalism. It presents itself as a 'natural' element in the process of constructing and maintaining the nation and the state; it is about belonging and the definition of a 'good citizen'. Political homophobia is in fact one of the manifestations of present-day populism, which is based on ethno-religious, patriarchal and nationalist construction of 'the other', the internal enemy who represents a threat to 'our nation' from the cultural, gender or sexual point of view. It is also closely intertwined with enduring patterns of gender (but also class and racial) inequality and is illustrative as a strategy of political actors who either maintain existing power relations or intervene by acquiring positions of power (Bosia and Weiss 2013). Most often, this is achieved by creating a 'homosexual threat' against which the proponents of political homophobia organise their efforts while at the same time maintaining their own (legal/symbolic/political) privileges. Political homophobia can take the form of episodes of moral panic, as the Family Code debate in Slovenia has witnessed.

Counter-Strategies to Populism

Our field work included the analysis of how activists against discrimination, hate speech and racism understand the populist landscape in Slovenia and in particular what strategies they use to oppose populist discourse in practice. Most of our interviewees have been actively involved in referendum campaigns on single women, erased and same-sex families. We also interviewed victims of populist discourse and practice who are actively fighting for their rights: two victims of erasure, (one is also an activist of the Civil Initiative of the Erased and one is engaged in the fight for the rights of migrant workers); and a lesbian mother who, together with her family, publicly defends the rights of same-sex families.

Populism is defined by our interviewees as a simplistic and misleading (also egoistic and egocentric) interpretation of issues and realities which, however, successfully addresses the feelings of many. According to the interviewees the populist block in Slovenia consists of several right-wing political parties, with the SDP and the Catholic Church playing a leading role in the 'fascismisation' of society. What seems to be new in comparison to research findings in the 1990s is the emergence of various influential civil initiatives (such as the CIFRC) giving the impression that opposition to equal rights is not orchestrated but comes from the will of 'the common people'. Within this triangle, the Church enjoys a special status: one of the interviewees was visibly afraid of publicly criticising the institution, while its representatives perceive every criticism directed towards them as "christianophobic".

While it has become commonplace for human rights issues to be referred by populist parties to public referendums, proponents and opponents also frequently build coalitions in an attempt to influence public opinion. The interviewees emphasised that right-wing actors are very well organised with access to financial and other resources, while NGOs have to defer their regular work in order to take part in referendum campaigns. Activists report that at the peak of referendum campaigns they attended several discussions, interviews, round tables and other public events every day, and on these occasions they faced questions about the extent to which they are instrumentalised by (left-wing) political parties when advocating which do not entirely meet their objectives, yet are better than nothing.

In this way activists come to criticise the inconsistent and half-hearted defence of human rights by parties on the left of the political spectrum.

All interviewees agreed that it is extremely hard to cope with right-wing populism; communication strategies are predominantly built around the use of rational argument and evidence-based research. Populist discourse is also a challenge because it seeks to provoke emotional reactions through personal attacks and manipulative interpretations. The activists' tactic is to avoid emotional reaction and refuse to play the 'victim'. They also refuse to use populist tactics when addressing the public, even though they have often been advised to do so. An LGBT activist we interviewed explains the reasons:

> We have decided [not to angrily respond to opponents and] to follow a strategy of advocacy in the sense of presenting same-sex families and partnerships and lifestyles as something that is OK, something that is not related to anything else. I think this is important, because we have decided to do it in order to protect the victims—same-sex families, couples and individuals. ... It means: we did try to win the referendum, but at the same time we knew that the day after the referendum life would go on and there is no point in fighting opponents, better to promote the lifestyle as something that can make people's everyday life easier.

If the discourse of populist political actors is compared to that of activists, 'mirror accusations' can be observed. Both sides claim to defend human rights and democracy, while accusing each other of being populist and using hate speech. This adds to the complexity of populist discourse which can fill up different empty signifiers with content that is often neither consistent nor even rational. The success of such discourses has caused many activists to become disillusioned.

> [All this] has shown me that there are a lot of people who do not think like me. It was very interesting to see this, especially because some of them based their rhetoric on human rights—just like I did. Even today, I find it fascinating ... I am astonished by the arguments, because I see how they contradict each other. ... You look at your 'opponents', who are defending the opposite viewpoint, and you just cannot believe what they are willing to say just to preserve their traditional beliefs.

Conclusions

The political constitution of contemporary populism in Slovenia can be traced back to the end of the 1980s. As it occurred within the dominant nationalist-democratisation movement, populism entered mainstream politics through open doors and became an established part of the newly established nation state and democracy. Considering that in the 1990s Slovenia did not shy away from openly ethnocentric policies and exclusivist practices that discriminated against minority groups, we can observe that populism became embedded in the state and its institutions. In the national political context of the last 25 years the processes that led to an independent nation state, democratisation and accession to the EU played a particularly visible role. We have shown in this chapter that in the populist imaginary these processes are thought of as breaking with the communist past, and as the de-balkanisation and Europeanisation of the nation. The populist vision of the world is built on the idea that Slovenia is a state of 'true Slovenians', who are constructed on the intersections of nationality, ethnicity, religion, sexual orientation, political affiliation and so on.

Various groups of 'others' are imagined as endangering the future of the nation and its people. The erased, LGBT, migrants, Muslims and Roma are the usual targets of populist anti-politics. Populist 'othering' is most visible within the block of right-wing political parties like the SDP, the Catholic Church and civil initiatives such as the CIFRC. These actors act along the lines of ethno-nationalist and ethno-religious populism and are also related organisationally. Just recently (in 2014), the president of the CIFRC, Aleš Primc, was one of the leading figures on a committee that organised daily demonstrations in support of SDP leader Janez Janša, who had been convicted of bribery in the Patria case (later the verdict was annulled by the Constitutional Court). As our analysis has shown, populist organisations and actors such as the SDP and the CIFRC frequently refer to democracy and patriotism; love of country, nation and people is used to defend exclusionary and discriminatory politics against minorities. In this chapter we have analysed the populist othering strategies practised by the SDP and the CIFRC, with the racist consequences for minority populations. It is striking that these policies have become largely accepted by the public as a valid patriotic defence mechanism allegedly working for the good of the nation and its people.

References

Bajt, V. (2011). The Muslim other in Slovenia. Intersections of a religious and ethnic minority. In K. Górak-Sosnowska (Ed.), *Muslims in Poland and Eastern Europe: Widening the European discourse on Islam* (pp. 307–326). Warsaw, Poland: University of Warsaw.

Baskar, B. (2004). Rasizem, neorasizem, antirasizem: Dvojni esej o tranzitivnosti navidezno protislovnih pojmov. *Časopis za kritiko znanosti, 32*(217/218), 126–149.

Bosia, M. J., & Weiss, M. L. (2013). Political homophobia in comparative perspective. In M. J. Bosia & M. L. Weiss (Eds.), *Global homophobia: States, movements, and the politics of oppression* (pp. 3–45). Urbana, IL: University of Illinois Press.

Bugarič, B. (2008). Populism, liberal democracy, and the rule of law in Central and Eastern Europe. *Communist and Post-Communist Studies, 41*(2), 191–203.

Butler, J. (1990). *Gender trouble: Feminism and the subversion of identity.* New York: Routledge.

Dedić, J., Jalušič, V., & Zorn, J. (2003). *Izbrisani: organizirana nedolžnost in politike izključevanja.* Ljubljana, Slovenia: Mirovni inštitut.

Dolar, M. (1995). Pohod desnega populizma. *Mladina, 30*, 18–23.

Hrženjak, M. (2001). Legitimiziranje neenakosti. *Poročilo skupine za spremljanje nestrpnosti, 1*(1), 104–113.

Kerševan, M. (1996). Cerkev v postsocializmu. *Družboslovne razprave, 12*(21), 43–56.

Kogovšek, N. (2010). Iskanje pravnih razlogov za priznanje enakih pravic isto-spolnim partnerjem in njihovim družinam. *Socialno delo, 49*(5/6), 319–330.

Kogovšek Šalamon, N. (2012). *Izbris in (ne)ustavna demokracija.* Ljubljana, Slovenia: GV Založba.

Kuhar, R. (2006). Hočva ohcet: o nezadostnosti registriranega partnerstva. In Z. Kobe & I. Pribac (Eds.), *Prava poroka: 12 razmišljanj o zakonski zvez* (pp. 107–134). Ljubljana, Slovenia: Krtina.

Kuhar, R. (2010). Populizam rulz: Zloupotrebe znanstvenih istrazivanja u raspravi o novom Obiteljskom zakonu u Sloveniji [Populism rules: Misuse of scientific research in the debate on family code in Slovenia]. *Queer.hr.* Retrieved April 3, 2013, from http://queer.hr/1401/populizam-rulz/

Kuhar, R. (2015). Playing with science: Sexual citizenship and the Roman Catholic Church counter-narratives in Slovenia and Croatia. *Women's Studies International Forum, 49*, 84–92.

Kuzmanić, T. (2002). Post-socialism, racism and the reinvention of politics. In M. Pajnik (Ed.), *Xenophobia and post-socialism* (pp. 17–36). Ljubljana, Slovenia: Mirovni inštitut.

Kuzmanić, T. (2003). Razumevanje desnic: Nove in drugih vrst. In C. Oberstar & T. Kuzmanić (Eds.), *Nova desnica* (pp. 7–31). Ljubljana, Slovenia: Mirovni inštitut.

Kuzmanić, T. (2005). An attempt to distinguish nationalism from Volkish populist movement, practices and ideologies—The Yugoslav case. In M. Pajnik & T. Kuzmanić (Eds.), *Nation-states and xenophobias: In the ruins of former Yugoslavia* (pp. 9–21). Ljubljana, Slovenia: Mirovni inštitut.

Lešnik, B. (2010). Sovražni govor v psihoanalitični perspektivi [Hate speech in pyschoanalitic perspective]. *Socialno delo, 49*(5–6), 299–304.

Mikuž, J. (2010). Populizem pod Alpami. *Pravna praksa, 29*(49/50), 42.

Mudde, C. (Ed.). (2005). *Racist extremism in Central and Eastern Europe.* Milton Park, England: Routledge.

Mudde, C. (2007). *Populist radical right parties in Europe.* Cambridge, England: Cambridge University Press.

Paternotte, D. (2014). Christian trouble: The Catholic Church and the subversion of gender. Retrieved January 3, 2015, from http://councilforeuropeanstudies.org/critcom/christian-trouble-the-catholic-church-and-the-subversion-of-gender/

Rajgelj, B. (2010). Razmerja v istospolnih družinah—kje smo in kam lahko gremo? *Socialno delo, 49*(5/6), 305–318.

Ramet, S. P. (1999a). Defining the radical right: The values and behaviors of organized intolerance. In S. P. Ramet (Ed.), *The radical right in Central and Eastern Europe since1989* (pp. 3–27). University Park, PA: The Pennsylvania State University Press.

Ramet, S. P. (Ed.). (1999b). *The radical right in Central and Eastern Europe since 1989.* University Park, PA: The Pennsylvania State University Press.

Rizman, R. (1999). Radical right politics in Slovenia. In S. P. Ramet (Ed.), *The radical right in Central and Eastern Europe since1989* (pp. 147–170). University Park, PA: The Pennsylvania State University Press.

Švab, A. (2010). Kdo se boji (raznovrstnosti) družin? *Socialno delo, 49*(5/6), 341–350.

Weeks, J. (1998). The sexual citizen. *Theory, Culture and Society, 15*(3–4), 35–52.

7

The Post-Communist Rise of National Populism: Bulgarian Paradoxes

Anna Krasteva

Introduction

National populism made a spectacular entrance on the Bulgarian political scene—with surprises, forcefulness, and aplomb. In 2005, Volen Siderov literally burst out of a television show into Parliament with 300,000 votes (8.14 per cent) and with such *élan* that he did not even manage to register his party. This breakthrough caught politicians, journalists and political scientists unawares. The media vastly multiplied the shock of the political quake, presenting a burlesquely unbalanced picture: a single representative of the new extremist party Ataka (Attack) against seven or eight moderate politicians, NGO members, journalists. Both the enormous media coverage and the numerous opponents of the handful of Ataka supporters simply reinforced the symbolic capital of the new political player. Ataka's emergence caused a spike of journal publications which reached a peak in 2007 and 2008 (Malinov 2007; Krastev 2007; Smilov

A. Krasteva
Department of Political Sciences at the New Bulgarian University,
Sofia, Bulgaria

© The Editor(s) (if applicable) and The Author(s) 2016
G. Lazaridis et al. (eds.), *The Rise of the Far Right in Europe*,
DOI 10.1057/978-1-137-55679-0_7

161

2008; Kabakchieva 2008), but scholarly literature on the subject is still thin (Linden 2008: 5).

Two questions formed the centrepiece of media and academic debate. Was Ataka a comet-like phenomenon? After the initial tremor on the political scene, would radical nationalism disappear as swiftly as it had emerged? The subsequent decade offered a picture which recalls waves rather than an arrow, an ebb-and-flow pattern rather than continuous ascent. This chapter looks for answers in two directions. Its first aim is to explore the factors that made the Ataka phenomenon possible and shaped the ups and downs of its turbulent history. Gaining an insight into Ataka transcends the party itself and encompasses all of Bulgarian radical nationalism. Even after the decline of its pioneers, nationalism has not shrunk like shagreen, but has demonstrated resilience and a lasting presence on the post-communist political scene. The other aim is to analyse Bulgarian national populism through the prism of its political actors' proliferation and diversification, its defining factors, and the periods in its evolution.

The second question is about Ataka's ideological identification: far left or far right. Bulgarian debates on this dilemma have been ideological rather than theoretical: leftist intellectuals have relegated Ataka's identification to the far-right spectrum, whereas rightist ones have placed it on the far-left pole with the same pathos and finality. Western debates have been calmer, but similarly polarised: most researchers focus on Ataka's extremism and othering (Kriesi 2014; Ibroscheva 2013), while some emphasise the radically leftist, neo-totalitarian elements and far-left political agenda (Ghodsee 2008). These controversies are not among the paradoxes to be analysed here. I believe that both groups of researchers are at once right and wrong. They are right, because Ataka's heterogeneous platform contains both far-left ideas such as nationalisation, and far-right extremism, nationalism, xenophobia and racism. They are wrong, not merely because they have selectively isolated the elements that would support their own conclusion; they are fundamentally wrong because they have measured national populism by the obsolete yardstick of structuring the political scene into left or right. My proposition here is that both of them miss the point. If Ataka occupies such an eclectic position along the classical socio-economic and political cleavages, it is because the party seeks to place itself along a new type of cleavage; it is transitioning from party politics to symbolic politics, from ideological to identity politics, from socio-economic and political to cultural cleavages.

I will elaborate on this proposition from two perspectives. The first is the party perspective. It focuses on the political proposal, on the role of elites in the generation and 'sale' of the national populism project. Here, I will introduce the genesis of Bulgarian national populism, reconstructing its history from its emergence, through its ascent, and to the diversification of its instances. The spotlight will be on Ataka: the first and most emblematic national populist party in Bulgaria. Another important entity is the Bulgarian National Union: one of the largest, most prominent and representative radical nationalist organisations. The theoretical question in this first part is which theoretical model is more appropriate to explain Bulgarian national populism. 'Is East-Central Europe backsliding'—which is the title of the special issue of the *Journal of Democracy* (2007, vol. 18, No. 4)—formulates the question all scholars of the Eastern European far right aspire to answer. The answers gravitate around two poles. The first is more populated; Hockenos summarises it: 'EU new comers are "illiberal democracies", systems that have all the trapping of constitutional states but lack the liberal political culture to make them function as healthy democracies' (Hockenos 2010: 18). Polyakova challenges this interpretation: 'EE today is not the backward hinterland that some scholars feared it would become. In terms of popular support for exclusionary ethnic nationalism, it is the West that appears more backward. The fear for the "new Europe" is no longer about the integration of the East, but rather the disintegration of the West' (Polyakova 2015: 71).

The second perspective refers to symbolic cartography and will map the poles and axes of othering and identity politics. The theoretical question is how Ataka has succeeded in building its own symbolic map out of copy-and-paste images and imaginaries from Western far-right parties and how it has attracted Bulgarian voters.

Far-right populism is—and often wants to be—a paradoxical phenomenon. My conclusion will summarise the democratic paradoxes of Bulgarian national populism.

Ataka: The Radical Party—Pioneer with an Emblematic Name

National populism emerged on the Bulgarian political scene in the form of a democratic paradox. In the 1990s, democracy was fragile, but there were no extremist parties; once democracy was consolidated, extremist parties appeared and achieved success.

The democratic paradoxes of Bulgarian national populism will be explored in detail in the final section of this article. Here, I will summarise the history of Ataka. Ataka is representative of the mixture of European and national reasons for the advent and ascent of radical extremism. It also offers a symptomatic view of the palette of strategies—from renunciation to alliances—employed by moderate parties with respect to radical ones, as well as the Bulgarian process of experimentation with and acquisition of these strategies in an environment lacking both a mature political culture and experience interacting with non-system actors. Due to the journalistic pen and speeches of leader Volen Siderov, who has produced a copious amount of text in the form of books, party programmes longer than 100 pages each and countless television talk shows, the symbolic cartography of national populism is most elaborated precisely in the region occupied by Ataka.

2005, Bulgaria. The country has recovered from the economic catastrophe brought about by the 1997 socialist government, the economy is relatively bouyant, the crisis is still beyond the horizon. Bulgaria is on the threshold of its EU membership. Roma integration has been given a chance[1] thanks to the Decade of Roma Inclusion, and the refugee crisis will not take place until 2013. As expected, Simeon Saxe-Coburg-Gotha has not lived up to the great hopes he created, but neither has he pushed the country into hyperinflation and stalled the economy as did socialist Prime Minister Zhan Videnov. In this comparatively calm, moderately optimistic situation, there emerges the first radical party with the emblematic name Ataka. What is the political rationale behind that, given the absence of the 'usual suspects': severe economic crisis, political

---

[1] The Decade did not bring any tangible results, but in 2005 this was not known.

instability, waves of refugees? All of these will occur later and cannot be held responsible for the genesis of the first radical party. I will seek the reasons in the interaction of three factors: foreign, domestic, and personal.

Among the foreign factors, the key one is the simultaneous (Reynie 2013) ascent of the radical right in Western Europe during the 1980s and 1990s: from the National Front in France to Freedom Party in Austria, from the Danish People's Party to the Party for Freedom in the Netherlands, from Northern League in Italy to True Finns, etc. Far-right parties have been one of the two[2] greatest innovations on the European political scene since World War II. The post-communist bloc does not lag behind: from Fico (Slovakia) to Siderov (Bulgaria), from Tudor (Romania) to Gabor Vona (Hungary) and Šešelj (Serbia). The trends can be summed up by two statements: far-right parties firmly ensconce themselves on the political scenes of both Western and Eastern Europe; and their share of the vote, at 10–20 per cent, is not to be underestimated. This trend will later continue, reaching 25 per cent in France, the UK and other countries during the 2014 EU elections.

Domestic factors consist of seeking alternatives to the established parties. This search has been catalysed by the lack of trust in the major political parties: the Bulgarian Socialist Party (BSP), Union of Democratic Forces (UDF), National Movement Simeon II (NMSS); by a growing dissatisfaction with the clientelism and omnipresence of the Movement for Rights and Freedoms (MRF)[3] and a conviction that, 'No matter who you vote for, you always elect MRF'; by a muffled discontent, which will erupt in the fury of protests much later, but is already festering and seeks expression in a contestatory vote. From the very start of the post-communist transition, all elections have obeyed the same logic—'ping pong game between the BSP and the UDF, with power shifting perennially back and forth between them' (Ghodsee 2008: 26): BSP (1990), UDF (1991), BSP (1994), UDF (1997). The Bulgarian electorate was evidently dissatisfied with the parties in power and looked for alternatives. When there are no new actors, the only solution is to alternate between the available ones,

---

[2] The others being Green parties.
[3] These parties structure the political scene: BSP on the left, UDF on the right, NMSS and MRF in the centre.

as Bulgarian voters systematically did in all parliamentary elections in the 1990s. When a new actor appeared in 2001—ex-Tsar Simeon Saxe-Coburg-Gotha—he predictably capitalised on the enormous expectations of change. In 2005, Simeon joined the camp of those who need to be replaced, and the hunger for new players arose again.

The third set of factors are personal and related to Volen Siderov himself. Siderov had already been on the political stage for 15 years, since the beginning of the democratic transition. He has gone through a number of political roles,[4] but it is precisely during this period that he puts on his perennial scowl and leather jacket and begins to chew people out from the TV screen: an efficacious rehearsal for the scandals from the parliamentary tribune. This new role that he takes on successfully—after a string of unsuccessful ones—is neither original nor innovative. It has long been played in Europe, where it has even started evolving: shortly afterwards, Marine Le Pen will begin the *dédiabolisation* of the Front National in France, steering away from the extremist fascistoid image of her father, Jean-Marie Le Pen. However, Siderov is not drawn to this later and more moderate stage of far-right populism, but to the early one of clamorous, aggressive, fierce extremism, because he can use it to capture the political breakthrough he has been craving for so long.

The intersection of these three axes—foreign, domestic and personal—forms the political alloy that crystallises into Ataka and illustrates the proposition that Ataka emerges for opportunistic reasons, as an imitation of Western radical parties, a political project to fill a potential electoral niche.

The name 'Ataka' spells clearly and emphatically radicalism and extremism. No other party name—before or since—is a match for this confrontational identity. The name's strong message plays a performative role in two directions: it sweeps over the radical right-wing segment of the political scene and presents the party leader and party activists as 'fighters.' Volen Siderov describes himself as a valiant warrior: 'As always, I am part of a combat coalition. Since its establishment, Ataka has been subject to severe criticism. Hence I have acquired the reflex to be always combat-ready' (Siderov 2013). This militant rhetoric manages to win

---

[4] Editor-in-chief of *Demokratsia*, the UDF newspaper; unsuccessful candidate for Sofia mayor; fan of Simeon II; assistant editor-in-chief of *Monitor*, another national newspaper.

Table 7.1 Votes for Ataka in parliamentary, presidential and European elections, 2005–2014

Year	Election	Number of votes	%	Result
2005	National Assembly	296,848	8.14	21 out of 240 seats in the National Assembly
2006	President, first round	597,175	21.486	Volen Siderov reaches the second round
	President, second round	649,387	24.052	Volen Siderov loses to Georgi Parvanov
2007	European Parliament	275,237	14.2	3 out of 18 seats for Bulgaria in the EP
2009	European Parliament	308,052	11.96	2 out of 17 seats for Bulgaria in the EP
2009	National Assembly	395,656	9.36	21 out of 240 seats in the National Assembly
2011	President	122,466	3.64	Fourth place in the first round
2013	National Assembly	258,481	7.297	23 MPs
2014	European Parliament	66,210	2.9	0
2014	National Assembly	148,262	4.52	11 MPs

over electors in record time, to carry out the second major innovation on the Bulgarian post-communist political scene and to achieve the first radical breakthrough in the party system. The decade after the establishment of Ataka is characterised by two opposing trends: continuity—from its inception, Ataka has always been a parliamentary party (Table 7.1 and Fig. 7.1); and radical discontinuities with regard to political partners, coalitions, internal composition. Five periods in the party's short and turbulent history can be identified.

I 2005–2009: Establishment and Consolidation

Volen Siderov presents Ataka's political strategy, which is focused on three priorities: stopping the Islamisation/Turkisation of Bulgarian citizens, getting a grip on Roma crime, and taking Bulgaria out of the hands of foreign companies. He founds Ataka two months before the general election in 2005; he wins almost 300,000 votes, or 8.14 per cent and 21 out of 240 seats in the National Assembly, which makes his party fourth

% Votes

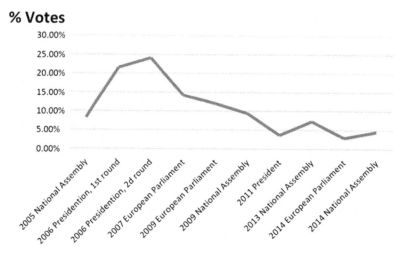

Fig. 7.1 Votes for Ataka in parliamentary, presidential and European elections, 2005–2014

among the parliamentary forces. Siderov is the pioneer of a parliamentary rhetoric that mixes harsh anti-elitism, anti-Europeanism and hard nationalism, which he introduced in his very first address to the opening of Parliament:

> After fifteen years of national betrayals, frauds and criminal plundering, after the arrogant demonstrative policy of genocide towards the Bulgarian people carried out by several parliaments and governments at the dictation of foreign powers, at last the hour of the Bulgarian Renaissance has come.

In the presidential election of October 2006, Siderov eliminates the right-wing candidate and reaches the second round, where he faces the incumbent president, socialist Georgi Parvanov. In the second round, Siderov gathers 649,387 votes, or 24.05 per cent of the popular vote the highest ever result for the party and for Siderov personally. In the European election of 2009, he almost reaches the 2005 figure (275,000 votes), winning three MEP seats and consolidating Ataka's fourth place among the political parties.

II 2009–2011: Informal Coalition with the Ruling Party GERB and 'Tamed' Extremism

Ataka assumes the new role of a party that plays the parliamentary game in informal coalition with the governing party GERB (Citizens for European Development of Bulgaria). This period is characterszed by a more moderate, bland discourse, limited controlled nationalism and 'taming' of extremism. Ataka illustrates the general trend: 'Their initial success makes them downplay their populism' (Rooduijn et al. 2012: 563). Nationalism is tamed, yet not forgotten: Ataka suggests that GERB should stage a referendum on the issue of Turkey's accession to the EU, but the idea is categorically rejected by the European People's Party.

III 2011–End of 2012: Internal Divisions, Splits, Resuscitated Extremism, Violence at Muslim Prayers

Many MPs leave Ataka[5] and join the ruling party GERB. After the splits, three new nationalist parties are established: GORD (Civic Union for Real Democracy), National Front for the Salvation of Bulgaria and National Democratic Party. Not only is extremism resuscitated, but it reaches new heights and switches from words to action: praying Muslims are assaulted by Ataka activists in a mosque in downtown Sofia. On 20 May 2011 Ataka's activists attacked Muslims at prayer in the biggest mosque in the capital. The assault produced ugly scenes of clashes, burning prayer mats and cut fezzes. Siderov labelled the policemen involved 'Janissaries'. Five policemen and five Muslims were wounded. In 2015, the European Count of Human Rights sentenced Bulgaria for the assault, drawing attention to the slow reaction of the Bulgarian authorities.[6]

---

[5] Political nomadism—leaving one party to join a ruling one or create a new one—is a widespread phenomenon in Bulgarian parliamentary politics, but it is particularly illustrated by Ataka's MPs. The party twice loses the right to have a parliamentary group (with a minimum of ten MPs) because of nomadism in favour of the governing party GERB.

[6] Европрисъда заради „Атака'и боя пред джамията Баня Башъ (Eurosentence on Ataka for the clash at Bania Bashi Mosque) in Webcafe.bg 24.02.2015, http://www.webcafe.bg/id_1327055544

IV 2013–2014: Mass Street Protests and Early Parliamentary Elections on May 12, 2013

In February and March 2013, thousands of Bulgarians take to the streets; Boyko Borisov's government falls, and Ataka's rating rises considerably. Despite the split and the multitude of new nationalist parties, Ataka has managed to consolidate its electorate, making capital of the 2013 winter protests. In the 41st Bulgarian parliament, Ataka shifts its coalition politics from right to left and informally supports the governing coalition of the Bulgarian Socialist Party and the Movement for Rights and Freedoms.

V Mid 2014–Present: Decline and Exacerbated Competition with NFSB, but Still in Parliament

Within a single year—from the early parliamentary elections in 2013 until those of 2014—Ataka loses over 100,000 of its voters (from 258,481 down to 148,262). While it sent three MEPs to Brussels in 2009, it sends none in 2014.

Four reasons explain Ataka's decline and the shrinking of its electoral support. The main one is the overpopulation of the political space with parties from the national populist spectrum. Two former Ataka MEPs— Dimitar Stoyanov and Slavi Binev—found their own parties: NDF and GORD[7] respectively. The second reason is the leadership conflict between Volen Siderov and Valeri Simeonov and the fierce political rivalry with NFSB. The third has to do with Siderov's damaged image: media disclosures about his luxurious lifestyle and love affairs have undermined the public perception of Siderov as a protector of the poor and the weak. The fourth reason is similarly important: the negative effects of Ataka's status as a ruling party and supporter of Plamen Oresharski's failed government. Despite this downfall, Ataka maintains its reputation as a phoenix rising from the ashes of great losses and travails; it enters the 43rd Bulgarian parliament, although barely passing the 4 per cent electoral threshold.

---

[7] NDF and GORD are 'copy and paste' from Ataka; they express the leadership ambitions of their leaders and have not gained significant electoral support. NDF is no longer present on the political scene, GORD is part of the 'Patriotic coalition' in the current parliament.

Both informal coalitions—with right-wing GERB and left-wing BSP—have catastrophic consequences for Ataka. Ataka is a typical example of radical parties that are punished by the electorate for any—formal or informal—coalition with the mainstream parties and survive only by adversarial strategies.

***

How to measure Ataka's impact? Rizova (2013) stresses that none of Ataka's legislative proposals to curtail minority rights in the National Assembly were approved, and concludes that 'Ataka has little impact on the Bulgarian legislative and political process' (Rizova 2013: 160). The argument is correct, but the conclusion illustrates the misunderstanding of the real impact of radical nationalism, which is less about policies and more about politics, less about improving pay and pensions and more about identity and anger. The political impact of Ataka can be measured by three aspects of the restructuring of the scene: introducing a new ethno-cultural cleavage, a new type of politics—identity politics, and a new type of party—radical nationalists. These fundamental changes, which will be analysed in the next section, do not depend on the survival of Ataka itself. They have already 'produced' the political actors required to sustain them.

The Genesis and Rise of Bulgarian National Populism

The history of Bulgarian national populism is more complex than that of Ataka, since it involves a multitude of political actors. I will summarise it along three axes: factors; diversification of far-right political parties; and periods.

Factors

The factors that proved conducive to the emergence and rise of post-communist far-right populism have various hues: external and internal;

social, ideological, and political. External factors include the absence of a Cold War, and globalisation. It is these factors that François Eisburg defines as essential to understanding the new elements in the landscape that has evolved on the soil of today's populism (Eisburg 2007). The end of the Cold War has rearranged political priorities. During the Cold War period, there was also corruption, but this issue was not so much at the centre of public awareness; today it is one of the top five issues in Bulgaria as well as in many other countries. For Bulgarians, globalisation has coincided with Europeanisation. In the first decade of the transition period, both were perceived positively, as an alternative to the closed society of communism. Paradoxically, when European integration was no longer a project but a reality, Euroscepticism began to rise.

Four groups of internal factors are significant: social, ideological, political and communication.

The social factors are rooted in a growing perception of the transition as unjust, disregarding the people, and benefiting criminals: 'Levels of distrust are particularly high in Bulgaria, Romania … Perceptions of corruption and feelings of unfair treatments by authorities explain the lack of support for the regime. There is a deep-seated disenchantment of citizens with democratic politics' (Kriesi 2014: 374). Disappointment with the transition and with the failure of elites to build a functioning state provides the social basis paving the way for populism: 'Bulgarian society is in a populist situation' (Kabakchieva 2008: 3).

Ideological factors. The clear-cut oppositions of communism vs. anti-communism, and radical change vs. gradual transition which left their indelible imprint on political confrontations and set the pattern for the political scene in the first decade of the new century, are now beginning to erode. There is a reconciliation of the political poles; the right–left distinction is fading; symbolic politics is playing an increasingly essential role; and nationalism and anti-Europeanism are becoming powerful mobilisation resources. 'Political competition is being shifted from the socio-economic realm to the realm of identities and moral integrity' (Smilov 2008: 26).

Political factors. In the course of two decades, the post-communist political scene has seen several transformations: from reformist vs. conservative, to the division between left and right, to configurations with a populist orientation. 'The main collision does not involve left-wing and right-wing, reformers and conservatives; the fundamental collision involves elites that share growing misgivings about democracy and an enraged society with increasingly anti-liberal attitudes' (Krastev 2007: 112). In an accelerated political temporality, post-communist democracies are experiencing the converging trends characteristic of European political scenes: erosion of the representative function and the role of parties as intermediaries between the citizen and polity. This dysfunction of the party system takes different forms: Western European parties are no longer adequately representing their constituencies, whereas Eastern European parties have not yet produced adequate representation (Kriesi 2014: 373). The paradox is that Eastern European citizens feel exactly the same as Western Europeans: after the first years of democratic enchantment, the distrust and disillusionment with parties is conceived not as 'not yet' a horizon, but 'no longer' an impasse. Radical parties capitalise on this disenchantment: a quarter (26 per cent) of Ataka's electorate in 2005 had not bothered to vote in 2001, 'a figure significantly higher than for any other party. Ataka had reached out to a new constituency, giving voice to a political agenda hitherto ignored by the Bulgarian political elite ... Right-wing rhetoric could inspire otherwise apathetic people to go to polls' (Ghodsee 2008: 31).

Communication factors are important but overrated. Ataka was conceived within the media and cannot exist outside it.[8] In 2003, Siderov started the ten-minute Ataka talk show on TV Skat; in 2005, the new party borrowed its name from the show. A common joke in political folklore claims that TV Skat has its own party. The argument that media logic has prevailed over that of politics has both folklore and academic versions: 'How the Bulgarian ultranationalist party Ataka engineered its political success using electronic media' (Ibroscheva 2013). However, the media are neither Ataka's demiurge nor its saviour: despite its constant levels of media presence, the party has undergone various ups and downs. Two tendencies account for the significance

---

[8] Volen Siderov's first priority after the split with TV Skat was to create TV Alfa.

of communication factors. The first is national and concerns the poor, ineffective regulation of hate speech in Bulgarian media. The second is general: it is about tele-politics, de-ideologisation of political rhetoric, charismatic personalisation of power, people-isation of the public sphere (Miscoiu 2014). The personalisation[9] of power and the mediatisation of politics has placed a double emphasis on leadership: 'The success of the party increasingly depends on the communication qualities of its leader' (Kriesi 2014: 366).

Periodisation

First Period 1990s–Mid-2010s: Fragile Democracy and 'Shy' Nationalism

The major parties are moderate. The political scene is structured around three poles: anti-communist, socialist/reformed communist, and minority representation, exemplified by the UDF, BSP and MRF respectively. None of these parties have overt nationalist claims. Nationalism is not forgotten, but it is 'outsourced' to small allies of the two large parties: IMRO for UDF, and the United Block of Labour for BSP.

Second Period Mid-2000s: Consolidated Democracy and Emergence of Political Extremism

According to most criteria for democratic consolidation—free elections, circulation of elites, changing roles of governmental and opposition elites by peaceful means, etc.—Bulgaria can be considered a democratic post-communist country. Despite the lack of an extremist tradition during the post-communist transition, Ataka achieves immediate success (Fig. 7.2).

---

[9] Ataka's manifesto bears the arrogant title 'Siderov's Plan against the Colonial Yoke'.

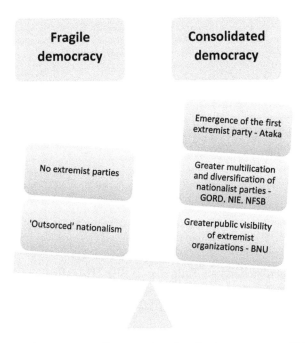

Fig. 7.2 The Bulgarian populist paradox: fragile democracy and 'shy' nationalism versus consolidated democracy and political extremism

Third Period Late 2000s–2015: Diversification and Multiplication of Nationalist and Extremist Actors and Discourses

The proliferation of far-right nationalist formations is largely due to Ataka's fragmentation: Volen Siderov's closest allies and partners create their own parties with an identical profile, reaching for the same electoral niche.

Diversification and Multiplication of Nationalist Actors and Discourses

The overpopulation of the far-right political scene reaches impressive proportions. Over an extremely short period, there appears a plethora of nationalist parties: GORD, NIE, National Democratic Party (NDP),

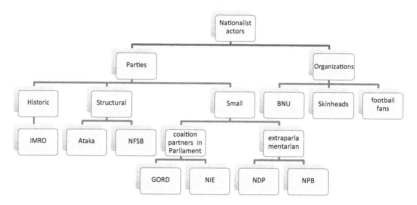

Fig. 7.3 Diversification and multiplication of nationalist actors

NFSB, Nationalist Party of Bulgaria (NPB). This diversity is illustrated in Fig. 7.3.

The first group of political parties includes three types: historical, structural, and peripheral.

IMRO is a historical party, created in 1919 and re-established in 1990. IMRO's coalition policies seem to be extremely opportunistic and chaotic: it would be hard to find a right-wing party that IMRO has never allied itself with: UDF (1997), Gergyovden (2001), Bulgarian Agrarian People's Party (2005), GERB (2007), Order, Law, Equity (2009), NFSB (2014). This political opportunism bespeaks a certain ambiguity in IMRO's political identity: on the one hand, the party has always identified itself as patriotic; on the other hand, its political allies hold diverse views on nationalism: some are definitely non-nationalist, such as UDF, others exhibit moderate nationalism, such as GERB.

Ataka and the National Front for the Salvation of Bulgaria (NSFB)[10] are the two key nationalist parties in the current political system. They have 'tailored' their coalition policy: Ataka has oriented itself towards left-wing coalitions, NFSB towards right-wing ones. Currently, NFSB supports the ruling coalition made up of GERB and the Reformist Bloc.

---

[10] National Front for the Salvation of Bulgaria was founded in 2012. It is supported and publicized by the Skat TV channel, which used to be Volen Siderov's launch vehicle.

The group of peripheral parties consists of two sub-types: the 'happy' ones that are part of successful coalitions in the 43rd Bulgarian parliament, such as GORD and NIE,[11] and those with no coalition and no influence, such as NDP[12] and NPB.[13]

What is the electoral rationale for this proliferation of nationalist parties? Have the demand and the nationalist electoral niche grown? Or has it been the supply and the leadership appetite for this relatively new niche? Election results point to the latter explanation. Far from increasing, nationalist votes have in fact decreased, because these votes have become distributed among a greater number of contenders: Ataka (148,262), NFSB and IMRO (239,101) have netted a total of 387,363 votes, fewer than Ataka's results at the 2009 parliamentary elections (395,656) and far fewer than the second round of the 2006 presidential elections (649,307).

The second sector of the nationalist political scene is composed of a key organisation, the Bulgarian National Union, and a more amorphous periphery with other actors: football teams, skinheads, xenophobic formations such as the Movement of Tangra's Warriors, National Resistance, etc.

The Bulgarian National Union (BNU) is an organisation with an explicitly aggressive extremist nationalist profile. It was established in 2001 by Boyan Rasate,[14] an active player at the extremist end of national populism, who maintained a characteristic media profile: he hosts a TV show on the former Bulgarian military channel which became a private television network. A recent quotation on the occasion of the seventieth anniversary of the end of World War II (9 May 2015) illustrates the narrative characteristic of Rasate and BNU:

Today, millions of nitwits celebrate 'Victory Day', never bothering to reflect that, without this victory, Europe wouldn't have been what it is now! Without this victory, Negroes would be in Africa, Muslims in Arabia,

---

[11] The NIE (National Ideal for Unity) was set up by Slavcho Atanasov, former mayor of Plovdiv, in 2010 after a split within IMRO.

[12] The National Democratic Party was established on 2 June 2012 by Volen Siderov's ex-wife Kapka Siderova and his adopted son Dimitar Stoyanov, former Ataka MEP; both of whom were Siderov's closest associates;the split was for family rather than political reasons.

[13] Not registered so far.

[14] Later, Rasate left BNU because of a leadership conflict but remained active in extremist politics.

faggots in the Medical Academy, and pushers in jail. To say nothing of paedophiles.[15]

They see a world overpopulated by hostile others of various kinds: racial (black people), religious (Muslims), sexual (gays), all of them in the close company of a variety of criminals: drug dealers and paedophiles.

The most visible activity of the BNU has been the Lukov March, glorifying a controversial military general from Bulgaria's fascist anti-Semitic past; the event has instigated the revival of a number of nationalist slogans. The theatricality of the march, with its neat, disciplined rows of participants, burning torches in the gathering dusk, the power of a mobilised and united group, has proved particularly attractive to young nationalists. Military imagery forms the core of BNU's symbolic universe. It is fuelled by videos of drills with young activists and photo sessions with uniforms resembling Bulgarian fascist youth before World War II.

The BNU represents the non-party actors on the radical scene, part of the same nebula as skinheads and football fans. They all operate in the political space between xenophobic discourse and violent activism. The 'civic patrols' in the capital against illegal migrants at the beginning of the refugee crisis illustrate the latter. Paradoxically, they attacked a person who happened to be not a migrant, but a Bulgarian citizen. Regardless of the citizenship of the victim, violence is violence. Yet, it took time before the authorities declared these patrols unlawful.

The similarities and differences between the far-right parties and organisations can be summarised from three perspectives: agency, politics and power.

The *agency* is the main unifier, because of the similarities in profile and numerous joint activities. The profile of the radical right activist resembles the authoritarian personality of Adorno with strong anti-minority, anti-migrant, anti-elites attitudes. The far-right activists function as a nebula with variable geometry configured in different ways for the different activities.

---

[15] http://www.rassate.bg/blog/id_6566/?fb_action_ids=824249427611427&fb_action_types=og. comments.

The *politics* of fear and the overproduction of othering is the common denominator of all far-right political actors. The politics of post-secularism and the religionisation of nationalism is the brand of Ataka. Most far-right actors adhere to the politics of sovereignty and statism, despite the virulent criticism of elites, but do not invest so much symbolic effort as Ataka in fighting the 'neo-colonianism' of global and EU forces.

The test of *power* is crucial for any right-wing party. Ataka and the National Front for the Salvation of Bulgaria pass it differently: Ataka fails it, while the NFSB is struggling to pass it. Ataka's place in the ruling coalition with the Bulgarian Socialist Party and the Movement for Rights and Freedoms had a disastrous effect on its political health. The NFSB has succeeded so far in remaining in coalition with GERB and the Reformers without losing its hard nationalist profile.

Three trends have emerged through the proliferation and diversification of nationalist actors and discourses. The first is the political impact of the intense rivalry in the overpopulated far-right space, which has led to radicalisation of nationalist actors. IMRO provides the most interesting example: during the 1990s, it maintained an image of a patriotic party open to moderate coalitions. After Ataka's appearance, IMRO became increasingly radical, competing in extremism with its new rival. And if IMRO illustrates the radicalisation of an old party, we have also witnessed a trend that is opposite in terms of party entities but identical in nature: the emergence of new increasingly radical formations. They are founded by the most extremist leaders, who leave their former party in order to create a new, even more extreme one. A typical example is Simeon Kostadinov, who was initially part of Ataka, transferred to BNU, and finally became one of the founders of the Nationalist Party of Bulgaria. His over-aggressive media behaviour replicates Volen Siderov's entrance into extremist politics.

The second trend is the greater public visibility of nationalist events, organisations and parties. The Nationalist Party of Bulgaria has received enormous media coverage, and its establishment was turned into a major political event by the media; football fans were employed by mainstream parties to radicalise the 2013 protests; and the media's love of scandals and controversial politicians has guaranteed a permanent large audience for extremist leaders and activists.

The third trend is the proliferation of extremist discourses and their authors, no longer restricted to extremist parties but also penetrating mainstream parties and institutions. Alarmingly, Bulgarian audiences have increasingly witnessed xenophobic discourse by 'moderate' politicians, and hate speech from the High Tribune of the parliament and various cabinet ministers. The most egregious example was the current Minster of Health Petar Moskov, a medical doctor and a member of the moderate right-wing Reformist Bloc. Moskov recently launched an avalanche of hate speech against the favourite target of all extremist parties, Roma people: 'Those who choose to live like beasts will be treated as beasts.' Emblematic of the normalisation of xenophobia in the Bulgarian political discourses is the statement of prime minister Boyko Borisov, qualifying the Bulgarian people as 'bad raw material': 'This is our population—1 million Roma, 700–800 000 Turks, 2.5 pensioners …'[16]

Symbolic Cartography

Nativism, authoritarianism and populism are the three pillars of the radical right parties (Mudde and Kaltwasser 2013: 497). All are present in Ataka's symbolic universe. The latter, however, could be better understood via another triad: identitarianism, post-secularism and statism. The idenititarian pole concentrates the overproduction of othering and expresses its politics of fear. Religionisation of politics is a fundamental post-communist trend of the political instrumentalisation of religion. It is even more central in the symbolic nationalist map, acting as its second pillar. 'Orthodox solidarity' has been the title of Ataka's manifesto at the last three elections[17] and it is crucial to the post-secularist message. Bringing the state back into politics and revitalising it against neoliberal weakening is the core of the third pole, statism and the politics of sovereignty. It takes the paradoxical form of an 'international nationalism',

---

[16] http://www.marginalia.bg/analizi/patevoditel-na-politicheskiya-stojkadzhiya/. If Boyko Borisov apologised for his statement, health minister Moskov emphasised he would not apologise to anybody (ibid.).

[17] 2013 parliamentary, 2014 European, 2014 parliamentary.

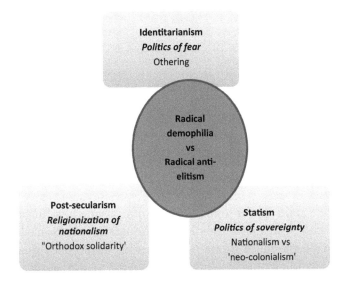

Fig. 7.4 Ataka's symbolic cartography

of Bulgarian nationalism closely tied to Russia.[18] The people—the *sine qua non* of any national populism—is in the centre of the three-pole map. Radical demophilism is defined and defended through radical anti-elitism (Fig. 7.4).

Identitarianism or the Politics of Fear

The overproduction of 'others', the politics of enemies, is the core of any national populist symbolic universe. Ataka's politics of fear is no exception: we see all the 'usual suspects'. This analysis has two goals. The first

---

[18] Ataka is the most Russophile party in Bulgaria, standing even closer to Russia and Putin than the BSP. These close relations are reinforced along the axes of Orthodox Christianity (Figure 7.5), pan-slavism, anti-Europeanism and anti-globalisation. There are two factors in the Russoplile orientation of Ataka: electoral and economic/geopolitical. There is an electoral niche for Russophile voters in Bulgaria and Ataka aspires to occupy most of it. The second reason combines energy policy, geopolitics and electoral strategy. Ataka is among the strongest defenders of Russsian energy interests in Bulgaria, but communicates them to the electorate not in geopolitical, but in social terms, translating them into slogans for affordable electricity bills for citizens.

Fig. 7.5 Ataka's vision of Orthodox Christianity: 'all-inclusive' polices and politics

is to provide an insight into the specifics of othering in a Bulgarian context. Numerous foreign far-right leaders indulge in anti-Roma discourses, yet the establishment of Roma people as a key scapegoat requires a specific understanding of post-communist conditions. The second goal is to structure identitarianism. The ethnicisation of otherness forms the major cluster, overpopulated by ethnic figures and overproducing anti-Roma, anti-Turkish, anti-Semitic and anti-refugee discourses. The sexualisation of otherness has a single favourite target: LGBT people. Other aspects, such as anti-elitism, will be reviewed in the section 'Radical Demophilism versus Radical Anti-elitism'.

Roma: The Archetypal Post-Communist Scapegoat

'If the Roma did not exist, post-communism would invent him.' I allow myself to paraphrase Sartre, because his insightful observation[19] provides the subtlest description of the mechanism for transforming Roma people into a key, archetypal figure of otherness in post-communist Bulgaria. We must note the radical change from communist to post-communist othering. Communism perceived others in political and class-based terms: imperialists, the bourgeoisie, *kulaks*, enemies inside the Party. Post-communism redesigned symbolic cartography from politics and class to ethnicity. In this new ethno-cultural universe, Roma people have drawn

---

[19] 'If the Jew did not exist, the anti-Semite would invent him.'

the short straw of serving as the universal culprits for all failures of the transition.

'Putting an end to Gypsy crime in the countryside' is one of the items on Ataka's manifesto. It is reinforced by even more extremist language: 'Gypsy gangs'; 'Gypsy aggression'; 'offenders of Gypsy origin'; 'Gypsies beat a policeman'. These anti-Roma, politically incorrect expressions are all quotations from the party's manifesto. The public speeches, statements, and appeals of its leaders are even more radical. They all resort to two discursive techniques with interwoven effects: ethnicising crime and criminalising the Roma community. Another landmark of anti-Roma rhetoric is the demographic argument: studies sponsored by Ataka indicate that within the next decade, the Roma population will reach 3 million[20] out of a total population of 8 million. Ivan Krastev, a lover of paradoxes, has identified the greatest one: in Bulgarian populist rhetoric, there are no significant distinctions between the elites and the Roma. 'Neither the former, nor the latter are like us: both groups do not pay taxes; both rob the honest majority; both benefit from Brussels support' (Krastev 2007: 112).

The anti-Roma pathos is so intrinsic that it is the only manifestation of hate speech in Ataka's program. The rest of the discursive figures of othering unfold mostly in the variegated spaces of verbal performance: rallies, marches, slogans, speeches and interviews.

Turks: The Historical Other for Bulgarians

A picture shows the Eiffel Tower topped by an onion dome, surrounded by four minarets, and decorated with the caption, 'That's what it would have looked like today if it hadn't been for us Bulgarians. Let's stop the fezzes again! Let's send *Bulgarians* to EU!' It is a single placard—but what ambitious messages, boldly rewriting history and promising a bright future. Never mind that there are few Bulgarian nationalists who believe that it was we who saved European culture from Islamisation and Europe

---

[20] According to the last census of 2011, the number of Roma is 325,348 (4.9 per cent of the population). This figure refers to those who identify as Roma. Roma identities are diversified: some identify as Bulgarian, others as Turks. Estimates put the number of Roma in Bulgaria at about 700,000–800,000.

from the Ottoman invaders; it doesn't stop Ataka from claiming that. Or urging us to be the anti-Turkish, anti-Islamic shield in Brussels.

The vociferous anti-Turkish discourse has two different targets: political and religious. The first is the MRF: Ataka's Bulgarian nationalism asserts itself in contradistinction to the Turkish party elite, the MRF, believed to be 'Ankara's fifth column' (Kapel-Pogacean and Ragaru 2007). The two parties are like communicating vessels: the MRF mobilise their electorate by emphasising the danger of Ataka's radical nationalism, and Ataka pushes the same buttons to mobilise nationalist voters by vehemently attacking nepotism and corruption among the MRF's elite. The religious target, Islam, is analysed in the 'Post-secularism' section.

Extremist Anti-Semitism Versus Bulgarian Tolerance Towards Jews

The anti-Semitic discourse occupies a peculiar space. Siderov started his career with books on world conspiracy and the Zionist plot to eradicate Eastern Orthodox Christianity: *The Boomerang of Evil* (2002), *Bulgarophobia* (2003)[21] and *The Power of Mammon* (2004). His language reaches incredible heights of intolerance and xenophobia. The Jews are 'represented as the enemy in a complex manner in that they are both to blame for communism, for the post-communist transition here and now, and for the predatory capitalist order' (Kabakchieva 2008: 4). The most visible manifestation of anti-Semitism is the annual Lukov March: 'Behind the mask of patriotism, by commemorating and glorifying General Lukov, the organisers of the march seek to rehabilitate and legitimize Nazism and fascism.'[22] These organisers are the BNU, supported by their 'friends' from Ataka, IMRO, and football firms.

The anti-Semitic rhetoric sounds paradoxical in a Bulgarian context. In 2013, there were national and international events commemorating the salvation of Bulgarian Jews during World War II; Bulgarians are very proud of this glorious chapter in their history. Against this

---

[21] An outline of the later manifesto 'Twenty Principles of the Ataka party'.
[22] This is a quote from an invitation by No to Neo-Nazi Marches, an informal citizen group.

background, Siderov's fierce anti-Semitism and the anti-Semitism of the Lukov March, concealed under the mantle of nationalism, seem somewhat strange and imitative, which does not make them any less troubling.

Refugees and Immigrants: The New Others

'The common Bulgarian is no racist, but there are such organizations— 'New Nazism', 'Extremism'—which are always active. For the time I have spent living in Bulgaria, I haven't met a black person who has not been attacked or has had a problem, who has not been offended' (Acts of Violence against Refugees and Immigrants 2007: 11). This is how a Cameroon refugee describes everyday racism. Another incident that illustrates the insensitivity of the media and public opinion in this respect occurred on 30 January 2007, when a refugee from Nigeria was severely beaten up in a café in downtown Sofia. The media coverage was rather scarce, and the institutional response even more so.

Despite everyday racism towards refugees and immigrants, for a long time the central target of hate speech was minorities rather than immigrants. The Syrian refugee crisis radically changed this situation, and Bulgarian nationalists gladly embraced their new target, which synchronised their discourses with those of their Western role models. The wave of Syrian refugees could be perceived by the general public as a humanitarian problem and presented in terms of international solidarity to victims of civil war. The nationalist discursive effort concentrates on dispelling these possible interpretations by transforming the humanitarian problem into a threat. Several discursive strategies are used for this purpose. The first treats asylum seekers as 'illegal' immigrants, presenting them as radical Islamists and terrorists: 'over 2,000 Islamists invaded our country and applied for asylum.'[23] The second discursive strategy treats illegal immigrants as a threat to national security: 'The wave

---

[23] http://www.vestnikataka.bg/2013/11/%D0%BF%D0%BB%D1%8A%D0%-B7%D0%BD%D0%B0%D1%85%D0%B0-3-%D0%B3%D1%80%D1%83%D0%BF%D0%B8-%D0%B8%D1%81%D0%BB%D1%8F%D0%BC%D1%81%D0%BA%D0%B8-%D0%BC%D0%B0%D1%81%D0%BE%D0%B2%D0%B8-%D1%83%D0%B1%D0%B8%D0%B9%D1%86/

of illegal immigrants threatens the security and public order in our State.'[24] Both contribute to increasing the sentiment of threat, insecurity and lack of protection. Two contradictory images are associated with the refugees/Islam threat: criminality and unfair privileges: 'The Jihadists and other criminals who illegally entered our territory will be given entire Bulgarian villages and land.'[25] This statement is typical of the extremist discourse of mixing fear and anger: it constructs the figure of the refugee as a radical foreigner who is a dangerous terrorist, yet receives privileges.

LGBT: De-Ethnicising and Sexualising Otherness

'Gay parade allowed! Smoking forbidden! What is more harmful for the nation?' Curiously, this billboard belongs to the regional NIE party in the city of Plovdiv, whereas the gay pride takes place in Sofia. This blurring of the boundaries between the problems of Plovdiv's citizens and the anti-gay message illustrates the centrality of the LGBT issue in the symbolic map of nationalist populism. 'Gay' is used as a universal attribute, charged with the power to invalidate any political entity it is applied to. 'Gay Europe' is a pet phrase in Ataka's rhetoric. It has no specific referent, but its connotations are clearly negative. The other semantic amalgam has been homosexuality/paedophilia. Its ambitious goal is to present the former, not as a sexual identity, but as a perversion and a violation of natural, moral and legal norms. The anti-LGBT rhetoric draws symbolic strength from two sources. The first contrasts it with the traditional family, put on a pedestal by nationalist discourse. The second is masculinity as a key sexualised and aestheticised ideal of the nationalist 'body'.

---

[24] http://www.ataka.bg/index.php?option=com_content&task=view&id=6766&Itemid=66 (Text 12).
[25] http://www.vestnikataka.bg/2013/12/80-%D0%BE%D1%82-%D0%BD%D0%B5%D0%B7%D0%B0%D0%BA%D0%BE%D0%BD%D0%BD%D0%B8%D1%82%D0%B5-%D0%BF%D1%80%D0%B8%D1%88%D1%8A%D0%BB%D1%86%D0%B8-%D0%B1%D0%B5%D0%B7-%D0%B4%D0%BE%D0%BA%D1%83%D0%BC%D0%B5%D0%BD%D1%82%D0%B8/%D0%BC%D0%B5%D0%B7-%D0%B4%D0%BE%D0%BA%D1%83%D0%BC%D0%B5%D1%82%D0%B5/ (Text 2).

Elastic Post-Secularism or Religionisation of Nationalism[26]

I coined the term 'elastic (post-)secularism' (Krasteva 2015) to conceptualise the eclectic, diverse and often contrary forms of the nationalist uses of religion in the post-communist context of religionisation of politics and politicisiation of religion which stretch in some cases toward secularism[27] and in others toward post-secularisation. Inspired by the interactionist notion of 'elasticity of ethnicity', the concept describes the redesigning of identities in the ever changing contexts of interacting with Significant Others. Kristen Ghodsee was fascinated by the oxymoron 'orthodox atheist' mentioned by her Bulgarian respondents (Ghodsee 2009). Unlike Ghodsee's symphonic secularism, which considers the relation between religion and politics from the point of view of religion, elastic secularism considers it from the point of view of politics. (Krasteva 2015)

'People was the church and the church were the people' (Friedland 2001: 142). Nation, identity and Church are inseparable both in Bulgaria and throughout the Balkans. As argued in Krasteva 2015, there are structural affinities between nationalism and Orthodox Christianity.

> Religious nationalism locates the agency in the disciplined self-bound to God, not a sacralized, self-interested monad; constitutes society not through the abstract disembodied individual of the market but through the erotic and gendered flesh of the family. (Friedland 2001: 142)

Orthodoxy lies at the centre of the symbolic cartography of Bulgarian national populism. Negation, dismissal and rage need a positive counterbalance, and populism pins it down in religion. The strong bonds between nationalism and religion are being forged on all levels: biographical, symbolic and programmatic. Siderov has a degree in theology. It is no accident that he chose this subject after he became a political leader; his diploma is part of his nationalist toolkit, along with the boxing gloves that he flaunted

---

[26] Original research taken from Krasteva, A. (2015). Religion, politics and nationalism in post-communist Bulgaria. Elastic (post)secularism. Nationalism and Ethnic Politics, 21 (4), 422–445.

[27] Muslim girls are not allowed to wear headscarves in secular public schools, but the same schools are being encouraged to introduce Orthodox Christianity as a compulsory subject.

in the video promoting his candidacy in the 2013 campaign. Ataka's campaigns synthesised this religious pathos in the emblematic motto 'Orthodox solidarity'. The campaign itself was designed as a charity event: the leader, accompanied by local activists, provided people experiencing financial difficulties with scholarships, funds for medical treatment and so on. The campaign has been completely replaced by a strategy that exchanges debate for donation, autonomous citizens for powerless individuals. (Krasteva 2015)

Bulgarian nationalism still lacks the symbolic and political power to transform into a religious nationalism in the sense of Roger Friedland (2001),[28] but it is working on various pieces of its 'patchwork': religionisation of national identity; turning the family–religion–nation triad into an organic whole, united by memories, roots, and martyrs; and offering social assistance as part of its strategy to marginalsze the state and forge direct and strong bonds of solidarity between nation and nationalists.

Statism or Politics of Sovereignty

'A nationalism whose roots go back 7,000 (!) years and a civilization more ancient than the Sumerian and Egyptian ones' (Ataka 2013a: 70) possess a miraculous power and deserve a strong state. Nationalism is perceived as a universal panacea and a magic tool. 'We the nationalists demand …', and there follows a lengthy list of forceful wishes ranging from salaries equal to those in Belgium to the demand that 'Bulgarian entrepreneurs should be in charge of Bulgaria's industry, trade, and banks, rather than foreigners who treat us with contempt and discriminate us as a nation' (Ataka 2013a, b: 26). This text, featuring a full page of underlined demands, is indicative of the style of national populism, where the leader's will and nationalist pathos are considered so persuasive and self-sufficient that there is no need for policies to be implemented. Although it offers such policies, they

---

[28] Roger Friedland defines religious nationalism through a set of characteristics: it provides a specific ontology of power that is demonstrated and sanctioned by its politicised practices and the central place its political aims and ambitions take; it localises social solidarity in the 'organic' space of the family and the community, rather than in the 'negotiated' space of abstract citizens; and it provides 'an alternative welfare state to their members, its services are offered and consumed as a condition of and within a context of community, unlike the distant, bureaucratic, and often officious state' (Friedland 2001: 142).

are symbolic rather than economic, chosen for the semantic proximity of their name: which policy would suit nationalism better than nationalisation? Ataka is the only Bulgarian party that has overtly and systematically raised the far-left slogan of the nationalisation of major enterprises.

Radical Demophilism Versus Radical Anti-Elitism

Bulgarian national populism is 'copy and paste' in nature and willingly applies all the main characteristics of the Western predecessors that inspired it. Politics must follow the common will of the people or their common sense (Mudde 2007). Society is divided into two rival wings, each of which is absolutely homogeneous: the immaculate common people and the venal elite (Mudde 2007). Radical anti-elitism and radical demophilism are two faces of the same message:

> As far as the political elite is concerned, rhetorical figures exceed all limits. It would be insufficient to say that the elite does not deserve to direct and govern: the elite does not even have the right to think of itself as the people's equal. Even more radically, the elite is inferior to the people, which in turn are morally sounder, and in some mysterious way, more competent than their elite. The ultimate phase of this logic is hard to articulate, and yet I will make an attempt: in fact, the people are the true elite. This species of ANTI-anti-egalitarianism puts the very limits of language to the test. (Malinov 2007: 83)

Anti-elitism takes three forms: anti-establishment, anti-globalism, anti-Europeanisation. The performativity of the anti-elitist discourse is predictable: each accusation against the elites translates into electoral support for the accuser. The political capital of anti-elitism draws from two sources: the genuine referent—the high level of corruption among Bulgarian elites has been unequivocally proven by all international surveys; and the broad consensus—mistrust of elites is not limited to the electorate of radical parties but is common to the general public.

During the first decade of the post-communist transition, globalisation was conceived as an escape from the controlled and closed communist world, synonymous with openness, liberation and freedom. Disenchantment with it is a late post-communist phenomenon. National populism is the first champion of the 'new structural conflict that opposes globalisation 'losers' to globalisation 'winners" (Kriesi 2014: 369). Ataka is one of the most vociferous proponents of anti-globalism and anti-capitalism. The politics of dismissal (Eisburg 2007) are radical and categorical: (Krasteva 2015)

> Globalism has failed. Monetarism has failed. The liberal politics of 'less government, the market has the final say' has failed. The worldwide financial crisis, caused by the US, is a clear sign of this. Market fundamentalism, transformed into a religion by the financial and political establishment of the US, has suffered an abysmal defeat. We say no to the world's speculative capital, no to supranational corporations, which destroy market economies, no to Wall Street, and we say yes to more common sense, balance, and equity. (Ataka 2013a, b: 2)

The discourse of negation makes use of three techniques: it equates capitalism with monetarism, as well as monetarism with financial crisis, promoting an alternative recipe that Ataka itself has failed to live up to: 'common sense and balance'. The populist rage is targeted mostly at international capital, which 'drains' the national wealth: Ataka has estimated that 28.257 billion leva have been diverted from the pockets of Bulgarian taxpayers into the treasuries of foreign companies selling food, clothing, electricity, banking services, etc. 'All institutions, all ministries, the culture, healthcare, and education sectors altogether, receive 10 billion leva less than the foreign colonizers!' (Ataka 2013a, b: 8). (Krasteva 2015)

Anti-Europeanism is the other topic to attract the critical pathos of populist negation. It strikes out in three directions. The first is the neo-colonialist accusation: the EU 'is becoming a new Soviet Union, functioning by force and against the constitution' (Ataka 2013a, b). Ataka's manifesto begins with the story of 'how we were enslaved after the fall of the Berlin Wall'. The second criticism is institutional: 'The Euro Pact invalidates the Parliament and the government, elections, and democracy at large'. The third direction has to do with Europeanisation as a form of globalisation: 'The Euro Pact reinforces the power of the supra-national and corporate oligarchy'. These criticisms converge in a cluster whose core conveys the message 'The EU is a threat to national identity, sovereignty and dignity'; 'Bulgaria is threatened with a loss of identity and with extinction'; 'Bulgaria is losing its sovereignty'. Post-accession euro-scepticism could be explained by variety of factors, two of which are significant: the inability of national elites to articulate EU integration in a meaningful political way, different from 'European funds', and the inability of Brussels to convincingly connect integration and democratisation: 'The EU and the external constraints that it imposed on the accession countries contributed to the perception of the transition regimes as "democracies without choices", and thus fuelled the current backlash against consensual politics' (Krastev 2007: 60–61).

In foreign affairs, even extremists cannot oppose everyone. The geopolitical alternative that Ataka suggests is Russia,'an economic giant' (Ataka 2013a, b: 32). While in identity politics, Ataka and the whole of Bulgarian national populism is a 'copy and paste' of its Western counterparts, Ataka's particular hallmark is Russophilia. Siderov launched Ataka's campaign at the most recent parliamentary elections in 2014 in Moscow. This shows the paradox of international nationalism. Incoherency and eclecticism are not an oversight or a weakness of extremists; they are a strategy that allows them to form the most baffling but politically effective mixtures. Ataka's overt, unconditional support for Russia, much more resolute than that of the BSP, makes sense in terms of elections and turns the party into a (near-)monopoly of Russophile votes, which constitute a considerable amount in Bulgaria. In the far-right three-pole system 'instrumentality, identity, ideology' defined by Klandermans and Mayer (2006), Ataka has managed to subordinate identity and ideology to instrumentality and to transform internationalism, in its specific Russophile variety, into one of the most powerful electoral resources of nationalism.

Combating Political Extremism: From Civil Society to Acts of Citizenship

As we already know, far-right extremism appeared relatively late on the Bulgarian political scene. Has civil society accumulated the strength to oppose it? It was Ralf Dahrendorf who mapped out the agenda of post-communist democratisation. The three objectives—creating the institutions of parliamentary democracy, the transition from planned to market economy, and building a civil society—have different temporalities: six months, six years and six decades. This ironic symmetry indicates that building a strong and vibrant civil society is the most challenging and long-term task of the three-sided post-communist democratisation. While the topic of the civil counteractivity to far-right extremism remains political, its analysis further asks a theoretical question about which conceptual framework is the most adequate to study and understand civic mobilisations. The present analysis argues that the concept of 'civil society' is adequate when looking at the first generation of civil organisations, while the second generation of protests and volunteers is better conceptualised through the prism of citizenship and acts of citizenship. If today the concept of citizenship is trendy, it is because of the powerful processes of re/de/construction, of redefining its scope and agency, of looking for new sources of invention and revitalisation. The current study understands citizenship as a bricolage of belonging and participation, of membership and engagement, with an emphasis on the latter—on the construction of the citizen through commitment, activism and involvement. Engin Isin and Grec Nielsen conceptualise this approach in terms of 'acts of citizenship' aimed at understanding 'how subjects become citizens as claimants of justice, rights and responsibilities' (Isin and Nielsen 2008: 18).

The present study questions civic agency from two perspectives:

- *New political agenda or mirroring the extremist one?* Who defines the agenda of civic activities and engagement? Do the anti-bodies succeed in defining their own agenda or do they follow the extremist one by counteraction and anti-discrimination activities?
- *New mobilisations or new actors?* Do we observe the emergence of new types of NGOs and other civic actors or experimentation with new forms of mobilisation? How do new actors and new mobilisations overlap?

The study presents three civic organisations against violence—Bulgarian Helsinki Committee, People against Racism and Friends of Refugees. They represent different types of institutionalisation of civic activism and different generations of NGOs.

The Bulgarian Helsinki Committee (BHC) was founded on 14 July 1992. In early 1993, it became a member of what was then the International Helsinki Federation. The activities of the BHC include systematic monitoring of the human rights situation in Bulgaria. Since 1995, the BHC has also included a legal programme offering legal assistance to victims of human rights violations through consultations and the pursuit of lawsuits before national or international courts. The BHC has won a series of cases in the European Court of Human Rights and other bodies. During the transition to democracy, one of the key objectives of the Bulgarian state is the acceptance of international and European standards in the fields of non-discrimination, respect for human rights and the fight against hate speech. The BHC plays a key role as both corrective to the post-communist state and catalyst for the harmonisation of Bulgarian legislation on anti-discrimination. It is an emblematic example of the emergence of the first NGOs and the role of civic voices against hate speech and violence in the new post-communist public space.

HORA (Hora Sreshtu Rasizma; People against Racism) was created to counteract an act of violence committed by skinheads. On 6 June 2010 in Sofia, masked aggressors on a number 20 tram armed with metal rods, brass knuckles and knives brutally attacked four young people who were heading to a peaceful protest against the illegal detention of foreigners in the Busmantsi Special Detention Centre. The Tram 20 case became one of the turning points and may be linked to the creation of informal initiatives and associations fighting against violence, violation of human rights and hate speech. The very protests against the illegal detention of foreigners in Busmantsi were among the first informal instances of the protection of foreigners' human rights. HORA includes people of different ideological views, all united by the human rights cause. Here is what they say of the attack in Tram 20:

> The attack on protestors demonstrating for foreigners' rights was the culmination of a disturbing trend which threatens fundamental freedom of expression and civil activity! This is a provocation against the freedom of expression and association and we cannot allow it to remain with impunity. Violence of political or racial origin is a problem not only for the victims and people assaulted Attempts to threaten and restrict the right of

expression through terror and violence are a harsh challenge to the principles of democracy in Bulgaria and this makes them a problem for all people of democratic thinking. Everybody is in danger! If today assaulters try to shut the mouths of activists or to 'cleanse' their city of ethnically, racially, religiously or sexually 'irregular' people, tomorrow the victim can be any of us who express the 'wrong'opinion. LET US SAY IT! Silence against fascist violence is what makes this violence possible. For this reason, we, the citizens who participated in the protest against Busmantsi, irrespective of our different political convictions, stand up in defence of the four people who became victims of political violence, and against the racism, xenophobia and neo-Nazism which are starting to gain ground in Bulgaria.[29]

Friends of Refugees is a volunteer citizen movement, spontaneously created in June 2013 as a response to the refugee crisis in Bulgaria and the anticipated inability of the government to manage it appropriately. The turning point in their work came in September 2013 when a member of the Friends organised a big media campaign to gather food, clothes, supplies and medicines for refugees in need: 'Back then the official programme of the Red Cross Bulgaria wasn't yet in place and the Bulgarian office of the UNHCR wasn't responding or working on the problem. The citizens were faster and more mobile in their reaction compared with the administration and the bigger organisations despite their international impact and resources'.[30] A small group of committed citizens succeeded in an impressively short time in attracting several other very different types of civic, humanitarian, business and media actors, such as Syrian and other Arab organisations, the Red Cross, business partners from immigrant and national business, numerous small human rights groups and a large number of individual citizens. Instead of an articulated structure Friends of Refugees functions through loose networking. They concentrate on three activities: humanitarian help; mobilisation against extremism such as the November 2013 demonstration against the increasing number of xenophobic attacks against refugees; and the symbolic fight for words—nationalist actors and some mainstream politicians constantly sought to impose the term 'illegal immigrants',

---

[29] Interview with Vanya Ivanova.
[30] Interview wirth Vanya Ivanova.

while human rights activists fought for the legitimacy of the term 'refugees'. They have a dual agenda: the first part is to counteract that of the extremists; the second is autonomous with a strong emphasis on humanitarian solidarity.

The three case studies illustrate two different types, and, respectively, two generations of civic agency. The role of NGOs has been crucial in building a democratic culture at the beginning of the post-communist transition. These 'first-generation' post-communist civic organisations promoted European human rights and anti-discrimination standards and discourses. The Bulgarian Helsinki Committee is typical of this first generation with its triple impact: professionalisation of NGO experts; the sustainability of the most respectful ones such as BHC; and their visible and important role in the post-communist public space.

In recent years civil society's outlook and the sources of its vitality have changed and we have witnessed the emergence of second-generation post-communist civic actors. HORA and Friends of Refugees are emblematic of this second generation. They demonstrate the enormous potential of citizens' self-organisation and the strength of solidarity in a situation of acute crisis and complete blockage of the state. They reveal the crucial importance of the new figure of the volunteer for the vitality of civil society.

The first-generation anti-bodies became professionalised and institutionalised in the form of NGOs and think tanks aimed at developing civil society. The second-generation post-communist civic actors are less organised, less professionalised and more spontaneous. The new mobilisations introduced another type of civic actor—the amateur, willing and able to experiment, to search, to propose new, 'rough' ideas, to make mistakes, to act, to innovate. The volunteer is a relatively recent phenomenon in the civic agency's development. The emergence of volunteers, their role in dealing with the refugee crisis and combating extremism is both an expression of the vitality of the civic agency and a catalyst for innovation and dynamisation of militancy. The synergy between the spontaneity of the initiative/movement, civic agency, the human rights logic and their unprecedented impact demonstrates that the Friends of Refugees and Hora movements are acts of citizenship.

Concluding Remarks, or How National Populism Takes Advantage of Paradoxes

Paradoxically, Bulgarian national populism is a democratic phenomenon. During the first decade of democratic transition, Bulgaria enjoyed a 'shy' nationalism; once democracy had been consolidated, radical national populism emerged.

Bulgarian national populism is 'left wing, right wing, everything' (Ghodsee 2008: 26). Like foreign far-right parties, it is not afraid of paradoxes; on the contrary, it creates and takes advantage of them. It is eclectic and inconsistent, not because it cannot, but because it does not want to be coherent. First, this distinguishes it from its opponents—liberalism, socialism, etc. Second, the 'ideological empty heart' (Taggart 2000) enables national populism to combine diametrically opposed appeals: from the aggressive exclusion of large groups such as Roma to the claim that it represents the entire Bulgarian people. We should also point out the paradoxical similarity between populism and technocratic governance. At first glance, they look mutually exclusive, but they are both premised on the assumption that there is only one right solution to a particular political challenge. In the technocratic vision, it is the experts who articulate this exclusive solution; in the populist version, it is the people. Both are at odds with liberal democracy, which 'understands things differently: it is a space for diverse viewpoints and political alternatives' (Muller 2013).

Among the numerous paradoxes of Bulgarian national populism, here I will elaborate on five. The first is that Bulgaria and Eastern Europe have been the 'usual suspects' of every extreme populism, yet such populism does not affect a larger electorate in Eastern Europe than it does in Western Europe. Perceiving Eastern Europe as the 'usual suspects' stems from two factors: the absence of a developed and ingrained democratic political culture, and deep mistrust of elites, institutions and procedures. However, these factors have not—so far—yielded catastrophic election results. Polyakova (2015) demonstrated that far-right voting is actually less prominent in Eastern than in Western Europe. The proliferation of radical political parties in Bulgaria has not—so far—led to an expansion of the electoral niche of national populism.

The second paradox is that despite the young age of Bulgarian national populism and its fierce leadership battles, it has succeeded in building a solid structure with two pillars and a volatile periphery. The pillars exemplified by Ataka and NFSB have opposite profiles in two crucial areas—coalition potential and experience of government. Ataka has specialised in left-wing coalitions, NFSB in right-wing ones. Ataka is typical of extremist parties that survive better in opposition than in government. NFSB is building an image of a more acceptable governmental partner. The two rivals have secured the future of national populism in that there is a potential partner for any government; even if one of them disappears, the other will assure the continuity. The future of national populism is also assured by the volatile periphery of small extremist parties, organisations and politicians ready to join the winner of the moment.

Democratic illiberalism[31] is among the most discussed paradoxes (Kriesi 2014; Rupnik 2007; Krastev 2007). Post-communist populism is an expression of the growing tension between democratic majoritarianism and liberal constitutionalism. 'The rise of populism is an indication that the liberal solutions in the realm of politics, economics, and culture are increasingly losing their appeal, whereas the policies of exclusion are increasingly gaining popularity' (Krastev 2007: 108). I would supplement its multiple interpretations with two more: the first has to do with the post-communist context, the second, with a general trend in Europe. Post-communist elites embraced neoliberalism without justifying it or 'translating' it into the language of democracy; furthermore, they quickly discredited it through irresponsible neoliberal policies that have been rejected by large sections of the general public. The second, broader trend has been the transition from cold to hot ideologies, from liberalism/socialism/conservatism to nationalism, from ideological to identity politics.

The third paradox holds the greatest danger for democracy: the proliferation of acts of hate speech and violence has not been solely due to

---

[31] 'If democracy means political legitimacy, premised on the popular vote, as well as constitutionalism (separation of powers), then populists accept the former and dismiss the latter (i.e. the idea that constitutional norms and representative democracy have a priority over values and the people's 'legitimate' anxieties)' (Rupnik 2007: 130).

the proliferation of extremist actors. It has been also caused by the radical populist 'contagion' (Rooduijn et al. 2012), the penetration of Ataka's topics and theses into the political rhetoric of mainstream political parties: 'the political system is becoming 'Atakized,' whereas the prototype is being 'normalized" (Coen 2007: 5). When an extremist leader speaks in a racist way, this is a threat to democracy that could be positively marginalised by a strong civil society and moderate mainstream parties. When a minister of health from a moderate party speaks in a xenophobic way without any sanction,[32] this challenges the actual core of the democratic system. The normalisation of extremism and the radical populist contagion of mainstream parties is a threat graver than the threat of radical national populism itself.

The fourth paradox has to do with Rosanvallon's third simplification[33]: structural simplification by maintaining that the social cohesion of society is provided by an identity, usually defined in negative terms, and not by the quality of social relations (Rosanvallon 2011: 7). Post-communism destroyed the collective communist project but failed to construct a new collective meaningful one. Bulgaria's geopolitical priorities—NATO, the EU, Schengen—absorbed the entire energy of the political class, leaving a void in the sense of living together as a community. National populism is the most strident and aggressive response to the need to fill this vacuum. It is also virtually the only response by a political party. There are no parties that have set 'the quality of social relations' as their priority.[34] Instead, there are innovative civil initiatives—pro-diversity, green and others—that have been weaving the threads of togetherness. The antagonism between these two projects—extremist versus civic, nationalist versus green—will determine the future of post-communist democracy.

---

[32] On the contrary, Petar Moskov's anti-Roma statements received support from the leaders of the Reformist Bloc (Radan Kanev) and many public figures.

[33] Rosanvallon formulates a triple simplification: a *political* simplification by considering the people as an obvious subject; a *procedural* simplification by maintaining that the established elites are corrupt and that the only real appeal to democracy is the direct appeal of the people; and a *structural* simplification (Rosanvallon 2011: 6–7).

[34] The Reformist Bloc, which rose to power after the wave of civil protests in 2013, offered some hope but quickly deteriorated into 'politics as usual'.

References

Acts of Violence against Refugees and Immigrants. (2007). Насилията над бежанци и мигранти. *Objectif Journal, 218*. Retrieved September 15, 2015, from http://www.bghelsinki.org/bg/publikacii/obektiv/blgarski-khelzinski-komitet/2007-02/nasiliyata-nad-bezhanci-i-imigranti/

Coen, E. (2007). Ataka's music—part of the repertoire of other political 'orchestras' (Музиката на Атака—част от репертоара на други политически 'оркестри'). *Objectif Journal, 218*. http://www.bghelsinki.org/bg/publikacii/obektiv/emil-koen/2007-10/muzikata-na-taka-chast-ot-retoara-na-drugi-politicheski-orkestri/ (Accessed 15 Sept 2015).

Eisburg, F. (2007). The old one and the new one (Старият и новият). *Critique and Humanism Journal, 23*, 101–106.

Friedland, R. (2001). Religious nationalism and the problem of collective representation. *Annual Review of Sociology, 27*, 125–152.

Ghodsee, K. (2008). Left wing, right wing, everything. Xenophobia, neo-totaliatariansm and populist politics in Bulgaria. *Problems of Post-Communism, 56*(3), 26–39.

Ghodsee, K. (2009). Symphonic secularism: Eastern orthodoxy, ethnic identity and religious freedoms in contemporary Bulgaria. *Anthropology of East Europe Review, 27*(2), 242.

Hockenos, P. (2010, May 24). Central Europe's right-wing populism. *The Nation*, 18–21.

Ibroscheva, E. (2013). A different kind of massive attack: How the Bulgarian Ultranationalist party Ataka engineered it political success using electronic media. *Central European Journal of Communication, 1*, 51–86.

Isin, E., & Nielsen, G. (2008). *Acts of citizenship*. London: Zed Books.

Kabakchieva, P. (2008). Is there a soil for national-populism in this country? (Има ли почва националпопулизмът у нас?). *Objectif, 157*, 3–4.

Kapel-Pogacean, A., & Ragaru, N. (2007). Romania Mare and Ataka in a comparative perspective: National-populism and Political Protest in Romania and Bulgaria (Романия Маре и Атака в сравнителен план: националпопулизъм и политически протест в Румъния и България). *Critique and Humanism Journal, 23*, 149–159.

Klandermans, B. and Mayer, N. (eds) 2006. *Extreme right activists in Europe. Through the magnifying glass* (Kindle Edition). London: Taylor and Francis.

Krastev, I. (2007). The strange death of the liberal consensus. *Journal of Democracy, 18*(4), 56–63.

Krasteva, A. (2015). Religion, politics and nationalism in post-communist Bulgaria. Elastic (post)secularism. *Nationalism and Ethnic Politics, 21*(4), 422–445.

Kriesi, H. (2014). The populist challenge. *West European Politics, 37*(2), 361–378.

Linden, R. (2008). The new populism in Central and Southeastern Europe. *Problems of Post-Communism, 55*(3), 3–6.

Malinov, S. (2007). Reflections on Bulgarian populism (Размисли за българския популизъм). *Critique and Humanism Journal, 23*, 71–84.

Miscoiu, S. (2014). Balkan populisms. *Journal Souteastern Europe, 38*(1), 1–24.

Mudde, C. (2007). Популисткият Zeitgeist в днешна Европа (The populist Zeitgeist in today's Europe). *Critique and Humanism Journal, 23*, 115–119.

Mudde, C., & Kaltwasser, C. R. (2013). Populism. In M. Freeden & L. T. Sargent (Eds.), *The Oxford handbook of political ideologies* (pp. 493–512). Oxford: Oxford University Press.

Muller, J.-V. (2013). Three myths on populism (Три мита за популизма). *Sega Newspaper, 23*(4), 13.

Polyakova, A. (2015). The backward East? Explaining differences in support for radical right parties in Western and Eastern Europe. *Journal of Comparative Politics, 8*(1), 49–72.

Reynie, D. (2013). *Les nouveaux populismes*. Paris: Fayard/Pluriel.

Rizova, T. (2013). The perils of populist radical right parties: The case of the Bulgarian party Ataka. *Jounral of Politics and Law, 6*(4), 160–175.

Rooduijn, M., de Lange, S. L., & van der Brug, W. (2012). A populist Zeitgeist? Programmatic contagion by populist parties in Western Europe. *Party Politics, 20*(4), 563–575.

Rosanvallon, P. (2011). *Penser le populisme*. Leçon inaugurale prononcée lors du 26ieme rencontre de Pétrarque 2011.

Rupnik, J. (2007). From democracy fatigue to populist backlash. *Journal of democracy, 18*(4), 17–25.

Smilov, D. (2008). The frustration of democracy (Фрустрация на демокрацията). *Objectif Journal, 159*, 26–27.

Taggart, P. (2000). *Populism*. Philadelphia: Open University Press.

Programs of Political Parties and Interviews in Media

Атака. (2013a). Планът Сидеров срещу колониалното робство (Siderov's Plan against the Colonial Yoke). Управленска програма на партия Атака. Пълен вариант.

Атака. (2013b). Планът Сидеров. Нов път за България (The Siderov plan. A new route for Bulgaria). Резюме на програмата на партия Атака.

Siderov, V. (2013, January 1). Герб извади бухалката срещу мен (GERB have taken out the Axe against me). Преса.

8

Posing for Legitimacy? Identity and Praxis of Far-Right Populism in Greece

Gabriella Lazaridis and Vasiliki Tsagkroni

Introduction

In order for a party to distinguish itself and generate political support, it needs a collective identity (see Bergbauer 2010). It is this identity that differentiates it from the rest and distinguishes it as a choice in the eyes of the electorate; it aims to address questions such as 'Why should I vote for you?' by proposing a profile with which the voter can identify and hence trust the party with their vote. Additionally, the intention of the political party is to create a 'sense of community', a 'we-feeling' (Easton 1965: 185) that could eventually motivate political participation from the perspective of the citizen. In this sense the parties aim to create a strong identity which the voters can identify with. The core of a party's identity can be centred on specific policies, ideologies or even charismatic leaders.

G. Lazaridis (✉)
University of Leicester, Leicester, UK

V. Tsagkroni
Queen Mary University of London, London, UK

© The Editor(s) (if applicable) and The Author(s) 2016
G. Lazaridis et al. (eds.), *The Rise of the Far Right in Europe*,
DOI 10.1057/978-1-137-55679-0_8

Over the last three decades, far-right parties in Europe have experienced a growth of electoral support and managed to turn those who have voted for the party once ('new voters') into loyal voters (creating a new voter profile) (Rensmann 2003). Since the early days of the parties' success studies have attempted to provide a model of classification according to the parties' characteristics and identity (see Betz 1998; Minkenberg 2004; Mudde 2004; Ignazi 2003). Betz (1998) argues that their success is due to their abandoning of traditional fascist ideology and the adoption of a more versatile profile that combines rhetorical radicalism and figurative policies, together with the adoption of a variety of communication techniques to make them more appealing to the electorate.

Scheuch and Klingemann (1967) have identified the manifestations of radicalism and extremism as a 'normal pathology of industrial societies', whose appearance they attributed to the structural and socio-economic changes, and the changes in value systems that are occurring in contemporary societies. Having said that, the boundaries between radical, extreme and populist are fluid and contested rather than fixed. The specific term 'far-right populism' is chosen as it characterises in a more meaningful way the parties under examination and gives a better explanation of their presence and position in the political arena and their attitude towards the political system.

Following Bergbauer (2010), whose work attempts to analyse ways in which collective identities are mobilised in the European context, and Bull (2003), who examines collective identities using the case of Lega Nord in Italy, the primary aim of this chapter is to identify far-right parties in Greece and to examine whether these parties share a common collective identity.

We concentrate on three political parties: Golden Dawn, LAOS and ANEL. First we assess briefly the concepts and definitions used in the analysis; we then explore the official material produced by the parties, such as manifestos and insignia, material which contributes to the construction of the parties' identity. The fieldwork consisted of interviews and ethnographic work (both offline and online), with 'populist groups' and their members. Content analysis has been adopted for methodological purposes, examining issues such as ideas of self-representation and identity, migration and Islamophobia, gender and LGBT rights, attitudes towards the elites and the EU. The main argument put forward is that despite the differences between the parties under examination (an argument that involves ongoing debate about definitions of the far-right family), the parties share a collective identity characterised by hate discourse against 'the others'.

Far-Right Populism: Demand, Context and Success

Since the late 1980s the far-right phenomenon has become a popular topic among scholars due to its increasing success in Europe. The emergence, the electoral success and the establishment of parties of the far-right family in the political scene of numerous countries, have captured the attention of the public. These parties have managed to launch themselves as significant players in the political field and have developed as a substantial challenge to established political agencies across several Western European countries (see also Betz 1998). Their emerging electoral success has often been seen as a compelling influence on government coalitions and policies (see Golder 2003). Discussions as to which parties belong to this particular political family, and the differences between the parties themselves have created an ongoing definitional debate. From radical to far-right populist and from extreme to anti-immigrant, a new scheme of classification has been created to identify the range of the far-right family (see among others Mudde 2004; Minkenberg 1998; Kitschelt and McGann 1995; Hainsworth 2004; Anastasakis 2000).

The most distinguishing characteristics that can be traced within the far-right populist parties are: advocating welfare and redistributive social policies; defending ethno-nationalism, which provides the basis for selective social-care policies; promoting demands for direct democratic enrichment of political expression and a wider plebiscitary form of political participation, while preferring authoritarian and hierarchical structures (see Georgiadou 2008); welfare chauvinism; anti-immigration policies; referendum policies and national priority (Hainsworth 2004); the decline of the established socio-cultural and socio-political system; and minimising the role of the state (Betz 1998: 4). For Betz (1998), the majority of these parties appear to combine liberal approaches to individual rights and the economy with elements of the socio-political agenda of the far-right parties in order to attract more potential voters. In addition, their closed structure gives them the advantage of responding more quickly to the preferences of the electorate (Evans and Ivaldi 2002). Charismatic leadership also plays an essential role in the positioning of these parties in the electoral arena.

As noted above, support for far-right populist parties varies across the countries. For Anastasakis (2000: 5–6), there are four approaches to 'the rise, resilience and nature' of the radical right parties: (a) historical, as a legacy of the fascist era, (b) structural, in terms of a socio-economic context, (c) political, as political actors, and (d) ideologico-cultural, as xenophobic rhetoric.

The fascist element can be traced back to the changes that occurred in the post-war era (Anastasakis 2000; Hainsworth 2004; Moufahim 2007). Additionally, the far-right parties successfully addressed such distress by focusing on issues related to, for example, socio-economic changes, unemployment and immigration of a part of the electorate, which eventually raised their support level. In the third feature, a vote can be translated as a protest vote against the political system but nevertheless a vote that also has ideological roots (Betz 1998). Mistrust of established political parties has created a climate of discomfort within the part of the electorate that has chosen 'to turn their back on politics or to use the ballot as a means of protest' (Anastasakis 2000: 14; see also Kitschelt and McGann 1995 on Scandinavia). Thus voters choose to project their dissatisfaction with the established political parties by voting for a party that is considered a pariah of the system (Coffe 2004). The final dimension concerns the xenophobic approaches of the far-right parties. According to Betz (1998), the far-right parties have exploited the opportunity created by the failure of established political parties to address critical issues, such as immigration—issues considered highly significant by a part of the electorate.

The success of radical parties in Western democracies is not only based on a favourable political environment, but also on leadership, organisational structure and political culture. The charismatic leadership and closed organisational structure of far-right parties has allowed them to rapidly react towards evolving issues (such as immigration), and take advantage of 'changing political opportunities' (see Hainsworth 2004). This chapter is not primarily concerned with the question whether the parties under examination can all be classified as far-right parties but rather with the characteristics that can argue for a common mobilised identity.

Far-Right Populism in Greece

More specifically, extremist elements of the right made their first appearance in Greece during the 1940s, with Organisation X (*Οργάνωση Χ*), a nationalist and anti-communist movement founded by Lieutenant Georgios Grivas during the Nazi occupation of 1941–1944. By the 1960s the far-right elements managed to become assimilated into the mechanisms of the state while the military junta (1967–1974) succeeded in extracting the nationalist right from its marginal position of the past. In the meantime, in 1960 Constantinos Plevris founded the Organisation of August the 4th (*4η Αυγούστου*), one member of which would be the later leader of Golden Dawn (GD), Nikos Michaloliakos. Plevris would also be an influence on George Karatzaferis, leader of LAOS (*Λαϊκός Ορθόδοξος Συναγερμός*) and a key figure in the far-right scene in Greece, founding numerous organisations, engaging in hate speech against 'the others' and rhetoric in favour of fascism and anti-Semitism. He also briefly participated in LAOS until 2004 and was regularly hosted as a guest on Karatzarefis' private TV channel TeleAsty (*ΤηλεΑστυ*).

With the restoration of democracy in the country in 1974, several organisations and parties made their appearance with minor electoral success. In 1977 National Alignment (*Εθνική Παράταξη*), a nationalist-conservative party with strong elements of law and order and militarism gained 7 per cent of the popular vote, electing five MPs to the national parliament. For decades, National Alignment (NA) would be the only party of the far-right family to be represented in Parliament until the 2009 elections and the electoral success of LAOS.

EPEN, founded in 1984 by the former leader of Junta, George Papadopoulos, was a nationalist party seeking the release of the imprisoned members of the military junta; it managed to elect one representative in the European elections of 1984 but only achieved its highest percentage of 0.3 per cent at national level in 1989. The party last participated in the elections of 1996, gaining 0.24 per cent of the vote. By 2000 several new parties had made their appearance: but First Line (Πρώτη Γραμμή) led by Constantinos Plevris and National Front (Εθνικό Μέτωπο), a far-right, nationalist and anti-Semitic party led by Emmanouil Constas, both failed to attract the attention of the electorate. According to Pappas (2003: 93) the 'existence of a strong far right party discouraged the emergence of smaller parties in the same area or additionally the political competition prevented them from becoming legitimate', an approach that may explain the lack of support for far-right representatives before 2000.

The first party to claim the 'people's voice' in the Greek political system was LAOS. The party, which is also a pun on the Greek word 'people', was formed in 2000 as a splinter group from the main conservative party ND (New Democracy), led by ND's former MP and journalist Georgios Karatzaferis. The electoral debut of LAOS took place on 13 October 2002. In the following years, although the party's ratings were very promising and it performed well above exit polls and opinion polls, it did not manage to acquire the necessary percentage to enter Parliament. In the European Parliament (EP) elections of 2004 LAOS gained 4.12 per cent of the vote and managed to elect its president Karatzaferis as an MEP. In 2007 LAOS passed the threshold for election to the national parliament by winning 3.8 per cent of the votes and electing ten members to the parliament. In 2009 LAOS managed to elect two representatives in the EP, with 7.14 per cent of the vote, and fifteen members of parliament, winning 5.63 per cent in the national elections. However, the growing electoral success did not last for long, unlike other far-right parties in

Europe, which have experienced a growth in support especially during the last ten years.

LAOS slipped below the 3 per cent threshold in the 2012 national elections, reaching a low of 1.6 per cent in June 2012 and failing to win any seats in the Greek parliament. One explanation for the party's performance is its decision to participate in the coalition government while supporting the initial bailout packages, a decision that proved controversial among its members and voters. In addition, there was a rise in support for GD and ANEL, which attracted a large section of the electorate that used to vote for LAOS. Similarly, in the general elections of 2015 the party received only 1.03 per cent. Its decision to enter the interim coalition government of Loukas Papademos in November 2011, itself a confirmation that LAOS had gained the respectability it coveted, proved fatal. As of now, the party, left with no seats in Parliament, is in disarray—with some of its former MPs (including the two Ministers under Papademos) having joined the New Democracy party.

LAOS began as a party with not only an Orthodox Christian religious identity, but also a radically nationalist political identity, 'in line with the constitutional requirement that everything undertaken by the state must serve the Nation' (LAOS 2004). It sponsored a novel synthesis of 'anti-establishmentarianism', hyper-nationalism and reverence for the Greek tradition. Although it has since allegedly tried to 'moderate' the nationalist part of its appeal, the party now officially declares that it supports patriotism and social solidarity. Finally, the party placed immigration issues at the centre of its populist electoral platform, calling for a total ban on further non-EU immigration and for the expulsion of illegal immigrants: 'we will see to their return to their homeland, even if funding is required to resettle them in their countries' (LAOS 2007). It also adopted a highly emotive language of national sovereignty and defence of national identity.

The results of the 2012 national elections may have been largely determined by the degree of public anger at the EU/IMF rescue package for Greece and the desire to deliver a shock protest vote against the two main established parties, the conservative New Democracy and the socialist

PASOK. Nevertheless, immigration also featured very prominently in most party manifestos and public discourses as a fundamental security concern. Golden Dawn was the most spectacular beneficiary of the securitisation of the immigration debate, its share of the vote rising from 0.29 per cent in 2009 to almost 7 per cent in 2012.

The origins of GD go back to the 1980s when Nikos Michaloliakos founded The Popular Association Golden Dawn. At the same time Michaloliakos launched the magazine *Golden Dawn*, self-identified as a platform of social nationalism. With Michaloliakos as editor, the magazine hosted articles on Adolf Hitler, expressed support for Nazism and had the swastika as a symbol on its cover. The publication of the magazine was terminated in 1984 and in 1993 GD was recognised as a political party.

For years GD was unable to gain any electoral success. However, in the local elections of 2010 the party managed to elect Michaloliakos as representative to the City Council of Athens, gaining 5.3 per cent of the vote. In the national elections of 2012, GD gained 6.92 per cent and managed to elect eighteen representatives to the national parliament. Despite the fact that in 2013 the Greek High Court of Annulment (Άρειος Πάγος) indicted the leader, deputies and members of GD based on Art. 187 of the Greek Penal Code, which penalises the formation of and participation in a 'criminal organisation', in the national elections of 2015 and with most of its leadership members in jail, the party gained 6.3 per cent and managed to maintain its representation in the parliament.

GD, often characterised as a neo-Nazi, fascist, racist xenophobic party, has several times been associated with hate speech and crime incidents which draw on people's national, ethnic, religious, sexual and political identities. In 2012 the party ran a campaign for the national elections based on concern about unemployment, austerity and the economy, as well as virulent anti-immigration rhetoric. As stated in its manifesto of 2012, GD opposes 'the demographic alteration, through the influx of millions of illegal immigrants, and the dissolution of Greek society, which is systematically pursued by the parties of the establishment of the so-called left' (GD 2012). Nationalism is seen as the 'absolute and genuine revolution' (GD 2012), and support is needed for the establishment of institutions originating in this ideology. The party 'equates the state with the nation, citizenship with ethnicity and demos with ethnos' (Ellinas 2013: 549).

The last party to be considered here is ANEL. Just before the legislative elections of 2012, in a period of severe economic depression and high anti-immigration rhetoric, a new party was launched as a splinter group from the conservative party of New Democracy, as a result of the disagreement of Panos Kammenos (the leader of ANEL) with New Democracy's support for the EU/IMF rescue package for Greece. With a strong anti-immigration agenda, the party's manifesto introduced the notion of a 2.5 per cent quota for non-Greek population residing in the country and advocated maximum-security detention facilities for mass expulsion of illegal immigrants (ANEL 2012). In the elections of the same year the party gained 7.5 per cent at national level and elected 20 representatives to the parliament. Since the last elections, when ANEL gained 4.8 per cent of the vote, the party has paradoxically been participating in the coalition government of the left-wing pro-migrant party SYRIZA, which agreed in summer 2015 to play ball with the European Central Bank, the European Commission and the IMF in order to avoid a 'Grexit' from the Eurozone.

The political identity of ANEL is not so clear and there is some discussion about whether the party can really be characterised as far right. The composition of the group is a mixture of neo-liberals, nationalists, conservatives and even former socialists. After the 2012 elections, their anti-immigrant rhetoric was considerably reduced (for example in their last manifesto there was no mention of migrants) in an attempt to differentiate themselves from the extremist rhetoric of GD. In the last elections of 2015 ANEL emphasised its disagreement with the EU/IMF-imposed austerity measures and the memoranda in Greece, but even though the party has been officially invited by GD to constitute a common front against the tripartite coalition government, especially on issues such as immigration, it has never replied positively to this request. Having said that, it is the party's national conservative approach, with the combination of a demand for stricter measures on immigration and its support for patriotism and the values of the Greek Orthodox Church that places ANEL on the far right of the Greek political spectrum.

Before trying to establish a general profile of the parties, it is necessary to identify their characteristics and ideology as well as their aims and purposes. Following Bull's argument that collective identities can be 'constructed around specific traits' (2003:42), an analysis of the parties' ideology can provide more detailed evidence of their communication tactics and traits and thus an opportunity to understand the parties' identity through their rhetoric.

Discourse on 'Ethnos', 'Nation' and the 'Others': The Ideology of Far-Right Populism in Greece

The narrow core of nationalism includes, apart from the concept of nation, an idea of community, national self-determination and a political identity. In other words nation can be perceived as 'a special and unique cultural entity which has the natural, inalienable right to political self-determination' (Lekkas 2001: 24).

Since national independence the Greek state has according to Triandafyllidou et al. (1997) 'engaged in a process of construction in which its ethnic origins have been in remote antiquity' where 'any changes which mark the past and the history of the national community has been re-constructed in such a way that the nation is represented as a homogeneous and compact unit'. Smith (1991) in his study on nations and national identities identified ethnic identity as a pre-modern form of collective cultural identity:

> Collective cultural identity refers not to a uniformity of elements over genera-
> tions but to a sense of continuity on the part of successive generations of a
> given cultural unit of population, to shared memories of earlier events and
> periods in the history of that unit and to notions entertained by each genera-
> tion about the collective destiny of that unit and its culture. (Smith 1991: 25)

Since nation is conceived as a community territorialised and politicised by ethnic and cultural traditions, nationalism promotes the idea of a consolidated community where multiculturalism creates an increasingly complex environment due to the differences and diversities that exist in contemporary societies. With the focus on 'identity', multiculturalism refers to these community diversities, whether ethnic or racial, and contributes to the emphasis of the 'other' distinct groups and identities. The Greek national identity is strongly linked to language, history, culture and traditions along with the religious consciousness of Christian Orthodoxy (Veremis and Koliopoulos 2006). Therefore the notion of the nation in the Greek case adopts the two concepts of a homogeneous ethnic community and a political community, where people share 'a set of cultural and ethnic features…. characterized as a nation, an ethnos, regardless of their possession of a state' (Triandafyllidou et al. 1997). The nationalist feelings of the population have been manipulated by political parties as a campaigning device, specifically as a means of discrediting one another while distracting voters from internal economic and social problems (Mouzelis 1978: 135).

In the cases under examination the notion of nation and national identity appear strong in the parties' discourses, something that strengthens the argument of a collective identity for the far-right populist scene in Greece. In LAOS' 'ideological platform' released in 2004, the founding of the party is identified as meeting a historical need to address a nation's needs and the 'self-identification' of the party emphasises that it is, above all else, a Greek party, focusing on the long-term interests of the country and the Greek people. Similarly, its policies are inspired by the 'Greek spirit, values and culture' (LAOS 2004). Its main priority has been the restoration of the sovereignty of the people and the overthrow of the 'rotten status quo' that is seen as oppressing the country and leading to the gradual 'de-Hellenization and enslavement of the nation' (LAOS 2004). Its main purpose is to gain 'power through democratic and legal means' (LAOS 2004). From the beginning, LAOS wanted to make clear its democratic identity in order to distinguish itself from existing far-right movements in Europe, such as Greek GD or the British BNP. Pursuing a 'double strategy'—initially a strategy 'of bile', in which LAOS functions as a stirrer of prejudice (against the Jews, Muslims, immigrants, the political establishment, etc.) and subsequently, since 2005, a 'Trojan horse' strategy, in which it seeks to soften its positions, (not in terms of their content but in terms of their public presentation)—the party has a twofold objective: first, to rally the hard core of far-right supporters, by revealing its political-ideological profile, and second, to draw on the pool of protest votes, by concealing that same profile.

The political rhetoric of ANEL focuses mainly on the termination of the Economic Adjustment Programme (also known as the First Memorandum signed by the government of PASOK in 2010), but also involves elements of ethno-nationalism and patriotism, populism, xenophobia and anti-liberalism that can be traced to similar far-right parties across Europe. At the party's official launch in 2012 it was stated that the party identifies with Greek citizens' anger and resentment created by the economic crisis and the policies of the government. For ANEL the negotiations and agreements that took place are illegal, which supports the argument for obtaining justice and punishing those who 'politically, legally and socially' (ANEL 2012) are responsible for the country's predicament and the economic crisis. Additionally, the party calls for a patriotic uprising to save Greece from the neo-liberal storm and support the protection of small property and small enterprises that are in danger due to the memorandum policies. Thus spoke ANEL until the January 2015 national elections, when it formed a coalition with SYRIZA. Although the party has not since changed its manifesto, the reality is that it has formed a government with the party that succumbed to the neoliberal reforms that Europe demanded in order not to face a Grexit from the Eurozone.

The party also supports a strong state which could intervene decisively to protect the minimum standards of living, freedom, access to basic goods, or the defence of the country, the security of citizens, unimpeded access to sources of knowledge and education and elementary medical insurance and social care (ANEL 2012). National security is also high on the agenda for ANEL. As stated in the manifesto of 2013, the party's official line is to strengthen aspects of national defence 'with maximum use of all local and international actors, such as geostrategic and geopolitical position of Greece, the military diplomacy, the network of international security and cooperation organisations (UN, NATO, OECD, OSCE, etc.)' (ANEL 2013). With strong beliefs in the Greek Orthodox Church and the values of country, family and education, the party opposes multiculturalism, calls for anti-immigration policies and highlights the significance of Greek history and culture. National, ethnic, cultural, and religious difference is seen as a threat to the Greek nation and identity.

The proposals of Golden Dawn (GD) cover the whole range of Greek political issues and problems. In principle, it has denounced the memorandum and loan agreements to which the country is committed and has remained faithful to this pledge. In the manifesto of 2012 the GD party stated that it is at the forefront of the struggle against 'ethnocide Memorandum' and underlines its opposition to 'the demographic alteration, through the influx of millions of illegal immigrants, and the dissolution of Greek society, which is systematically pursued by the parties of the establishment of the so-called left' (GD 2012). In contrast, the party proposes a national policy to address the exit crisis and emphasises the importance of 'struggling for a Greece that belongs to the Greeks'. For GD, 'nationalism is the only absolute and genuine revolution because it pursues the birth of new moral, spiritual, social values' (GD 2012). It underlines the activity of multinationals in the country, which seek to serve their own needs and not the national interest, and asks for a redefinition of the Exclusive Economic Zone (EEZ) (GD 2012).

Illegal immigrants, crime and security have been important issues for GD. The party demands the immediate implementation of laws to deport all illegal immigrants, proposes the deportation of foreign criminals with inter-state agreements to serve sentences in their countries of origin, and calls for a restructuring of the prison system and modernization of prisons with a clear division in type and severity of crimes (GD 2012).

Despite their differences, LAOS, GD and ANEL all appear to have common approaches especially on the issue of immigration, engaging with a securitisation discourse and rhetoric of fear against the 'other'. However, although LAOS and ANEL appear to have the ability to disguise their far-right rhetoric under the recognisable principles of state and nation towards a collective identity around nationalism, GD appears to be more extreme (see below for detailed discussion).

One common theme that kept re-appearing in our interviews with the LAOS and ANEL representatives was their insistence on differentiating between the terms 'nationalism' and 'patriotism', claiming that they are patriots and not nationalists. As an active LAOS party member told us,

'Our party is basically a patriotic party, and I do not use the word 'nationalist', because the word 'nationalism' has per se or has been interpreted by us, human beings, as having a dark connotation. We are a patriotic party, we care for our country and want it to get more developed and get out of this dark era. We are a party that cares above all for the Greek citizen … the average person …the farmer. We are interested in education … we want to be free both practically and literally [laughs] and figuratively. We are patriots … whatever the term 'patriot' means.

These views correspond to the analysis of Kosterman and Feshbach (1989), according to which nationalism represents the negative side of positive in-group evaluation, since it includes the view that one's country is superior to others and hence should be dominant. However, patriotism is understood as an essentially valuable aspect, because it represents feelings of attachment to one's country (see also Blank and Schmidt 1993).

Unlike LAOS and ANEL, GD has been branded by the Greek judicial authorities as a criminal organisation and its leaders were arrested in late September 2013. In political terms, it has also been characterised as a neo-Nazi, fascist, racist and xenophobic political organisation, although the party officially rejects these labels and refers to itself as a nationalist party based on popular support. However, as a GD ideological supporter stated, 'the focus should not be on labelling e.g. neo-Nazi, old Nazi, but on National Socialism that is on the core ideology of GD'. In addition, the term 'national socialism' was used by the majority of Golden Dawn interviewees as representing their party's ideology, but it was disconnected from Nazi Germany. As one of our interviewees pointed out,

In no way can we identify with the Nazis, when our grandparents fought against them. The Nazis for us represent foreign domination. We reject anything foreign, wherever it comes from, it is a threat to Greek sovereignty.

Another GD activist commented:

You could say that the ideology of the party is national socialism, but because unfortunately in modern political history, Europe learned to say that National Socialism is what Hitler did in Germany …. clearly there are some common elements ... but in any case we do not identify with them for one simple reason: they are Germans of the 30s and we are Greeks of 2010.

As far as ANEL is concerned, all interviewees refused to accept any connection with the family of the far right. A considerable number of the interviewees, when it come to the right-left spectrum of Greek political life, place ANEL to the left of the conservative party of New Democracy. When we asked whether ANEL is a nationalist party it appeared that the interviewees, like LAOS' supporters, preferred to be labelled patriots rather than nationalists; this is because nationalism has been associated with the family of the far right.

GD can be characterised as a 'majority identitarian populist party' that places the 'identity' of the majority, i.e. ethnic Greeks, at its centre. It claims to represent only Greeks and claims to defend them from external threats to their identity. These threats can come from two places: the 'other' and an 'elite'. Golden Dawn MPs often accuse powerful elites of favouring or being complicit with the 'other'. This can lead to strong anti-elitism.

Ideas About Self-representation

In the case of LAOS, the party insignia is more than simply a logo; it is about its political message; it is about the name; it is about the personalities. According to article 4 of the LAOS manifesto (2004): 'This Party's name is LA.OS', meaning 'People'. The emblem of the party consists of four white crossing arrows with a green wild olive wreath in the middle. The arrows and the wild olive wreath are embedded in an azure square while the whole complex is surrounded by a red circle (LAOS 2004, 2007, 2012). The symbol refers to the Greek Orthodox tradition, as some of our interviewees suggested; it is a direct reference to the cross, the blue and white colours of the Greek flag, and the red colour signifies the need for some revolutionary change in Greek politics. The wreath in the centre refers to Greece's glorious past and is reminiscent of ancient Greece.

In modern use the symbol has become associated with extremist right-wing organisations such as the leading Hungarian fascist political party,

NyilaskeresztesPárt. The symbol has also been used by neo-Nazi organisations in England like the League of St. George (1974) whose symbol appears to be almost indistinguishable compared with the emblem LA.OS. Additionally, numerous racist organisations including Golden Dawn (where the expanding cross was used as the initial symbol on the cover photograph of the first issue of its magazine) have used the symbol. The underlying meaning of the arrow cross is to express expansion in all directions. In this, it is synonymous with all Christian crosses used to represent world evangelization, the effort to spread the doctrines of the Christian faith in all directions. In an interview entitled 'I am not a nationalist, Place me with Peron!' When asked about the similarities of the party's logo compared to KKK's, Karatzaferis commented on the emblem as follows: the circle represents 'ancient Greece, red is Byzantium', (as LA.OS stands in favour of theocratic Byzantium) and the four arrows expanding to east, west, north and south are a concept structured on the basis of *Μεγάλη Ιδέα* ('Great Idea', meaning the aim of recapturing the old Greek-inhabited areas). He also adds that any similarities with KKK are mere coincidence.

GD's flag closely resembles the Nazi swastika, and many of its leaders proudly unleash the Nazi salute, while they carry out squad attacks on immigrants, homosexuals and political opponents (Psarras 2012). Moreover, the slogan used in public gatherings by GD's supporters is 'Blood, Honour, Golden Dawn' which rhymes in Greek (*Αίμα, Τιμή, Χρυσή Αυγή*).[1] All Golden Dawn interviewees however, have claimed that the symbol is the meander, an ancient Greek symbol, and that as Greeks they have every right to use it. To our suggestion that there is a connection with the Nazi swastika, they answered that the Nazi Germans took their symbol from the Ancient Greeks: 'it is them that copied us and not us that copied them'. Regarding the Sieg Heil salute, they claim that this is an ancient Greek, especially Spartan, salute that was also used by the Romans and 'it is the Germans that took it over from us'.

---

[1] Listen to their song http://www.youtube.com/watch?v=JoEGH60Y8JI.

ANEL's symbol is a drawing of a bird with the word 'Independent' underneath, underlined in red and below the word 'Greeks' in capital letters. The symbol is used as a reference to a book called *Jonathan Seagull*,[2] suggesting that innate need of any seagull to escape from the other seagulls and search for a better future. As far as the colours of the symbol are concerned, the blue refers to the colour of Greece and the red represents dynamic radicalism, which signifies the need for change at the political level, thus suggesting that ANEL is more of a movement than a political party.

Construction of the 'Other'

Race and Identity

As Rothenberg underlines, racism is best understood by theorising about 'difference' and 'othering'. In fact, 'the construction of difference' and the 'process of assigning value to difference' are key elements in the understanding not only of racism but of many other forms of oppressive beliefs (Rothenberg, in Harris 1998: 281). Migrants have become the scapegoats for socio-economic problems alongside the threat arising from cultural differences. The securitisation of migration via the fabrication of cultural differences into a threat, has become a prominent discourse of the far right who propagate the homogenisation and essentialisation of Greek culture and identity, thus establishing an antagonistic relationship between 'us', the Greeks, and 'them', the migrants. The far right in Greece build their racist framing of certain groups on this binary opposition. If, according to Diken (2001: 8) 'racism is a constant movement and constantly mutates itself', in Greece at different times different cultures have become the victims; the 'dangerous others' have shifted from being the Albanians in the 1990s to being the Mulsims, Iraquis and Afgans today.

Recent attempts to legislate in this field have all failed. In December 2011, a law on 'Combating Racism and Xenophobia' was drafted, which

---

[2] Bach, R., *Jonathan Livingston Seagull*, Scribner, 2006.

would incorporate into Greek law the Council of the EU Framework Decision 2008/913/JHA on combating certain forms and expressions of racism and xenophobia by means of criminal law. The draft law, however, was not introduced for a vote before the plenary session of the Greek Parliament for more than a year, and was finally introduced for a vote in the parliament in late March 2013. The draft legislation provided for the first time for hate crime and hate speech as separate crimes . The law was finally passed in September 2014 but was not supported by the majority party New Democracy in the then tripartite government.

When asked their opinion of the proposed anti-racist legislation, most of our interviewees in all three political parties under study were against its adoption. One of the arguments that re-appeared in the interviews was that the existing legal framework is enough to protect people from racism.

One of the common responses from GD interviewees when they were asked about accusations of racism against their party, was: 'There is racism against the Greeks'. All GD interviewees expressed concerns about Zionism and many of them openly denied the term 'holocaust', arguing that the figure of the death toll of the Jewish population in the Nazi concentration camps during WWII has been largely fabricated. On the other hand, LAOS and ANEL representatives openly accused GD of being the only racist and neo-Nazi political party currently in parliament, and they categorically denied any connection between their party and any racist ideology.

Immigration and Islamophobia

All the parties under study are in favour of stringent migration controls in Greece. However, their positions differ. GD members were for eliminating any illegal entry into the country, and for sending back all immigrants (legal and illegal) to their home countries. LAOS and ANEL representatives showed a more moderate view on the issue. They were in favour of sending back to their home countries illegal immigrants, but they were not in favour of prosecuting legal ones who pay regularly their taxes. On the matter of securitisation of migration LAOS seems to have made a political turn after the 2012 national elections, in which it did not elect any members to the national parliament. The views of the party on this issue have become more moderate, possibly in an attempt to dissociate LAOS' rhetoric from that of GD, which is widely accused of hate speech and crime against immigrants.

Moreover, when GD interviewees were asked about their social action programme which is designed 'only for Greeks' and includes distribution of food, blood supplies, job centres, history lessons for school children, neighbourhood watch, protection against crime etc., they replied: 'There is racism against the Greeks', 'it is the Greeks we need to protect'.

Influenced by Simmel's (1950) work, Levine (1979) created a continuum of strangers based on the two variables of 'compulsive friendliness' and 'compulsive antagonist' of the host community. His analysis shows a close relationship between the host's perceptions of strangers and attitudes towards them. Levine argues that typically this response to all strangers is a mixture of friendliness and antagonism. Some 'strangers' are likely to be treated as guests, to be welcomed and treated more favourably than those strangers who are seen as 'intruders' or inferiors. These strangers can, and often do, experience open hostility from the host community. In Greece anti-Muslim sentiments have strong links not only to religion but to history. Muslims are often identified with Turks, the major 'national enemy' of the Greek state, dating back to the Ottoman rule. Even in modern years of secularisation, Greek nationalism has drawn upon religious discourse to articulate itself. All Golden Dawn interviewees were against the creation of a mosque in Athens and they expressed concern at the increase of Muslim immigrants in the country; similarly all interviewees from LAOS agreed that no mosque should be built in Athens and certainly not with Greek funding. Most ANEL representatives agreed with this view, referring to the problem of illegal immigration as a problem connected to EU immigration and asylum policy. Among both Golden Dawn and LAOS members, there has been a convergence of views connected to allowing Muslims to exercise their religious beliefs in a mosque, since Muslims are perceived as a threat to Greek national identity and culture. 'A process of differentiation ranks the "others" into hierarchies, with "Muslims" at the bottom, whether or not they come from states where Political Islam is ascendant. They are perceived as inferior, untrustworthy, suspect' (Lazaridis and Wickens 1999: 642).

Gender and LGBT

Gender-equality legislation in Greece was first introduced by the socialist PASOK government back in 1983. When Greece became a European Economic Community (EEC) member in 1981, it undertook to conform to the Community's standards on gender-equality issues. Since then, Greece has had some of the most progressive family laws in Europe. Just being a member of the then EEC (later EU) transformed its whole legal system, even if the traditional Greek society of the times was not ready to embrace gender equality. Golden Dawn is the first political party in parliament since the 1983 reform to openly oppose gender equality. Counting its support by voters in the 2012 national elections and recent polls that foresee an increasing electoral basis for the party, one may assume that there is also a societal backlash regarding gender equality in Greece and a return to the more traditional values of the past regarding gender roles and family.

The gender issue is not included at all in the political agendas of LAOS and ANEL, and this was also revealed by the interviews we conducted with their members. However, a couple of older LAOS members stressed the importance of motherhood, without, however, denying the virtues of gender equality. ANEL members were in favour of gender-equality policies. However, the gender issue holds a prominent position in GD's ideology. GD promotes a certain kind of lifestyle for women in accordance with nationalist socialist ideals. A blog managed by the Women's Front of Golden Dawn, called 'Ideological Library of Women's Front' (http://ideology-studies.blogspot.gr/), openly denounces feminism and gender equality and explains that in today's world the values of family and motherhood have been supplanted by other values of a lower quality. Among others is the following post:

We believe that Motherhood is a holy task... the value of Greek woman as Mother, Partner and Co-fighter... it is the duty of any real Greek woman to bring up her children according to the role model of brave warriors relying on the ancient values of Hellenism which will honour our Homeland.

All the Golden Dawn members we interviewed confirmed the views of Women's Front, and discussed the prominent role of women as mothers and their contribution to the reproduction of the Greek race. Furthermore, all Golden Dawn members characterised abortion as 'murder'. Being framed within a heteronormative conception of gender that oversimplifies male–female differences and within the GD's machismo culture, the idealised form of manhood is strong and tough, risk-taking, heterosexual, competitive; it is the man's responsibility to provide for and protect his family, the woman's to nurture. It is not therefore surprising that within this 'hegemonic masculinity' (Connell 1987), most of their attacks against the 'other' are on migrant men rather than on women or gay men. Gay masculinity is the most conspicuous subordinated masculinity alongside heterosexual men and boys with effeminate characteristics.

Homophobia is 'existent but dormant' in Greek society (Hatzopoulos 2010: 25). According to Hatzopoulos (2010: 25–28), there are several reasons for this homophobic stance. First is the dominant role of the Greek Orthodox Church, which considers LGBT sexuality as a sin. Then there is the macho and homophobic discourse of several politicians, and the stereotyped and negative imagery of LGBTs promoted by the media. Another problem is the absence of sex education in schools, and the unwillingness of all governments to consider LGBT claims and legislate accordingly. On 10 June 2015, the Ministry of Justice, Transparency and Human Rights published a legislative initiative on the new civil partnerships which is still under review.

One should also consider the role of the police in Greece, which idealises 'manhood' as an absolute virtue among police officers. More alarmingly, however, several police manuals, dating back to the pre-WWII era, still present homosexuality either as a mental disorder or as an attribute linked with criminality (Hatzopoulos 2010: 27).

GD is the only political party in the Greek Parliament which is openly homophobic. In 2005, it demonstrated its hostility towards gay people by handing out homophobic flyers during the Athens Gay Pride. More recently, Golden Dawn openly threatened the gay community by leaving flyers in Gazi, a gay area of Athens, where one could read: 'After the immigrants, you're next'. In all cases of Golden Dawn interviewees homosexuality was considered an 'illness'. 'I wouldn't feel proud if I were a fag'. Nikos Michaloliakos, Golden Dawn's leader, made a speech about the 'abnormality' of homosexuals, who are obviously 'not welcome' in Golden Dawn. He also regretted the absence of a 'test' which would enable him to know with certainty who in his party is gay.[3] A GD activist, commenting on modern psychiatric studies which do not recognise homosexuality as a disease, said:

> Medical studies may be thousands … but there is a general principle … the principle of nature that says whatever is unnatural … leads to a result… which cannot be … be attuned to the moral and … with the optimal evolution of the species. People who are male marry women and they have children together and continue the nation.

As far as LAOS interviewees were concerned, there has been a divergence of views on certain issues depending on the age of the interviewee. Younger representatives of youth organisations (aged 25–35) were more reluctant to engage openly with othering while older members openly characterised homosexuality as sickness. The views of ANEL representatives on homosexuality were rather moderate and generally favourable to recognising different sexual identities. In one case, there were concerns about adoption by gay couples and homosexual marriage, without however disagreeing with the possibility of accepting a civil union for same-sex partners.

---

[3] Michaloliakos, N. (2012) Protagonistes. For the full interview please see: https://www.youtube.com/watch?v=hjHIOpJadqA.

Attitudes to the Elite and the EU

According to the social contract between the people and the state (Hobbes 1651; Locke 1689; Rousseau 1762), self-interested, rational, but equal human beings agree with one another to live together under common laws and create an enforcement mechanism managed by a civil authority or government (in the past the sovereign). Following the austerity measures this has started to break down in three ways. First, the social contract is being broken by the Eurozone mechanisms under the German umbrella, which preserve the neoliberal ideology of the free market, and whose response to the crisis is simply to apply more of the same and quicker privatisations, removing workers' rights, reducing pensions, increasing taxes etc., all of which formed the basis of the contract. Second, it is being broken by the workers and their union representatives and by working people in general, who see that the 'contract' is really one-sided, and fails to include them. Third, the Euro crisis is destroying not just jobs, but the very underpinnings of society. People who took actions that were prudent at the time are increasingly at the mercy of forces beyond their control managed by unknown economic centres, strong central European governments (mainly Germany) and European elites. At the same time, the Greek state during the management of the crisis has become an increasingly repressive force; its role is to ensure that the social contract remains in force, but the imposed austerity measures threaten its own existence and legitimacy. There is increasing mistrust not only of government but of the political system as a whole.

All interviewees from all three political parties under study were rather critical of the way consecutive Greek governments handled the economic crisis, especially after 2009. All the GD and ANEL representatives agreed that one of the reasons for their rapid increase in power and entry into parliament is the pathetic collaboration of the government with the EU and IMF during the crisis. They consider this collaboration as treason against the country and a blunt surrender of its national sovereignty to foreign interests. Interviewees from all three political parties share a common anti-memorandum policy (i.e. against the EU/IMF memoranda and rescue packages for Greece). Having said that, ANEL joined SYRIZA, which is now supporting implementation of the memoranda. Also, all the interviewees of all three political parties, when asked about their connection to other political groups or parties from abroad, denied any connection with any of them. Only LAOS representatives, asked if there is an ideological connection with UKIP in the UK, replied in the affirmative, as LAOS belongs to the same political group as UKIP in the European Parliament. In most cases, however, they confirmed that in reality they are not completely sure about UKIP's ideology, but they certainly do agree with its idea of a 'Europe of Nations'.

From Hate Speech to Hate Crimes: Acts of Violence

Members of Golden Dawn have been accused of carrying out acts of overt violence against the 'other'. As Lazaridis and Skleparis (2015) argued, 'their supporters—in some instances with the alleged cooperation of police—stand accused of unleashing an escalation of hate crimes since the party rose to national office, including the stabbing and beating of immigrants, ransacking an immigrant community centre, smashing market stalls and breaking the windows of immigrant-owned shops'. As the authors note, 'Golden Dawn has not only targeted migrants, they have also directed their anger and hatred at locals who disagree with their extreme ideologies and praxis' (ibid).

'The rise of Golden Dawn and extremism in Greece can be seen as part of a broader phenomenon of a culture of intolerance that is maintained and perpetuated through the Greek education system' (Halikiopoulou and Vassilopoulou 2013). As they underline, 'strong anti-immigration sentiments and the rise of the far right reveal a deeply nationalistic society which has been socialised towards violence and defiance from a very young age. As the perpetuation of a political culture favourable to extremism is maintained and reproduced through the education system, the most appropriate solution is educational reform' (ibid). As a representative of an anti-racist organisation told us: 'Racism can only be fought through education'.

The escalation of violence by Golden Dawn action squads in January 2013 resulted in a 27-year-old Pakistani, called Sahjat Lukman being murdered by two Golden Dawn members (who were later charged and convicted of the crime). Even before this, after the 2012 national elections, a leading activist from the Migrants' Social Centre in Athens told us, racist attacks in the centre of Athens reached a peak when Golden Dawn members were elected to parliament.

One of the victims we interviewed, Ali from Pakistan, who was brutally hit by a Golden Dawn action squad, told us:

> A year ago, I left home at seven o'clock in the morning to go to a friend's place. Suddenly, five or six people came behind my back and hit me on the head with a bat, or a crowbar ... I do not know what it was, for sure.... I fell down .. fainted .. uh ... fell down ... and then ... they did not stop there ... but they kicked me ... punched me. They deformed my face.

The attackers soon disappeared and there were no witnesses. After a while, he was found by some of his Pakistani friends who lived in the area and they called an ambulance. He was treated at the hospital, but he never went to the police. Ali said:

> I was afraid to go to the police, and I knew that the police would not do anything to help me. On the contrary, when someone goes to the police to report an attack against them, policemen shout at them, call them names, they terrorize people, they ask for their papers. There is a reason for this. The police are in collaboration with Golden Dawn.

He also said when he was asked about his feelings after the attack:

> After that there's a fear ... fear. I cannot go out alone late at night, and I don't want to go out alone at dawn. I don't go out so much, I stay there, in the same area, and I am scared! There is insecurity ... I feel insecure.

Another migrant, Aslam, told us:

> 'You go to a police station for help and the policeman there is Golden Dawn: 'We will hit you! Come on lousy bastard get out of here! You want to sue and ask for your rights and then what? Leave, otherwise we'll kill you, we will not leave you alone!'

To our question on how many such attacks he could account for, an activist we interviewed from the Migrants' Social Centre[4] replied that in the summer of 2012, they recorded 460 victims who were beaten by Golden Dawn action squads and went to hospital. As the Assistant Ombudsman confirmed, the victims of racist attacks are afraid to go to the police, or ask for protection by judicial authorities. In most cases they are illegal immigrants, and hence are frightened of deportation. They just go to hospital to be treated, and then they leave.

The Assistant Ombudsman, Vassilis Karydis, who was interviewed in July 2013, gave us advance information on a special report that the Greek Ombudsman was preparing at the time on racist violence, which was finally published in September 2013. He explained to us that only legal immigrants and Greek citizens can, in practice, make a complaint to the Ombudsman, especially in cases where the victim has been treated violently by public authorities, e.g. the police. Illegal immigrants, when attacked, rarely address any public authorities, but request protection from their own community or their own embassy. Thus, when we gave him the figures on recent attacks given to us by the representative of the Migrants' Social Centre, Karydis said that if a number of victims go to the Migrants' Social Centre, a much lower number will come to the Ombudsman.

As Lazaridis and Skleparis (2015), in their research on securitisation of migration and the far-right, state, 'the records that the Ombudsman has collected for a period of 16 months (from 1 January 2012 to 30 April 2013) from various sources   identify 281 cases of attacks connected to othering as far as nationality, colour, religion and sexual orientation is

---

[4] The Migrants' Social Centre participates in a Racist Violence Recording Network together with other parties and human rights organisations under the auspices of the UNHCR.

concerned. 253 out of the 281 attacks took place as recently as 2012, which is also the year of the national elections in Greece and the election of Golden Dawn deputies to parliament'.

There are cases of attacks against gays and lesbians. The interviewee in the Migrants' Social Centre mentioned an LGBT beach party that took place at the end of June 2013 in Athens, where LGBTs were attacked by fascists; as he told us, 'they arrived with motorcycles, surrounded them, hit them and destroyed everything, and the people that participated in the party were forced to run into the sea to save themselves. When the attackers were leaving, they said that they are patriots from Kalithea' (an area in Athens where a strong fascist group operates, according to the interviewee). When we asked him why we did not know about this event, and why it never went public, he replied that they were afraid to go to the police. When we approached gay and lesbian organisations that participated in the 16th Antiracist Festival organised on 5–7 July 2013 in Thessaloniki and asked them to give us an interview, they told us that they did not know of any cases of attacks against homosexuals, which is undoubtedly not true. We believe that the gay and lesbian movement in Greece is reluctant to go public on attacks against their members for fear of exposing their identities in a conservative society, and exposing them to future attacks by members of Golden Dawn.

In all the interviews from anti-bodies, lawyers and victims, the attackers were always identified as Golden Dawn members. There were no testimonials of attacks by members of any other political party. The LAOS and ANEL interviewees all condemned violence, and confirmed that their parties are not involved in any violent acts.

Paraphrasing Arendt's (1994) *banalité du mal* to *banalité de la violance*, such acts of everyday violence against the 'other' could be in a sense, called 'banal', in that for GD activists such crimes had become accepted, routinised and implemented without moral revulsion or political indignation and resistance and showed a failure to step away from the requirements that the blind adherence to internal party rules imposed upon them.

Opposition to Far-Right 'Othering'

The Greek anti-discrimination movement has a strong anti-racist, pro-migrant approach, focusing on intercultural contact and exchanges, the provision of specialist support services to vulnerable groups (especially migrant and refugees/asylum seekers), as well as on affirming human rights actions. Nowadays, public condemnation of racism is becoming more frequent in Greece, despite the fact that racist discourse still permeates a great part of the political spectrum and parties.

Since 2010 the civil society landscape in Greece has been strengthened considerably, as has the role of bottom-up NGO initiatives. Reasons for this can be found in a combination of factors, ranging from anxiety over economic strife, and mistrust of the ability and competence of government, to a need to respond to the rise of populist far-right parties able to tap into public anxiety induced by the framing of immigration as a security issue. Networks of associations of mainstream human rights NGOs (e.g., Hellenic League for Human Rights; Amnesty International Greece), state organisations (the National Commission for Human Rights (NCHR) and the Greek Ombudsman), cultural associations (Human Rights and Sexual Orientation Group; Rainbow Families; Homophobia in Education Group), pro-migrant organisations active in the protection of refugee and asylum-seeker rights (Greek Council for Refugees; UN Refugee Agency Greece; Group of Lawyers for the Rights of Migrants and Refugees; International Organisation for Migration) and anti-racism organisations (Racist Violence Recording Network; KEERFA-United Movement Against Racism and the Fascist Threat; Colour Youth) have created an increasingly vocal and active civil society. Lacking their own funding and organisational capacity, and maintained on a semi-voluntary basis, the civil sector operates in the context of an 'emergency-based assistance' strategy, while funding mainly derives from European funds.

Migrants are increasingly excluded and criminalised by the mounting neo-assimilationist and increasingly xenophobic public discourse and policy of, inter alia, the far-right populist parties discussed above. Vulnerability, abuse, injustice and denial of recognition and opportunities push many of them to seek the support of advocacy organisations that campaign for their rights and against an increasingly xenophobic public discourse and racist practices; such campaigns include the 2015 social experiment carried out by the NGO Action Aid to determine people's reaction when they witnessed racism on the streets on the International Day for the Elimination of Racial Discrimination. A representative of KEERFA (United Movement Against Racism and the Fascist Threat) told us that he was

> seriously concerned about the increase in racist hate crimes in Greece, which primarily targets migrants and poses a serious threat to the rule of law and democracy ... The Greek authorities ... [have to] use all available means to combat all forms of hate speech and crime and to end impunity for these crimes ... including penalties on political groups advocating hate crimes, such as Golden Dawn.

At the same time civil society organisations are taking action against the mistreatment and violation of human rights that are taking place in detention centres which have been set up across Greece as part of a coordinated immigration policy and in police stations like the one in the Agios Pandeleimonas area of Athens which has been allegedly infiltrated by Golden Dawn. 'The victims of racist violence are afraid. They are people with or without official documents, refugees or the institutions. All they care about is to heal the wound, physically and mentally. They are scared go public with their complaint to the authorities as they are afraid of further targeting' said another lawyer who deals with violent crimes against immigrants.

The anti-racist movement in Greece is characterised by a mainstream unified approach to anti-racism which blurs the specificity of the variety of marginalised experiences by collectively labelling them 'diverse'. Anti-racist movements and anti-racist activists do not seem to make a distinction between the diversity of experiences of discrimination. Against this context, scholars like Lentin (2011) have argued that it is not operable to speak of a

> unitary/unified anti-racist movement, a fact which hampers the cause of anti-racism; instead it is possible to speak of a variety of anti-racisms, often

competitive or even conflictual, the heterogeneity and disunity of which mirror the often painful transformation of European societies, from the myth of monoculturalism to the reality of diversity. (Lentin 2011: 4)

In Greece anti-racism has often been appropriated as a particularly malleable political discourse to encompass too many different experiences under one unitary anti-racist movement. In other words, the nuances of distinction in the practice, experience and ideology of anti-racist bodies and movements is lost in the blanket label 'anti-racism' under which diverse initiatives are grouped. For example the activism of the Human Rights and Sexual Orientation Group, which advocates against racial and gender discrimination alike, is resulting in the relativisation of the experience of discrimination and not only allows spokespersons to speak on behalf of any/all subjects of diversity, but it also fails to be specific about the true nature of their activism and political intentions.

Our respondents' standpoint seems to be that anti-racism seen as diversity politics offers a space, albeit problematic, to develop alliances, and a greater affinity between marginalised groups, activist organisations and individuals for whom a commitment to anti-racism is a common thread that runs through their particular struggle either as racialised immigrants, refugees, queer, Roma or Muslims, etc.

Greek anti-racist movements have indeed, on occasion, unified their actions at the national level in their counter-mobilisation against discrimination and racism. These unified national actions include the cooperation agreement set up in 2011 by 35 NGOs and other participating bodies coordinated by the NCHR and UNHCR, with the aim of filling the gap caused by the absence of a formal and effective system for recording incidents and trends of racist violence in Greece, in accordance with international and European obligations. The Racist Violence Recording Network (RVRN), set up in 2012,—one of the most recent campaigns of these 35 organisations—demonstrated that racist violence cannot be dealt with effectively without guarantees for the victims that they will not be held accountable at any stage in the process (i.e., for lack of legal documents, etc.). Several of our respondents from the RVRN stressed that attempts to report a racist crime by immigrant witnesses or victims of such incidents are made even more difficult as the protection of the person who files a report is not guaranteed if they do not possess legal residence or work permits to stay in the country and thus risk deportation on filing a report to the authorities.

At the heart of such unified actions is a constant concern among activists about what they call the 'long-term institutional tolerance' of racially motivated crime in Greece and the disturbing way racist crimes have been approached by the judiciary due to lack of effective, independent investigation mechanisms; this remains, according to them, an institutional deficit that needs to be addressed.

Concluding Remarks

The interviews and other data we collected revealed certain patterns that reappear horizontally in all three case studies. The issue of nationalism and patriotism and the preservation of Greek identity and culture are common themes in all three political parties. In addition, all three political groups are against EU migration policy, especially the Dublin II regulation on asylum seekers, support the deportation of illegal migrants and are against the creation of a mosque in Athens. This shows some sort of ideological affinity among these groups. However, in the case of the GD the party's symbols are directly connected to Nazism, they deny the Holocaust, and employ hate speech and crime against the 'other'.

Motherhood is praised by all Golden Dawn interviewees; there are gender-specific roles in family and society, and an implicit denial of gender equality. Homosexuality is openly characterised as an undesirable evil, a mental illness or at best abnormal behaviour. Similar views are shared by older-generation activists in LAOS, but not by its younger members, a fact that is revealing of a possible recent shift in the party's ideology to distance itself from that of Golden Dawn. ANEL interviewees do not share the same views and they show a more pro-gender equality and less homophobic approach.

A common pattern shared by all three groups appears to be the anti-EU, anti-memorandum, anti-systemic approach. They are closer to the idea of a 'Europe of nations' than a 'Europe of people', and they openly accuse Greek governments of the passive acceptance of the EU/IMF bailout, characterising it in some cases as treason. A recent development, however, shows that whereas GD's and LAOS' positions remain strong on this issue, ANEL has symbolically shifted by choosing to renew its coalition with SYRIZA, which was forced by the Troika (EC, ECB and IMF), to sign a new harsh austerity package. Another common pattern that reappears in the interviews of all three groups is the denial of any connection with other international groups or parties, with the exception of LAOS and UKIP.

GD shows a very well organised network of local and youth organisations around Greece and the interviewees stressed the internet as an important means of promotion of the party's ideology, since as all the interviewees have explained, the party is excluded from all mainstream media. Conversely, LAOS has limited presence on websites and official sites are maintained on a volunteer basis by the youth organisations. ANEL is, admittedly, a party created through the internet and is supported by young voters who are also users. ANEL has recently formed its own youth organisations.

Regarding hate speech and hate crime, ANEL and LAOS do not engage in such acts (LAOS especially after the 2012 elections), but GD is by definition the party that is openly accused of committing violent acts, something that LAOS and ANEL interviewees, but also victims, lawyers and representatives of anti-bodies underlined. The latter openly accuse the Greek police of collaborating with GD action squads both in committing and concealing violent attacks or even murders. After the arrest of the GD leader and members following the murder of the first Greek, Pavlos Fyssas, in September 2013, numerous reports stated that a Greek had to be killed, in order for public authorities and mainstream media to finally act. There has also been a major international outcry against Greece stemming from the EU, which apparently could not have Greece take over the presidency of the European Council in January 2014, with the country being at the same time accused by international media of being unable to combat hate speech and hate crime. As an anti-racist organisation activist told us 'Racism is not only the result of the economic crisis. It is, also, promoted through public policies followed by consecutive Greek governments for many years. Golden Dawn is the result of this governmental approach'.

The economic crisis of since 2009 is part of the explanation of the far right's upsurge. This effect has been essentially indirect, insofar as the crisis has exposed the ineptitude of the country's traditional two-party system and this, in turn, has pushed voters towards parties with a strong anti-systemic rhetoric. Focusing on the effects of the economic crisis on Greek political culture and society brings to mind the concept of 'underdog culture', used by Diamandouros (1994) to describe a type of political subculture in modern Greece that is marked by parochial, defensive, authoritarian and xenophobic elements. Diamandouros (1994) contends that Greece before the 1990s was characterised by this longstanding culture that tended to be inward-looking, suspicious of foreigners, statist and anti-market, and has been able to offer powerful resistance to any reforms that sought to modernise Greece. Among other things, one of the effects of the economic crisis was to enhance and project this 'underdog culture' in Greece which, in turn, ferments support towards racist and authoritarian parties like the ones under examination.

During the last decade, three parties of the far-right family have managed to be elected at national and European level. Despite the differences between these parties, especially regarding issues of terminology due to the radical profile of ANEL and LAOS against the extreme rhetoric of Golden Dawn, it is this 'underdog culture', along with the strong notion of nationalism, that argues in favour of a collective identity of the far-right populist parties in Greece. Inciting discrimination and hatred against the 'other' has created a mobilisation against racism, counteracting the far-right populist and nationalist turn in Greece. But is this opposition enough? This is not just a Greek phenomenon. Extreme ideologies—far-right populism, ethno-nationalism or xenophobia—can find fertile ground and impact on several aspects of life; supporters of these groups aim to create a network across the whole of Europe. This needs to be placed high on the agendas of agents of civil society with declared democratic principles, especially against racist acts and violence against the other. Anti-racist discourse and practice provides the opportunity to end racism. What is additionally required is to raise the alarm and strengthen the margins of tolerance in society through education and training.

References

Anastasakis, O. (2000). *Extreme right in Europe: a comparative study of recent trends* (Discussion paper No.3). The Hellenic Observatory, The European Institute London School of Economics and Political Science.

ANEL. (2012). Launching presentation of ANEL by Panos Kammenos. Retrieved July 12, 2015, from http://anexartitoiellines.gr/files/parousiasi.pdf

ANEL. (2013). Manifesto. Retrieved July 11, 2015, from http://anexartitoiellines.gr/gov_program.php

Arendt, H. (1994). *Eichmann in Jerusalem: A report on the banality of evil.* New York, N.Y., U.S.A: Penguin Books.

Bergbauer, S. (2010). The European Public Sphere and the Media: Europe in Crisis. In A. Triandafyllidou, R. Wodak, & M. Krzyżanowski (Eds.), *JCMS: Journal of Common Market Studies, 48,* 1161–1162

Betz, H. G. (1998). Introduction. In H.-G. Betz & S. Immerfall (Eds.), *The politics of the right. Neo-populist parties and movements in established democracies.* Basingstoke, UK: Macmillan.

Blank, T., & Schmidt, P. (1993). Verletzte oder vertletzen de Nation? Empirische Befunde zum Stolz auf Deutschland (Harmed or harmful nation? Empirical evidence on national pride in Germany). *Journal fur Sozialforschung, 33*(4), 391–415.

Bull, A. (2003). From the politics of inclusion to the politics of ethnicity and difference. *The Global Review of Ethnopolitics, 2*(3–4), 41–54.

Coffe, H. (2004). *Can extreme right voting be explained ideologically?* Uppsala: Paper for ECPR Joint Sessions.

Connell, R. W. (1987). *Gender and power.* Sydney, Australia: Allen, Mercer and Urwin.

Diamandouros, N. (1994). *Cultural dualism and political change in postauthoritarian Greece.* Madrid: Centro de Estudios Avanzados en Ciencias Sociales/ Instituto Juan March de Estudios e Investigaciones.

Diken, B. (2001). Immigration, multiculturalism and post politics after 'nine eleven'. *Third Text, 15*(57), 3–12.

Easton, D. (1965). *A Systems Analysis of Political Life.* New York: Wiley.

Ellinas, A. (2013). The rise of the golden dawn: The new face of the far right in Greece. *South European Society and Politics, 18*(4), 1–23.

Evans, J., & Ivaldi, G. (2002). 'Electoral Dynamics of the European Extreme Right', Translation of 'Les dynamiques électorales de l' extrême- droite européenne' in Revue Politique et Parlementaire, Juillet -Août 2002.

Georgiadou, V. (2008). *The far right and the consequences of consensus*. Athens, Greece: Kastaniotis Publications (in Greek).

Golden Dawn. (2012). Manifesto. Retrieved online May 12, 2015, from http://www.xryshaygh.com/kinima.

Golder, M. (2003). 'Explaining variation in the success of extreme right parties in Western Europe' *Comparative Political Studies, 36(4)*, 432–466.

Hainsworth, P. (2004). The extreme right in france: The rise and rise of Jean-Marie Le Pen's front national. *Representation, 40*(2), 101–141.

Halikiopoulou, D., & Vassilopoulou, S. (2013). The rise of the Golden Dawn and extremism in Greece can be seen as part of a broader phenomenon of a culture of intolerance, which is maintained and perpetuated through the Greek education system. Retrieved August 14, 2013, from http://blogs.lse.ac.uk/europpblog/2013/01/29/greece-golden-dawn-education/.

Hatzopoulos, V. (2010). 'Legal Study on Homophobia and Discrimination on Grounds of Sexual Orientation and Gender Identity - Thematic study Greece'. *Centre for European Constitutional Law, Fundamental Rights Agency*. Retrieved April 11, 2015, from http://www.econbiz.de/Record/legal-study-on-homophobia-anddiscrimination-on-grounds-of-sexual-orientation-and-gender-identitythematic-study-greece-hatzopoulos-vassilis/10009640792.

Hobbes, T. (1651). Leviathan. Retrieved from the 1651 edition on 29 April, 2013, from http://archive.org/details/hobbessleviathan00hobbuoft

Ignazi, P. (2003). *Extreme right parties in Western Europe*. Oxford, England: Oxford University Press.

Kitschelt, H., & McGann, A. J. (1995). *The radical right in Western Europe: A comparative analysis*. Arbor: The University of Michigan Press.

Kosterman, R., & Feshbach, S. (1989). Toward a measure of patriotic and nationalistic attitudes. *Political Psychology, 10*, 257–274.

LAOS. (2004). Manifesto. Retrieved May 11, 2015, from http://www.laos.gr

LAOS. (2007). Manifesto. Retrieved May 11, 2015, from http://www.laos.gr

LAOS. (2012). Manifesto. Retrieved May 11, 2015, from http://www.laos.gr

Lazaridis, G., & Skleparis, D. (2016). 'Securitization of migration and the far right: the case of Greek security professionals'. *International Migration, 54*, 176–192.

Lazaridis, G., & Tsagkroni, V. (2015). 'Modern Day Blackshirts': The strategies of hate against the 'other' in Greece and the UK'. *Journal for the Critique of Science, Imagination, and New Anthropology*, June/July, second edition 2015.

Lazaridis, G., & Wickens, E. (1999). Us and the others': Ethnic minorities in Greece. *Annals of Tourism Research, 26*(3), 632–655.

Lekkas, P. (2001). *The game with time, Nationalism and modernity*. Athens. Ellinika Grammata. (in Greek)

Lentin, A. (2011). What happens to anti-racism when we are post race? *Feminist Legal Studies, 19*(2), 159–168.

Levine, D. N. (1979). Simmel at a distance: On the history and systematics of the sociology of the stranger. In W. A. Shack & E. P. Skinner (Eds.), *Strangers in African societies* (pp. 21–36). Berkeley: University of California Press.

Locke, J. (1689). Second treatise of government. Retrieved 29 April, 2013, from http://www.gutenberg.org/ebooks/7370

Minkenberg, M. (1998). Context and consequence: The impact of the new radical right on the political process in France and Germany. *German Politics and Society, 48*, 1–23.

Minkenberg, M. (2004). *Religious effects on the shaping of immigration policy in western democracies*. Uppsala, Sweden: Paper for the ECPS Joint Session of Workshops.

Moufahim, M. (2007). Interpreting discourse: A critical discourse analysis of the marketing of an extreme right party. The Vlaams Blok/Vlaams Belang. Thesis submitted to the University of Nottingham for the degree of Doctor of Philosophy.

Mouzelis, N. (1978). *Modern Greece: Facets of underdevelopment*. New York: Holmes and Meier.

Mudde, C. (2004). The populist zeitgeist. *Government and Opposition, 39*(3), 541–563.

Pappas, T. S. (2003). 'The Transformation of the Greek Party System Since 1951'. *West European Politics, 26*(2), 90–114.

Psarras, D. (2012). *I Mavri Vivlos tis Chryssis Avgis (The black book of the golden Dawn)*. Athens, Greece: Polis (in Greek).

Rensmann, L. (2003). The new politics of prejudice: Comparative perspectives on extreme right parties in European democracies. *German Politics and Society, 21*(4), 93–123.

Rousseau, J.-J. (1762). The social contract. Retrieved April 29, 2013, from http://ebooks.adelaide.edu.au/r/rousseau/jean_jacques/r864s/

Scheuch, Erwin K., & Klingemann, H. D. (1967). 'Theorie des Rechtsradikalismus in westlichen Industriegesellschaften'. Hamburger Jahrbuch für Wirtschafts- und Gesellschaftspolitik, *12*, 11–29.

Simmel, G. (1950). The stranger. In K. Wolff (Ed.), *The sociology of George Simmel* (pp. 401–408). New York: Free Press.

Smith, A. D. (1991). *National Identity*. London: Penguin.

Triandafyllidou, A., Calloni, M., & Mikrakis, A. (1997). New Greek nationalism. *Sociological Research Online*. 2:1. Retrieved May, 2015, from http://www.arts.yorku.ca/hist/tgallant/documents/triandafyllidounewnationalsim

Veremis, Th., & Koliopoulos, J. (2006). Hellas: Continuation to the Present 0-From 1821 till today. Athens. Kastaniotis.

9

Majority Identitarian Populism in Britain

Gabriella Lazaridis and Vasiliki Tsagkroni

Introduction

In the 2014 European Parliament elections, Eurosceptic and far-right populist parties made an impact: the French Front National (FN) gained of 24.85 per cent of the popular vote, the Greek neo-Nazi Golden Dawn party 9.4 per cent, the Italian Five-Star Movement (M5S) 21.2 per cent, the Sweden Democrats (SD) 9.7 per cent and UKIP 26.6 per cent. Europe's vote pointed to a Eurosceptic surge challenging the already established mainstream parties in its member states.

Far-right populist parties as we know them today began to emerge in the 1980s, while parties that were linked with fascist ideology in the past (e.g. MSI[1] in Italy) started to evolve in order to create a more legiti-

---

[1] MSI (Italian Social Movement).

G. Lazaridis (✉)
University of Leicester, Leicester, UK

V. Tsagkroni
Queen Mary University of London, London, UK

© The Editor(s) (if applicable) and The Author(s) 2016
G. Lazaridis et al. (eds.), *The Rise of the Far Right in Europe*,
DOI 10.1057/978-1-137-55679-0_9

mate image and attract the electorate. By adopting a majority identitarian populist rhetoric and emphasising socio-cultural and identity issues,
these parties have experienced growing success. This form of populism
will be examined in this chapter as part of the rhetoric of the far (radical
and extreme) right representatives on the British political scene: namely
UKIP (UK Independence Party), the BNP (British National Party), and
the EDL (English Defence League).

With the Euro-crisis and the pronounced socio-economic issues that
ensued, far-right populist parties have sought to point out the potential threats to EU member states' national identities, based on a rhetoric
enriched with elements of authoritarianism, populism, ethno-nationalism
and welfare nationalism that often targets the 'other' (immigrants,
Muslims, homosexuals, the Roma, etc.) as one of the major threats to
'the nation and its people'.

In the UK, although the far right was not as popular as in other
European countries (such as the Nordic countries) in the late 1980s,
a combination of circumstances in the late 2000s brought a change to
the domestic political scene. Rising rates of immigration (see Migration
Observatory 2015) and general concern about multiculturalism (see
David Cameron's criticism on state multiculturalism,[2] 2011), together
with increasing Islamophobia and the economic crisis, created a fertile
ground for the support of far-right populist representatives.

UKIP, although active since 1993, managed to achieve a strong performance in the 2014 European Parliament elections, becoming the
strongest party at the time in the UK.[3] With its Eurosceptic discourse,
xenophobia and strong anti-immigration policies, UKIP managed to
make a breakthrough on the country's political scene and increase its
political influence (Ford et al. 2012). On the other hand, EDL, a protest

---

[2] David Cameron told the 47th Munich Security Conference in 2011, attended by world leaders,
that state multiculturalism had failed in the UK, echoing a similar argument put forward by Angela
Merkel who in 2010 declared that attempts at creating a multicultural society in Germany had
'utterly failed'.

[3] European Union electoral results for 2014: UKIP: 27.49 per cent, Labour: 25.40 per cent,
Conservative: 23.93 per cent (see http://www.europarl.org.uk/en/your-meps/european_elections.
html).

group formed in 2009, managed to create a sense of cultural alientation regarding ethnic minority groups in the UK, focusing mainly on anti-Islamic sentiments and pointing out cultural divisions within society. Finally, the BNP is another acknowledged representative of the far-right scene in the country that has managed to attract the attention of the public, especially under the leadership of Nick Griffin since the early 2000s.

Our research focuses on hate speech and crime, such that the overall research question might be conceived as the relationship between the activities of political groups and individuals, and incidents of hate crimes and 'othering'. We argue that although it seems questionable at present whether the existing far-right populist representatives can achieve greater electoral results (UKIP gained 12.6 per cent in the national elections of 2015), the decline of class identity and the loss of faith in traditional ideologies, along with controversy about Britain's future with the European Union, the ongoing extended rhetoric of securitisation of migration in Britain, and the economic crisis, can still foment and give a new impetus to such groups.

The chapter is structured in three main parts. The first section contextualises the chapter theoretically (which includes a discussion of 'majority identitarian populism' and its impacts), outlines the rationale for choosing EDL, BNP and UKIP as case-study groups, and the methods used for gathering our data. In this section a historical, socio-economic and political contextualisation is provided, which helps us understand the rise of such groups in the UK. The second section focuses on describing what they do and how they do it, raising questions of hierarchical control, response to opponents, and the difference between group and individual activists and supporters, and especially their diversity of thought and action. The third section focuses on counter-strategies by organisations that adopt the role of an 'anti-body' and ways they combat the phenomenon of majority identitarian populism.

Theoretical Context and Methodology

In recent studies the term 'populism' has created an ongoing debate between academics and has often been used as a synonym for far-right/extreme-right politics, e.g. Rydgren (2003) on radical right populism,

Mudde (2004) and Taggart (2000) on new populist right, Laclau (2005) on right-wing populism or Fella and Ruzza (2009) on populist parties.

For the purpose of the research this chapter is based on 'populism' which is approached as a 'thin ideology' (Stanley 2008) and a resultant style of politics which presents society in terms of a conflict between 'virtuous and homogeneous people' and 'a set of elites and dangerous "others"' (Albertazzi and McDonnell 2008: 3) who lie 'outside the heartland' (Zaslove 2008: 323). In addition, according to Canovan (1999: 3), populist movements along the political spectrum of left–right argue that 'the people' have been excluded from power by 'corrupt politicians and an unrepresentative elite' who purposely ignore the interests and opinions of the electorate.

Nevertheless, neither is this form of populism the sole preserve of particular groups and parties and nor is populism a synonym for the far right, extremism or fascism. 'Majority identitarian populism' (Johnson et al. 2005) can be identified with more clarity in the approaches of mainstream parties in relation to immigration and multiculturalism (Bale et al. 2011), with arguments that an out-of-touch elite has allowed changes to British society which advantage newcomers over settled Britons: these are sometimes, but not always, done as 'dog whistles'. Majority identitarian populism focuses on the concept of identity as a tool for determining who belongs to what they see as the 'majority group', based on a number of characteristics, e.g., religion, or ethnicity creating a status where the 'other' stands against the 'mass'.

Taken thus, such populism cannot be what defines a particular individual or group as far right or extreme right. The ideological heterogeneity (Anastasakis 2000) of far right has created a continuing discussion about the definition and terminology of this political family. The debate includes approaches on whether and how a particular group should be categorised as fascist, radical or extremist, with the 'ideological core' and/or the breaking of democratic norms (i.e., violence) as indicators (see Carter 2005; Eatwell and Goodwin 2010; Richardson 2011). Studies of the electoral success of groups like the BNP (for examples, see Ford 2010; John et al. 2006) are, however, more concerned with the populist politics part of their activity than with the core ideology or relationship to violence. For Eatwell

(2004) similarities with certain conservative policies raise questions about whether a clear line can be drawn between extremist and radical right. For Barker (1981) the reason is a form of 'new racism' that is not promulgating the old type of racism based on ideas of inferiority and superiority between racial groups but in contrast emphasises the group solidarity and exclusion of those seen as outsiders. This 'new racism' according to May et al. (2004: 223) does not 'construct an explicit racial hierarchy but rather an immutable fixed and organic belonging of specific people, territories and states that in effect excludes and racialises all "others"'.

That said, and given the research focus on populism and hate speech and crime, we raise the empirical question of the relationship between this populist politics and hate incidents. Any relationship could have multiple forms, including those practising populist politics moving towards illegal methods or inciting others, or the more diffuse possibility that populist calls (by mainstream or non-mainstream politicians) can give others a licence to express hate. Indeed, while some opponents of the BNP argue that BNP activity increases hate crime, others (Clark et al. 2008; Koopmans 1996; Painter 2013) argue that it acts as a safety valve, allowing racist and other discontent a democratic outlet that might otherwise be channelled into non-democratic activity. It is important here to also note that the UK has 'developed the most comprehensive and systematic approach to policing racist crime and violence' in the EU (Oakley 2005), such that some incitement can and is prosecuted as a criminal offence. We are therefore mindful of the narrow band of ambiguous activity that is not illegal but may create a climate of fear and distrust where violence becomes more likely (Smith 2008).

It is this context that makes the EDL, BNP and UKIP contrasting case studies. Anti-racist activists accuse all three of problematic activity, with organisations such as Hope Not Hate asking its supporters in 2013 whether UKIP should be added to the BNP and EDL as organisations it automatically campaigns against (Hope Not Hate 2013). At the time of writing, UKIP is both populist and popular. The EDL is populist but not popular, arguing that mainstream politicians ignore the threat from radical Islamism and Islam more generally, but EDL street demonstrations usually only attracting a few hundred people, and a maximum of 3,000 (Bartlett and Littler 2011). While UKIP and BNP[4] carry on their electoral activities, with occasional disruption from anti-racist or anti-fascist activists, the EDL demonstrations are heavily policed in order to avoid confrontation between EDL and opposition activists.[5] This too may have an impact on how these forms of populist activism develop, both on particular occasions and over time, and how they are viewed by those engaged in them, those opposing them and those merely observing them.

This chapter examines the selected cases through fieldwork that concentrates on the perspectives of those who are active within populist politics against the 'others'. Fieldwork included analysis of parties' websites, looking at discourses and symbols, participant observation and semi-structured in-depth face-to-face interviews with members of EDL, UKIP and BNP as well as with representatives of groups who work with minority populations, that is those who are 'othered', and 'anti-body' organisations.

Before examining the main factors leading to the increasing popularity of far-right politics in the UK, we will briefly look at the socio-economic and political context that provided fertile ground for the groups under analysis. We will then proceed with an analysis of their political mobility and ability to respond to the demands of the public by adopting a populist discourse and proposing aggressive policies on issues like immigration and the EU.

---

[4] BNP publicly promotes violence in order to gain 'institutionalized power' (Heitmeyer 2003: 406).
[5] As Hilary Pilkington writes in her blog (http://blogs.lse.ac.uk/politicsandpolicy/when-is-a-kettle-not-a-kettle-when-it-is-on-slow-boil/), a few years ago, during an EDL demonstration in Walthamstow, East London, around 600 EDL demonstrators found themselves on the receiving end of a barrage of eggs thrown by counter-demonstrators; they were surrounded for hours by police without access to water, food or toilets and, before finally being released, they were arrested en masse under Section 60 of the Criminal Justice Act (breach of the peace), regardless of whether there was any evidence that individuals had participated in any public order offence. The result was that many demonstrators declared they would never again attend a demonstration.

Economic and Socio-Political and Cultural Background in the UK: The Effect of Economic Policy Trends on Views on Diversity

It was by the early 1980s that Britain was arguably one of the most ethnically diverse countries in the world (see Jefferies 2005). As Jefferies (2005) underlined, the more recent waves of immigration have seen the terminologies of 'refugee' and 'illegal immigrant' become deeply engrained in the popular imagination and our actors, the press and popular polling have come to construct Muslim immigration on the one hand and Eastern European migration on the other as particular problems.

The major recession (1979 to the mid-1980s) prior to the 'big bang' of the devolution of financial services, next to the Great Depression of the 1930s and the financial crisis of 2008–2015, represented the deepest loss of industrial capacity and social cohesion in British history. Rapid and sustained de-industrialisation was accompanied by very substantial job losses and rapidly rising inflation. At the time, these economic pressures generated remarkably little ethnic tension. Indeed, the fact that the BNP was formed in 1982 as a splinter group from the fascist National Front, speaks to the fact that these conditions created real tensions amongst the ranks of far-right groups themselves.

The deregulation of financial services in the mid-1980s gave a widely acknowledged boost to local and regional economies; it laid the foundations for selective urban investment (the rebuilding of the urban centres of Liverpool and Leeds, for instance), low unemployment and a pronounced upward social mobility. Low average unemployment, notably in the south of England (see Demman and McDonald 1996) emboldened a political class to begin to move legislatively on LGBT issues. Inter-community tensions based on religion, skin colour or origin were moderate during this period. From 1999 the BNP dropped much of its rhetoric of biological racism and adopted a rhetoric which linked its core message to identity at the national and local levels (see Eatwell 2004).

With rising south Asian chain migration, towns and cities such as Leicester, Bradford, Burnley and Liverpool become both poor and visibly non-white. This has had long-term implications for the national psyche and underpins some of the campaigning agenda of modern far-right organisations which have focused both their resources and their national message on the threat posed in which 'whites' might become a minority before 2070, an opinion supported by David Coleman from the Migration Observatory (Coleman 2010).

Nevertheless, as in many European countries, the financial crisis is a dominant issue in UK politics, followed by the government's austerity-motivated policies.[6] Stripping out economic growth funded by the unsustainable accumulation of debt, the British economy barely grew between 1997 and 2015. The end of social mobility in the late 2000s created tensions within faith and migrant communities (between different ethnic groups and between the generations within ethnic groups) as it did between these groups and far-right populist groups. This does much to explain the sustained rise of groups such as UKIP, BNP and EDL, the latter focusing primarily on the threat that migration poses to 'our' (the British) state.

From the Past to the Present: Far-Right Populism in the UK

The most successful post-war representative of the far-right scene in the UK, the National Front (NF) was formed in 1967. Despite denying accusations of fascism, the party was linked with neo-Nazi movements within the UK (e.g. Blood and Honour UK and British Movement) and abroad and was associated with the strong xenophobic nationalist rhetoric advocating biological racism and opposed non-white immigration that still underlines that 'the multiracial Commonwealth is a farcical relic of an unfortunate past which should be disbanded' (NF 2015). Although NF managed to attract minority support at local level, the party would be proved incapable of gaining any form of electoral success (Eatwell 2004). In the general elections of 1979, with 303 candidates, the party managed to attract 0.6 per cent of the popular vote, which was to be

---

[6] For more, see David Cameron, Age of Austerity, 2009: http://www.conservatives.com/News/Speeches/2009/04/The_age_of_austerity_speech_to_the_2009_Spring_Forum.aspx.

the highest performance in the party's history. NF declined towards its gradual extinction in the mid-1990s, despite efforts to revive the party by Ian Anderson in 1995. Nevertheless, it was in the mid-1990s and early 2000s that the far-right populism mobilisation started to emerge on the British political scene.

Formed in 1982 as a fragment from the NF (Goodwin 2011), BNP under the leadership of John Tyndall, former leader of NF, and of Nick Griffin since 1999, dominated the far-right scene for almost a decade, by adopting a more moderate populist profile, abandoning extreme language and biological racist rhetoric (Halikiopoulou and Vasilopoulou 2010), similar to later efforts of other far-right parties in Europe e.g. Marine Le Pen and the French Front National or Gianfranco Fini and the Italian MSI (Movimento Sociale Italiano). However, despite the efforts of Tyndall to distinguish the newly formed party from its predecessor NF and from links to neo-Nazi movements, BNP would still be identified with neo-Nazism, racism, violence and rhetoric on denial of the facts of the Holocaust. The party started participating in the general and local elections in 1983 but it was not until 1993 that it achieved its first electoral success when Derek Beackon was elected as a councillor in Millwall, London.

The change of leadership in 1999 would signify a modernisation reform of the party, with Griffin isolating the extremist elements and transforming BNP into a more moderate version of the far right, closer to similar parties in other European countries, e.g., Italy and France. In the local elections of 2002 the party managed to gain three seats on Burnley Council and continued increasing its popularity in the following years; in the European elections of 2004 it won 4.9 per cent of the vote. It is between the years 2008 and 2010 that the party reached its highest rates of popularity, with Richard Barnbrook winning a seat in 2008 on the London Assembly, and in the following European elections of 2009 it managed to win two seats in the European Parliament by gaining 6.3 per cent of the popular vote.

BNP is self-identified as British nationalist with fundamental core values which call for national and cultural regeneration (BNP 2005). Under Griffin's leadership the party has focused its rhetoric on ethnic nationalism, anti-immigration policies and opposition to Islam and the alerting threat of multiculturalism, claiming that white people will be 'ethnically cleansed' and calling for an 'immediate halt to all further immigration' (BNP 2005). The economic policy of the party is to oppose globalism, economic liberalism and *laissez-faire* capitalism (BNP 2005). In addition, among other policies, BNP advocates harsher sentences for criminals, opposes same-sex marriage, embraces tradition, heritage and civility and is opposed to European integration (BNP 2005).

Nonetheless, regardless of the efforts to renovate it to a more modernist party, the BNP failed to maintain its success (see Goodwin 2011). For Hainsworth (2008), several reasons have managed to prevent an electoral breakthrough like that of far-right counterparts in other European countries, e.g., Denmark or the Netherlands: poor leadership, the anti-fascist tradition in Britain, internal divisions between representatives of the far right in the country and the associations of far-right groups with violence and street politics (Hainsworth 2008). Similarly, for Eatwell, despite the fact that there have been developments in the country that could have favoured racial and extreme nationalist policies, such as increasing migration rates, increasing unemployment, the decadency of urban centres and opposition to European integration, the conditions for possible success of far-right groups would include the legitimacy of the group, increasing personal effectiveness and a strong decline in confidence in the system, factors that have proved insufficient in the case of Britain (2004: 325–330).

Formed by Alan Sked in 1993, and successor to the Anti-Federalist League, UKIP was set up to oppose the 1992 Maastricht Treaty which was supported by all three main political parties (see Daniel 2005). By focusing on opposing European integration and by developing popular far-right policies, the party managed to steadily increase its support from 0.3 per cent of the vote in the general elections of 1997 to 12.6 per cent in the latest general election in 2015; in the European elections of 2014, the party gained 27.5 per cent of the popular vote to became the strongest party in the country at the time. After a series of changes in leadership the party, under Nigel Farage, successfully increased its visibility from what Ford and Goodwin described as 'a large angry bear', that 'would stumble out of hibernation once every few years, briefly stir up popular discontent with Brussels and Westminster political elites, and then return to their slumbers' (Ford and Goodwin, 2014: 2). With a mixture of xenophobia, nationalism, Euroscepticism and populist rhetoric,

UKIP managed to address the concerns of the electorate and provide a moderate alternative compared to the BNP, thereby establishing its place on the national scene.

UKIP's constitution states that the UK shall cease to be a member of the EU and shall not thereafter make any treaty or join any international organisation that involves in any way the surrender of any part of the UK's sovereignty in order for the country to 'be governed by her own citizens and that its governance shall at all times be conducted first and foremost in the interests of the UK and its peoples' (UKIP 2012). In addition to encouraging withdrawal from the EU, in its recent manifesto of 2015 UKIP argues in favour of a political reformation to ensure that the 'government answers properly to Parliament and that Parliament is accountable to the people' (UKIP 2015), invoking populist appeals to show that the party stands for the 'people's' interests. In addition to the party's positions in favour of a reformation of the political system, UKIP underlines its role as a challenger to the established political parties. In essence, UKIP's anti-establishment credentials are illustrated by the belief that all mainstream parties are the same (UKIP 2013).

More specifically, based on Abedi's (2004: 12) criteria, (a party that challenges the status quo in terms of major policy and political system issues, that perceives itself as a challenger to the established political parties and that asserts that a fundamental divide between the political establishment and the people exists), UKIP can be characterised as an anti-political establishment party. An anti-political establishment party puts emphasis on the argument that the organisation of the party should be based on democratic values and demand direct involvement of the electorate in the decision-making process. Self-identified as a democratic libertarian party, UKIP argues in favour of a liberal economy, demands the repeal of the Human Rights Act and the removal of Britain from both the European Convention on Refugees and the European Convention on Human Rights, embraces patriotism against the threat of multiculturalism and asks for a political reformation in order for politics to reconnect with the people (UKIP 2015). As Nigel Farage stated in 2006: 'We're going to be a party fighting on a broad range of domestic policies and together if we're united and disciplined we will become the real voice of opposition in British politics'. He continued arguing that 'on the big issues of the day you cannot put a cigarette paper between the three major parties' and played the populist card, emphasising that although people tend to 'place us as being right of centre, I would place us as being in the centre of public opinion' (BBC 2006).

The EDL was formed by Tommy Robinson in 2009, as a response to a demonstration against the war in Afghanistan, organised by the local Luton group of Al-Muhajiroun (an international and later banned organisation). The newly formed group focused its attention on two primary aims: to draw attention to the growing threat of Islamic extremism in the UK and work towards the elimination of such propensities. A single issue-oriented protest movement, focusing on anti-Islamic sentiments in a greater effort to 'protect the inalienable rights of all people to protest against radical Islam's encroachment into the lives of non-Muslims' (EDL's Mission Statement 2015). EDL since its emergence has conducted numerous demonstrations across the country and succeeded in sustaining the public's attention despite accusations of violent acts, anti-social behaviour, racism and hate crimes. For Pilkington (2014) EDL's slogan 'Not racist, not violent, just no longer silent' motivates EDL's supporters in 'speaking out' and 'standing strong' in contrast to the 'politics of silencing' supported by the social distance between 'politicians' and the 'people' and cultural limitations on 'acceptable' issues for debate.[7]

Following the argument of Betz (2007) who underlines the sustained focus on Islamophobia across numerous European far-right parties, e.g., Switzerland, the Netherlands and Denmark, EDL offered an alternative on the far-right scene in the UK, suggesting selective multiculturalism and engaging pro-LGBT approaches. That said, drawing in other issues besides extremism—'denigration and oppression of women, the molestation of young children, the committing of so-called honour killings, homophobia, anti-Semitism' (EDL Mission Statement 2015)—does lead to a focus on Islam more generally as these issues are not limited to radical Islamists, and of course not to Islam either. For Bartlett and Littler (2011: 11), EDL attempts to moderate its political agenda (by supporting Israel, deriding racism and employing human-rights talk) and

---

[7] Pilkington has conducted ethnographic research on EDL under the auspices of the MYPLACE project. For more information see https://myplacefp7.wordpress.com/.

style (by advocating for less violence), which some factions felt was a sign of weakness. Other early supporters of the EDL have left to join more aggressively anti-Islam groups, feeling that the EDL has lost focus on fighting Islamism.

What differentiates EDL from UKIP and BNP to an even greater extent is the use of media for the purpose of communicating to the public. By using a wide range of social media, especially Facebook, EDL has managed to organise campaigns, cultivate street protests and other forms of direct action and organise its supporters by using online culture to promote its populist nationalist ideology (Jackson 2011).

Communication Strategies, Charismatic Leadership, Insignia and Beyond

In terms of structure and leadership, there are noticeable differences between the three groups. While UKIP and BNP follow a more typical party-political structure, including democratic procedures such as elected leadership, annual conferences and a number of active committees accountable for the party's policies, EDL has no formal membership and thus, it is difficult to calculate the number of its supporters. When it comes to the leadership, since 1993 UKIP has experienced more than seven changes in its highest office, with former leaders often turning their back on the party, a reaction that can be found in both BNP and EDL former leaderships. In the case of EDL for example, the founding leaders (Tommy Robinson and Kevin Carroll) decided to leave the group and work with Quilliam, a Muslim-led counter-extremism think tank, itself led by ex-Hizb ut-Tahrir[8] activists, arguing that the EDL was becoming a home for far-right extremists (BBC News 2013). For all three, BNP, UKIP and the EDL, the group and the individual members change over time, with the degree of fit at least partially determining who leaves and who remains. This fit is, of course, relational: those leaving UKIP, for example, will include some like Alexandra Swann who see the party as too

---

[8] This is an international pan-Islamic political organisation founded in 1953. Their goal is for all Muslim countries to unify as an Islamic state ruled by *sharia* law.

'socially conservative' and others such as Paul Weston of Liberty GB (an anti-fundamentalist, anti-immigration political party formed in 2013)[9] who considers the party to be too soft on the issue of Islam.

Nevertheless, the public personas of Nigel Farage and Nick Griffin appear to be one of the most influential factors when it comes to attracting voters in the case of UKIP and BNP. The personality of the party leader is crucial when it comes to the identity of the party, as in the face of the leader the voter sees what the party represents; it appears that Farage and Griffin have managed to create a figure to which the electorate can relate. As strong charismatic demagogues and populist leaders, Farage and Griffin, in combination with a successful reformation of the public images of their parties, have led both UKIP and BNP to a new era and contributed to their electoral success. It is the perception of the value of the party leader, and the level of their effectiveness in convincing the electorate of their party's worth, that creates a strong factor at the disposal of the party's communication strategy.

Apart from the figure of the leader, a valuable element of the communication strategies of the groups under examination is their insignia, since what defines them is more than just a logo, a political message, a name or a personality, but rather a combination of all four.

The UKIP logo is a pound sign (£), with many activists wearing a gold lapel badge, opposition to the Euro being obviously necessary to the party's euro-scepticism. Another symbol used is the pint of beer and the fag (cigarette): a number of young activists we interviewed mentioned the pint as something that should be in one's hand. Party leader Nigel Farage's most obvious image is that of being in the pub with a pint of bitter or a cigarette in his hand, or both. With its references to elements of British culture, this plays into ideas of Britishness, the ordinary against the elite and freedom from bureaucracy (UKIP would repeal the smoking ban). On occasion UKIP have been described as the 'BNP in blazers' (Hinsliff 2004): in reality, party activists are largely to be seen in business attire.

Unlike UKIP, EDL (and its offshoots) has a plethora of distinctive symbols and imagery deployed by its activists. The EDL logo appears

---

[9] Its Facebook page describes it as 'patriotic counter-jihad party for Christian civilisation, Western rights and freedoms, British culture, animal welfare and capitalism'.

online and on pin badges and clothing, and is a Christian cross with the Latin *in hoc signo vinces* ('in this sign you will conquer') written below. Alongside this, their online presence often features images of medieval knights, a direct reference to the Crusades. Having said that, as stated earlier, an interesting point is that EDL has its origins in demonstrations against the radical Islamist Al-Muhajiroun,[10] which itself used images of the Crusades.

At demonstrations, the primary offline activity of the EDL, the most visible symbol is the flag of St George (red cross on a white background). This is combined with slogans and symbols which reference Islam ('No Sharia', 'No more mosques'), and the British military ('Support our troops') and sometimes slogans which aim to distance the group from racism and extremism ('Patriotism does not equal Nazism'). The references to the military reflect the fact that the British military are engaged in operations against Islamic groups overseas, and more importantly, are a response to al-Muhajiroun and its successor organisations' protests against the military. Thus, the use of the poppy image was a direct response to the radical Islamists' burning of a poppy on Remembrance Sunday 2010 (BBC News 2010b).

The BNP's logo, on the other hand, is a direct reference to the party's ethno-nationalist and British-nationalist character: a Union flag-infilled heart with the party's name. According to Griffin, the new logo 'illustrated exactly what the party is about' (BNP 2015), replacing the Union flag-infilled 'BNP' logo that was previously used. The new insignia, according to Derek Adams, 'softens the image a bit which is what we need'.

What is significantly important in all three cases is the contemporary use of new media and online spaces as part of their communication strategies, leading to what Jackson and Gable (2011) describe as a 'revolutionised extremist activity'. Online networks like Twitter and Facebook have been created, offering a space for public discussion, both measured and crude, and attract comments from all sides of the debate. In other words, a public forum is being created for policing by campaigners, defacement by opponents and disagreement within the groups' sup-

---

[10] This is a terrorist organisation that was based in Britain and has been linked to international terrorism, homophobia and anti-Semitism. It was banned in 2005.

port base. As Jackson and Gable (2011), in their research on *Nationalism extremism on the internet* point out, BNP encouraged members to engage with social networks in order to proclaim their political dogma and declare their party affiliation, whereas in the case of EDL, as previously stated, the group has managed to mobilise large parts of its supporters to participate in direct activities but has also explored the internet to create online networks with other organisations and groups.

Ideologies, Values and Rhetoric in Perspective

Mudde (2005) suggests that to identify as far right someone has to focus on key elements, such as nationalism, xenophobia, racism and immigration, that appear to be referenced more frequently than other elements in the discourse on right groups in Europe. Mudde's (2004) approach, along with Norris' (2005) theory on market-oriented elements of supply and demand in relation to the public's needs, could provide an extended explanation for the rise of far-right populist parties in the UK.

Our analysis of the three groups under examination and the interviews we conducted clarify the perception of the concept of cultural identity and its relations to the 'other'; in that sense, representation can be related to various versions of stereotypes such as gender (see de Beauvoir 1971), race (see Hage 2010) or religion (see Said 1978). In Gillespie's (2006) view, 'othering' leads people to differentiate in-group from out-group and Self from Other. In the case of EDL, UKIP and BNP, one of the main focuses in constructing the image of the 'other' is migrants, with an additional focus on Islam as a threat to British cultural identity. For Minkenberg (2002), radicalising ethnic, cultural and political criteria of exclusion serves to construct the nation with an image of extreme collective homogeneity (2002: 337). This perception addresses the elements of nationalism, xenophobia and racism, which are strong in all three cases.

> As I look ahead, I am filled with foreboding. Like the Roman, I seem to see 'the River Tiber foaming with much blood'. That tragic and intractable phenomenon which we watch with horror on the other side of the Atlantic

but which is interwoven with the history and existence of the States itself, is coming upon us here by our own volition and our own neglect. Indeed, it has all but come. In numerical terms, it will be of American proportions long before the end of the century. Only resolute and urgent action will avert it even now. Whether there will be the public will to demand and obtain that action, I do not know. All I know is that to see, and not to speak, would be the great betrayal. (Powell 1968)

In his 'rivers of blood' speech (1968), Powell underlined that Britain must be 'mad, as a nation to be permitting the annual inflow of some 50,000 dependents, who are for the most part the material of the future growth of the immigrant-descended population. It is like watching a nation busily engaged in heaping up its own funeral pyre.' Nigel Farage, in an interview in *The Guardian*, said of Enoch Powell: 'Enoch Powell was an extraordinary fellow. I admired him for having the guts to talk about an issue that seemed to be really rather important—immigration, society, how do we want to live in this country' (Farage 2009). Powell's approach summarises Barker's (1981) argument on 'new racism' and correlates with the understanding of a form of nationalism linked to a cultural sensibility in Britain. From this perspective, racism, although it started as an ideology forming prejudice against people of colour (Fryer 2010), has managed to evolve from biological inferiority to cultural racism, anti-immigrant racism and Islamophobia, focusing on cultural differences, an approach popularly engaged by British political discourse since the early 1980s.

There is no doubt that some UKIP interviewees exhibit 'othering' attitudes and behaviour, whether as part of political campaigning or not, but this is not unique to them. Surveys used to examine far-right supporters' attitudes find that those attitudes stereotypically associated with the far right are widespread among mainstream voters too. For instance a 2009 survey suggests that 13 per cent of UK adults—6.5 million—think that black people are intellectually inferior, and 26 per cent—13 million—opposed civil partnerships (Cutts et al. 2011). These numbers surpass the numbers voting BNP or even UKIP, and while they can be characterised as potential support for BNP or UKIP, they also demonstrate that such attitudes are compatible with mainstream voting.

Analysis of parties of the far right (see Mudde 2004) shows xenophobic sentiments, underlines the threat of mass immigration and the potential creation of a multicultural society, and proposes strict immigration control and asylum policies. In France, since the early 1970s the Front National has adopted an anti-immigration rhetoric and called for 'assisted repatriation' (Hainsworth 2008); comparable examples are found in the Belgian Vlaams Blok, in the Italian Lega Nord, in the Swiss Schweizerische Volkspartei and in the Austrian Freiheitliche Partei Österreichs, among others. Norris (2005) argues that immigration is the 'signature' issue of the far right, and the fear of the 'other' that drives policies on immigration, asylum seekers and multiculturalism (2005: 132). Rejecting any form of multiculturalism is essential within far-right ideology and is often the reason that far-right parties have been accused of racism. Nation and national identity along with an ethnic and religious homogeneity are seen as things that need to be protected and secured by any threat posed by, for example, asylum seekers, Muslims, immigrants. In addition, far-right groups 'postulate a homogeneous society where national identity is passed on through blood and heredity' (Hainsworth 2000 in Moufahim 2007: 31).

Having said that, as underlined by a number of interviewees, it is important to note that there is a difference between the feeling that Islam and/or Islamism are a threat to the British way of life and hating Muslims just because they are Muslims; focusing more on the threat of migration and more specifically of Muslims towards British cultural identity ('Englishness'), one of the EDL activists we interviewed said:

> Other people say 'I'm not particularly interested in the – in Englishness and that doesn't really bother me that much – I'm concerned about Muslims and them changing our way of life and so there's a whole – for some people Englishness is important, some it isn't, some think religion is important, some– 'ah- it's not so much about religion'- some people are really attached to the Christianity identity – some people see themselves as being atheists – so there's an interesting hotch potch of people who end up basically, becoming friends who become part of a network. (EDL4)

The official EDL website warns against 'the unjust assumption that all Muslims are complicit in or somehow responsible for these crimes' and describes Muslims themselves as the 'victims of some Islamic traditions and practices' (EDL Mission Statement 2015). Similarly to EDL's approach, although UKIP in its 2010 manifesto rejected 'blood and soil' ethnic nationalism, it promoted the notion of 'uniculturalism' in opposition to multiculturalism and political correctness; in other words a united British culture that embraces all the races, colours and religions (UKIP 2010). BNP also claims not to be 'against Islam per se' but additionally signifies the potential danger posed to 'democracy, traditions and freedoms by the creeping Islamification of Britain' (BNP 2005). Nevertheless, a video released by the youth of BNP in 2014 creates a clear perception of the immigrant as the 'other'.[11]

Immigration rhetoric incorporating strong sentiments of xenophobia is among the most characteristic themes of the far right, with a distinguishing popular appeal within the electorate, something that can be identified in the groups under examination. Xenophobia, literally reflecting the fear (phobia) of the foreigner (xenos), is the sentiment in which far-right populist parties invest and ground their proposals of welfare-nationalist policies and anti-immigration measures (see Davies and Lynch 2002 in Moufahim 2007).[12]

Since the majority of immigrants originate from non-Western European countries, as Mudde (2002) observes, they are regarded as a threat to the cultural identity of the host countries and, therefore, are often accused of exploiting the welfare system, taking jobs away from native citizens and being responsible for the rising crime rate. In the interviews we conducted, while some described themselves as against uncontrolled mass migration but not against immigration as a whole, others were calling

---

[11] BNP Youth—Real Version, Retrieved 2 May 2015 from https://www.youtube.com/watch?v=q2snwxSGn-Y.

[12] A detailed analysis of xenophobia and immigration can be found in Betz (1994), *Radical Right Wing Populism in Western Europe*. New York: St. Martin's Press. pp. 69–106.

for a stop to migration until issues such as access to health and education services and the cost of interpreters were resolved.

> The problem we have at the moment being in the EU, millions of people can claim benefits if they want. They haven't got a skill, they, they're not coming to work. (UKIP 4)
>
> If you're going to come here and work and benefit the country and your community, I don't have a problem. But if you're going to come here just to sponge benefits and demand your laws and start breaking our laws, that's what we've got a problem with. (EDL2)

In addition, the homogeneity of the nation reflects issues like welfare chauvinism. The socio-economic policy of welfare chauvinism introduces a notion of 'our own people first', an exclusionist approach adopted by the entirety of far-right parties. Based on this principle, the state's funds job opportunities should be used by natives, rather than immigrants, and along with that the state should protect the national economy against 'foreign competition' (Mudde 2002: 175).

Another approach to identifying their ideological content is to examine the slogans used by the groups. A common slogan in EDL's demonstrations, for instance, is 'No Surrender', or NFSE (standing for 'No Fucking Surrender Ever'). This harks back to the use of the phrase in Northern Irish politics (see Wallis et al. 1986) and its appearance in football songs in 1980s England as 'No surrender to the IRA'. This football song has been adapted to 'No surrender to the Taliban', and is sung at EDL demonstrations alongside other football-related songs, including 'England 'til I die'. Another EDL slogan, seen on the back of many EDL shirts, is 'Not racist, not violent, no longer silent'. The first two parts of this are a direct refutation of the accusations made by opponents such as Hope Not Hate and Unite Against Fascism, and mainstream commentators (see below). For the EDL, the people of Britain have been silent for too long on the question of the threat of Islam and/or Islamism, targeting the government which 'they perceive as pandering to Jihadis' demands, drowned in political correctness and marred by indefensible double standards' (Bartlett and Littler 2011: 12–13) and demanding direct action.

Similarly, UKIP's 'Believe in Britain' or 'Love Britain' (a slogan that was used also by BNP in 2010) are targeting the voter's sentimental attachment to the country and emphasising the element of nationalism. Defending ethno-nationalism, the representatives of the far right argue for a homogeneous environment in which the nation is consistent with the state (Eatwell 2000). Thus they disregard or belittle any foreign elements that are differentiated from it. This refers back to the idea that the nation, for EDL, UKIP and BNP, is perceived as a unit that shares identical cultural and ethnic origins, and individuals that do not share these features should not be considered as part of it.

What differentiates EDL, however, from both UKIP and BNP is the openness of the group to other issues, specifically to their Jewish, LGBT, Sikh and Hindu divisions (Lane 2012). This promotion has a triple meaning: first, these groups have been the target of Islamist groups globally (the latter two in Indian Gujarat), thus there is an expression of solidarity; second, EDL activists know that the rainbow flag and Israeli flag represent things that the radical Islamists hate, so it acts as a 'wind-up'; and third, it is also an attempt to demonstrate that the group is not fascist or extreme right. Although the genuineness of each motive can be questioned, the interviews showed that it appears to be enough to convince some gay EDL activists.

> Tommy and Kev told us, 'We don't care if you're black, if you're gay, if you're lesbian or whatever religious path you follow, if you want to join us to fight against Islamic extremism we'll take you' … I first met some lesbians and some gays and some bi-sexuals and transgenders, we all met up at London when Geert Wilders came over. And we thought to ourselves, why don't we set up an LGBT division? (EDL2)

Julia Gasper, the Oxford UKIP chairperson, made online comments on a private members' forum linking homosexuality and paedophilia and also claiming 'some homosexuals prefer sex with animals' (Moss 2013). However, the party's position on gay marriage is not necessarily homophobic. The party officially supports the civil partnership regime as a way of giving same-sex couples the same rights as all other couples, but fears a change to marriage law would pave the way for EU or UK law to interfere with the operation of religious bodies (UKIP 2015), an approach that the interviewees seemed to agree with. 'I mean a man, if two men want to go to the registrar and get married, it's a doddle, I mean it's the same with two women doing that, I can't see it as a problem—that's entirely up to them' (UKIP1).

Moreover, BNP also opposes same-sex marriage and wishes to ban what it perceives as the promotion of homosexuality in schools and the media, which it calls 'homosexual propaganda'. In 2014, the party's youth released a recruitment video claiming that 'militant homosexuals' are part of an 'unholy alliance' taking charge of the country in order to destroy families. According to the video, homosexuality is linked to ongoing attempts to eradicate the British cultural identity and therefore poses a threat to the traditional family model and the Christian values of British society (Pink News 2014). Following the referendum in Ireland on same-sex marriage, Jean de Valette (2015) of the BNP wrote an article on the party's website characterising same-sex marriage as a 'madness to equality', while Nick Griffin, in 2014, referring to the issue of same-sex marriage commented that:

> Same-sex marriage isn't about rights of gay people. It's fundamentally an attack by a Trotskyite Leftist and capitalist elite which wants the pink pound and the pink dollar. It's an attack on marriage. It's an attack on tradition. It's an attack on the fabric of our society. ... Teach them about homosexuality? That's not in any way for the rights of homosexuals. That's some dirty pervert trying to mess with the minds of my kids and I think it's great that a major European power has stood up and said: Leave our kids alone.[13]

Opponents and Opposition: Anti-bodies Against the Politics of Fear

The past 20 years have seen some consolidation of state and community-sector organisations against the politics of fear spread by the far right. The backlash against Muslims post-2001 prompted responses from ant-racist

---

[13] Germany: Ukrainian nationalists are being used by the EU—Nick Griffin. Retrieved May 2, 2015 from https://www.youtube.com/watch?v=Q6Ir2rWzkFk.

organisations and the government, notably with the 'community cohesion' agenda as a framework for addressing conflict.

While the asylum seekers issue, resulting in multiple pieces of legislation (Fletcher 2008), and the beginning of the debate over the treatment of Muslims and Islam (Khan 2000) were important aspects of the British experience of the 1990s, both were overshadowed by the enquiry into the racist murder of a 19-year-old black British man, Stephen Lawrence, which laid more blame at the door of public bodies than had previously been allowed, concluding that the Metropolitan Police was 'institutionally racist' and resulting in legislation which aimed to reform the public sector.

Previously, the government inquiry into the 1981 Brixton riots (the Scarman Report) had blamed the deprivation in the area (characterised by high unemployment, crime and poor housing) on some unwittingly racist police officers. An overly restrictive definition of 'institutional racism' as consciously set up to be racist cleared the Metropolitan Police. However, the 1999 Macpherson Report (which resulted from the public enquiry into the Stephen Lawrence murder) reassessed this judgement in the light of the failed police investigation into the murder (see Lea 2000 for a critical discussion). Bell argues that the state response to this was, in part, the 'mainstreaming' of 'ethnic equality issues' in the Race Relations (Amendment) Act 2000 which placed … public authorities under a legally enforceable duty to have due regard to the need (a) to eliminate unlawful discrimination and (b) to promote equal opportunity and good relations between persons of different racial groups. (Bell 2008: 47) A decade later, the 2010 Equality Act aimed to tidy up a number of pieces of legislation which did similar work for other sets of people with 'protected characteristics'.

After riots in various Northern towns and 9/11, 'race relations' more broadly was in effect reconfigured and rebadged as 'community cohesion' (Worley 2005). Of concern were both the state's relationship with the Muslim minority (mainly those with a sub-continental background) and the revitalised far right, which was focused on the same minority. The Cantle Report (Cantle 2001) cemented the notion of 'community cohesion' as the framework for addressing conflict, and an Institute of Community Cohesion was launched in 2005. As with the equalities work associated with equalities legislation, local bodies in the public and voluntary sectors have staff working in a variety of community cohesion interventions, including counter-extremism and counter-terrorism work which aims to reach those at risk of moving to violence. While this work has sometimes been characterised as Islamophobic and as stigmatising particular places and communities, recent years have seen attempts to conduct and demonstrate a balanced approach. In this vein, the state has also funded Muslim-led groups, such as TellMAMA, which monitor hate speech.

While hate speech and other hate crimes are dealt with in separate pieces of legislation for each characteristic, new laws have attempted to put different types of hate on a par, with laws made in 2006 and 2008 creating new offences of 'stirring up religious hatred' and 'inciting hatred on the grounds of sexual orientation'. Fella and Bozzini found that most respondents in the UK believe that EU anti-racist policy has had little impact on the UK as its 'legislation was clearly the most advanced in Europe' (Fella and Bozzini 2013: 72), with EU policy playing catch-up.

This, of course, begs the question of the impact of such laws. Seemingly part of the response to EU initiatives, in 2007 the Commission for Racial Equality (CRE) was merged with other equalities bodies to create the Equalities and Human Rights Commission (Fella and Bozzini 2013: 73). Similarly, many of the Racial Equality Councils—local versions of the CRE with links to local government—have been reconfigured to cover a range of discriminations, being renamed Rights and Equality Council or Equality Council. These bodies continue to provide legal and social support to those discriminated against in the workplace or elsewhere, and to the victims of harassment and crime. These changes, and the post-2001 focus on religious divides and discrimination, have led some activists to see race as sliding down the priority list.

The brief success of the BNP in the mid-2000s, and later the emergence of the EDL (see previous sections), also revitalised the anti-fascist movement. This includes the campaigning and research work of organisations such as Hope Not Hate (HnH[14]), and campaigning and counter-

---

[14] This is an advocacy group, created in 2004, that campaigns to counter racism and fascism.

demonstrations by Unite Against Fascism (UAF). The end of the 2000s also saw a number of Love Music Hate Racism events, continuing in the tradition of the Rock Against Racism events of the 1970s. However, the failure of the BNP to achieve long-lasting success has led UAF to focus on opposing the EDL, with the 'None Shall Pass' approach of the 1930s and 1970s, while HnH have broadened their work to oppose UKIP in Project Purple Rain; by combining research with community organisation, HnH aims to raise the profile of extremism and work against hate groups.

In parallel to these developments, the 1990s onwards saw the increasing demonisation of asylum seekers and refugees by mainstream media, together with 'pro-othering' activism anti-deportation campaigns, campaigns against the detention of asylum seekers, and promotion of the rights of migrants. National and local/grass roots organisations have continued to be founded for the purposes of one-off or longer-lasting campaigns, as in the work of the National Coalition of Anti-Deportation Campaigns.

Meanwhile, the diverse range of actors and actions that could be considered 'anti-bodies' to far-right 'othering' can be seen to be rooted in different histories, with differing motivations, rationales and tactics. Some of the anti-fascist activism is not based on a desire to defend people from 'othering' discrimination, but more rooted in the belief that fighting fascism defends working-class unions or is fighting for the soul of the working class or is defending democracy. Conversely, some justify anti-immigration legislation on the basis that 'it was for the good of race relations within the UK that the white population had to be assured that no large number of blacks would be coming in.' (Moore and Wallace 1975: 2). Other motivations may be less honourable, especially where electoral calculations mean that attacking racism or other 'isms', populism and extremism is designed to appeal to a population in the short term, or to undermine political opponents. The argument over the relative legitimacy and efficacy of 'liberal anti-fascism' and 'militant anti-fascism' (Olechnowicz 2005), also seems to include participants' feelings of moral superiority, as each side feels their approach is what will stop fascism.

Indeed, many commentators (and the state itself) see militant anti-fascist activity as more problematic than that of the BNP and EDL. 'Some strategies implemented by civil-society actors with good intentions against the far right, have ultimately caused more harm than good. Examples of this include combative or militant anti-fascist movements that go to extremes to prevent activity by far-right movements.' (Ramalingam 2012). These movements' activities in opposing the far-right both inflame passions on the day, increasing the risk of violence, while also—due to the connection to mainstream politicians—giving far-right activists the impression of a government-sponsored opposition.

Similar arguments can be made about the activities of the state and associated public bodies and charities, for if they are active against 'othering' by the far right, while ignoring the same 'othering' elsewhere, they appear to be politically motivated. 'From a government perspective, inconsistent implementation of the legislation has in some cases led to counter-productive results. For example, some experts argue that the ongoing "quarrel" about the ban of the NPD in Germany has lent legitimacy to the party.' (Ramalingam 2012). Just as the currents of far-right and populist 'othering' and the currents of political argument are in conflict with each other, so are the forces against them— sometimes along the same lines. Thus, some activists in the anti-fascist scene argue that Unite Against Fascism's politics are problematic due to its accommodations with Islamist activists (see Readings 2011). The inability of any one political force to capture an issue means that policy moves slowly: in the UK we are unlikely to see either a strong 'othering' nationalism, or a radical anti-'othering'. In the UK there is a palpable fear amongst campaigning groups/anti-bodies that their gains are fragile, notwithstanding that many of them have been inscribed into law and practice. While the evidence for this in terms of direct counter-demonstrations and anything but periodic violence is slim, activists we interviewed elaborated and events embodied a clear sense that an underlying but often unspoken culture needs to be challenged with direct action and a continuing campaign of mixed education and confrontation. There was a distinct sense in these engagements that racist and discriminatory discourse should not be isolated but rather confronted and engineered out of the social system through education, emblematic prosecution and the creation of a wider programme of support for the (often poor white, black and Muslim) communities that are the direct focus of extremist attention.

Concluding Remarks

In the UK, the far-right populist scene has struggled to maintain its support despite circumstances that created a fertile environment that could have contributed to their sustenance. As Eatwell (2004) notes, studies from the 1960s to the 1970s underlined the growth of nationalism in combination with anti-immigration sentiments. In the case of the UK, however, these sentiments did not necessarily lead to the support of the far right. By engaging hatred rhetoric, provocation and violence, far-right movements and parties in Britain failed to forge a respectable representation in the 1970s. Despite attempts at infiltration in the years that followed, this political family has yet to become electorally successful at national level. The strong bonds of loyalty that the established political parties have created with the electorate, along with the structure of the electoral system, makes it difficult for new parties to emerge; furthermore, the fact that the mainstream parties have managed to respond to the growing issues of immigration, scepticism over European integration and the adopted rhetoric of far-right representatives that are still associated with extremism and elements of hate speech, violence and discrimination against the 'other', are the major factors contributing to the low performance of the far right in the UK.

'Anti-body' activism can embrace a wide range of activity, come from multiple sources and have differing motivations and strategies. Opposition to far-right extremism and populism can be divided into three strands. The first is the more militant anti-fascist activity, which focuses on organised far-right politics and disrupts this activity, but at the risk of exacerbating problems. Second is the activity of the state itself, and the related mainstream political actors, which are both against racism and other discriminatory activities, but at the same time accept and contribute to some discrimination. This may be for electoral reasons and can also be justified on the grounds that, for example, restrictions on immigration are necessary to reduce racism. The third strand is the broad-based activity of civil-society organisations, some closely aligned to the state, which, at least some of the time, aims to address problems of 'othering' in society more widely, including that of populist and mainstream politics and the state.

References

Abedi, A. (2004). *Anti-political establishment parties: A comparative analysis.* London: Routledge.

Albertazzi, D., & McDonnell, D. (2008). Introduction: The sceptre and the spectre. In D. Albertazzi & D. McDonnell (Eds.), *Twenty-first century populism: The spectre of Western European democracy.* Palgrave Macmillan: Basingstoke, England, 1–11.

Anastasakis, O. (2000). *Extreme right in Europe: A comparative study of recent trends* (Discussion paper no. 3). London: The Hellenic Observatory, The European Institute London School of Economics and Political Science.

Barker, M. (1981). *The New Racism: Conservatives and the Ideology of the Tribe.* London. Junction Books.

Bale, T., Hampshire, J., & Partos, R. (2011). Having one's cake and eating it too: Cameron's conservatives and immigration. *Political Quarterly, 82*(3), 398–406.

Bartlett, J., & Littler, M. (2011). *Inside the EDL.* London: Demos.

BBC. (2013). UKIP is not a racist party, Lord Heseltine told. Retrieved October 3, 2013, from http://www.bbc.co.uk/news/uk-politics-24385139

BBC News. (2006). Farage elected new UKIP leader. Retrieved May 4, 2015, from http://news.bbc.co.uk/go/pr/fr/-/2/hi/uk_news/politics/5336126.stm

BBC News. (2010b). EDL founder charged with Muslim poppy protest assault. Retrieved October 1, 2013, from http://www.bbc.co.uk/news/uk-england-london-11744811

BBC News. (2013). EDL leader Tommy Robinson quits group. Retrieved October 15, 2013, from http://www.bbc.co.uk/news/uk-politics-24442953

Bell, M. (2008). *Racism and Equality in the European Union.* Oxford, England: Oxford University Press.

Betz, H. G. (1994). *Radical Right Wing Populism in Western Europe* (pp. 69–106). New York: St. Martin's Press.

Betz, H. G. (2007). 'Against the 'Green Totalitarianism': Anti-Islamic Nativism in Contemporary Radical Right-Wing Populism in Western Europe'. In Christina Schori Liang (Ed.), *Europe for the Europeans: The Foreign and Security Policy of the Populist Radical Right*. London: Ashgate.

BNP. (2005). Rebuilding British democracy. Retrieved March 13, 2015, from http://news.bbc.co.uk/1/shared/bsp/hi/pdfs/BNP_uk_manifesto.pdf

BNP. (2015). 'Securing our British Future'. Retrieved July 3, 2015 from https://www.bnp.org.uk/sites/default/files/bnp_manifesto-2015.pdf.

Cameron, D. (2011). *Speech at Munich Security Conference*. Retrieved April 11, 2015, from https://www.gov.uk/government/speeches/pms-speech-at-munich-security-conference

Canovan, M. (1999). Trust the people! Populism and the two faces of democracy. *Political Studies, 47*, 2–16.

Cantle, T. (2001). *Community cohesion : A report of the independent review team* (p. 79). London: Home Office. Retrieved June 1, 2015, from http://image.guardian.co.uk/sys-files/Guardian/documents/2001/12/11/communitycohesionreport.pdf

Carter, E. L. (2005). *The extreme right in Western Europe: Success or failure?* (p. xiv, 271). Manchester, England: Manchester University Press.

Clark, A., Bottom, K., & Copus, C. (2008). More similar than they'd like to admit? Ideology, policy and populism in the trajectories of the British National Party and Respect. *British Politics, 3*(4), 511–534.

Coleman, D. (2010). When Britain becomes 'majority minority'. Retrieved May 2, 2015, from http://www.prospectmagazine.co.uk/features/when-britain-becomes-majority-minority

Cutts, D., Ford, R., & Goodwin, M. J. (2011). Anti-immigrant, politically disaffected or still racist after all? Examining the attitudinal drivers of extreme right support in Britain in the 2009 European elections. *European Journal of Political Research, 50*(3), 418–440.

Daniel, M. (2005). *Cranks and Gadflies: The story of UKIP*. London: Timewell Press.

de Beauvoir, S. (1971). The Second Sex. Random House. Alfred A. Knopf.

de Valette, J. (2015). The madness of equality: Same sex 'Marriage'. Retrieved May 3, 2015, from http://www.bnp.org.uk/news/national/madness-equality-same-sex-marriage

Demman, J., & McDonald, P. (1996). Unemployment statistics from 1881 to the present day. Retrieved April 3, 2015, from http://www.ons.gov.uk/ons/rel/lms/labour-market-trends--discontinued-/january-1996/unemployment-since-1881.pdf

Eatwell, R. (2000). 'The rebirth of the Extreme Right in Western Europe?', *Parliamentary affairs, 53.*

Eatwell, R., (2004). 'The Extreme Right in Britain: The Long Road to 'Modernization''. In Eatwell & Mudde, (Eds.), *Western Democracies and the New Extreme Right Challenge* (pp. 62–81). London: Routledge.

Eatwell, R., & Goodwin, M. J. (2010). Introduction: The "new" extremism in twenty-first-century Britain. In R. Eatwell & M. J. Goodwin (Eds.), *The new extremism in 21st century Britain* (pp. 1–20). London: Routledge.

EDL's Mission Statement . Retrieved May 11, 2015, from https://www.english-defenceleague.org/?page_id=9

European Election Results for UK. Retrieved May 12, 2015, from http://www.europarl.org.uk/en/your-meps/european_elections.html

Farage, N. (2009). Nigel Farage, Ukip: 'Other party leaders live in a PC world'. Retrieved May 11, 2015, from http://www.theguardian.com/politics/2009/jun/05/nigel-farage-ukip-interview

Fella, S., & Bozzini, E. (2013). Fighting racism in the UK. In S. Fella & C. Ruzza (Eds.), *Anti-Racist movements in the EU* (pp. 53–81). Palgrave Macmillan: Basingstoke, England.

Fella, S., & Ruzza, C. (2009). *Reinventing the Italian right: Territorial politics, populism and 'Post-Fascism'.* London: Routledge.

Fletcher, E. (2008). *Changing support for asylum seekers : An analysis of legislation and parliamentary debates* (Working paper No. 49). Sussex, England: University of Sussex.

Ford, R. (2010). Who might vote for the BNP? In R. Eatwell & M. J. Goodwin (Eds.), *The new extremism in 21st century Britain.* London: Routledge.

Ford, R., & Goodwin, M. J. (2014). *Revolt on the right: Explaining support for the radical right in Britain.* Abingdon, England: Routledge.

Ford, R., Goodwin, M. J., & Cutts, D. (2012). Strategic Eurosceptics and polite xenophobes: Support for the United Kingdom Independence Party (UKIP) in the 2009 European Parliament elections. *European Journal of Political Research, 51,* 204–234.

Fryer, P. (2010). *Staying Power: The history of black people in Britain.* London. Pluto Press.

Gilroy, P. (2012). "My Britain is fuck all": Zombie multiculturalism and the race politics of citizenship. *Identities: Global Studies in Culture and Power, 19*(4), 380–397.

Gillespie, A. (2006). *Becoming other: from social interaction to self-reflection.* New York: IAP -Information Age Publishing.

Goodwin, M. (2011). *New British fascism*. London: Routledge.

Hage, G. (2010). 'The affective politics of racial mis-interpellation'. Theory, Culture & Society December 2010, *27* (7–8), 112–129.

Hainsworth, P. (2008). *The extreme right in Western Europe*. New York: Routledge.

Halikiopoulou, D., & Vasilopoulou, S. (2010). Towards a "civic" narrative: British national identity and the transformation of the British National Party. *The Political Quarterly, 81*(4), 583–592.

Heitmeyer W (2003). 'Right-Wing Extremist Violence' in International Handbook of Violence Research. Hagan J, Heitmeyer W (Eds); Dordrecht,Boston,London: Kluwer Academic Publishers: 399–436.

Hinsliff, G. (2004). It feels like the BNP - only in blazers. *Guardian*. Retrieved October 1, 2013, from http://www.theguardian.com/politics/2004/may/30/otherparties.immigrationandpublicservices

Hope Not Hate. (2013). Overwhelming response. Retrieved March 1, 2013, from http://www.hopenothate.org.uk/blog/article/2549/overwhelming-response

Jackson, P. (2011). 'The EDL: Britain's 'New Far Right Social Movement'' Radicalism and New Media group: Northampton. Retrieved March 2, 2015 from http://nectar.northampton.ac.uk/6015/.

Jackson, P., & Gable, G. (2011). *Far-Right.com: Nationalist Extremism on the Internet*. London: Searchlight Magazine.

Jefferies, J. (2005). 'The UK population: Past, present, future' in focus on people and migration. Retrieved May 2, 2015, from http://www.ons.gov.uk/ons/rel/fertility-analysis/focus-on-people-and-migration/december-2005/focus-on-people-and-migration---focus-on-people-and-migration---chapter-1.pdf

John, P., Margetts, H., Rowland, D., & Weir, S. (2006). *The BNP: The roots of its appeal*. Colchester, England: Democratic Audit, Human Rights Centre.

Johnson, C. A., Patten, S., & Betz, H-G. (2005). Identitarian politics and populism in Canada and the antipodes. In J. Rydgren (Ed.) , Movements of Ecclusion: Radical Right-Wing Populism in the Western World (pp. 85–100). Adelaide: Nova Science Publishers.

Khan, Z. (2000). Muslim presence in Europe: The British dimension—Identity, integration and community activism. *Current Sociology, 48*(4), 29–43.

Koopmans, R. (1996). Explaining the rise of racist and extreme right violence in Western Europe: Grievances or opportunities? *European Journal of Political Research, 30*(2), 185–216.

Laclau, E. (2005). *On populist reason*. London: Verso.

Lane, H. S. (2012). A study of the English Defence League: What draws people of faith to right-wing organisations and what effects does the EDL have on community cohesion and interfaith relations? Retrieved May 12, 2015, from http://faith-matters.org/images/stories/edl%20report.pdf

Lea, J. (2000). The Macpherson Report and the question of institutional racism. *Howard Journal of Criminal Justice, 39*(3), 219–233.

May, S., Moddod, T., & Squires, J. (2004). *Ethnicity, nationalism and minority rights.* Cambridge, England: Cambridge University Press.

Migration Observatory. (2015). Retrieved April 21, 2015, from http://www.migrationobservatory.ox.ac.uk/

Minkenberg, M. (2002). 'The Radical Right in Post-socialist Central and Eastern Europe: Comparative Observations and Interpretations'. *East European Politics and Society,* 335–362.

Moore, R., & Wallace, T. (1975). *Slamming the door: Administration of immigration control.* London: Wiley.

Moss, V. (2013). Ugly face of UKIP: Sunday Mirror exposes racist and homophobic views of party members. *Mirror.* Retrieved October 1, 2013, from http://www.mirror.co.uk/news/uk-news/ugly-face-ukip-sunday-mirror-1531879

Moufahim, M. (2007). Interpreting Discourse: A Critical Discourse Analysis of the Marketing of an Extreme Right Party. The Vlaams Blok/Vlaams Belang. Thesis submitted to the University of Nottingham for the degree of Doctor of Philosophy.

Mudde, C. (2002). *The Ideology of Extreme Right.* Manchester and New York. Manchester University Press.

Mudde, C. (2004). The populist Zeitgeist. *Governance and Opposition, 39*(3), 541–563.

Mudde, C. (Ed.). (2005). *Racist extremism in Central and Eastern Europe.* Milton Park, England: Routledge.

National Front. (2015). National Front policy. Retrieved March 13, 2015, from http://www.britishnationalfront.net/policy.html

Norris, P. (2005). *Radical Right: Voters and Parties in the Electoral Market.* New York: Cambridge University Press.

Oakley, R. (2005). *Policing racist crime and violence: A comparative analysis.* Vienna, Austria: European Monitoring Centre on Racism and Xenophobia.

Olechnowicz, A. (2005). Liberal anti-fascism in the 1930s the case of Sir Ernest Barker. *Albion, 36,* 636–660.

Painter, A. (2013). *Democratic stress, the populist signal and extremist threat.* London: Policy Network.

Pilkington, H. (2014) 'Loud and proud': Youth Activists in the English Defence League. XVIII ISA World Congress of Sociology. Facing an Unequal World: Challenges for Global Sociology. Yokohama, 13–19 July 2014. Retrieved May 30, 2015, from https://isaconf.confex.com/isaconf/wc2014/webprogram/Paper42549.html

Pink News. (2014). BNP Youth recruitment video: Militant homosexuals want gay marriage to destroy families. Retrieved May 2, 2015, from http://www.pinknews.co.uk/2014/05/13/bnp-youth-recruitment-video-militant-homosexuals-want-gay-marriage-to-destroy-families/

Powell, E. (1968). Rivers of blood speech. Retrieved April 16, 2015, from http://www.telegraph.co.uk/comment/3643823/Enoch-Powells-Rivers-of-Blood-speech.html

Ramalingam, V. (2012). *Countering far-right extremism*. London.

Readings, G. (2011). Too many on the Left are continuing to promote Islamist extremists. *Left Foot Forward*. Retrieved February 20, 2014, from http://www.leftfootforward.org/2011/05/too-many-on-the-left-are-continuing-to-promote-islamist-extremists/

Richardson, J. E. (2011). Race and racial difference: The surface and depth of BNP ideology. In N. Copsey & G. Macklin (Eds.), *British National Party: Contemporary perspectives* (pp. 38–61). Abingdon, England: Routledge.

Rydgren, J. (2003). 'Meso-level Reasons for Racism and Xenophobia: Some Converging and Diverging Effects of Radical Right Populism in France and Sweden'. *European Journal of Social Theory* 6(1):45–68.

Said, E. (1978). *Orientalism*. New York: Pantheon.

Smith, J. (2008). *Home Secretary's speech at the Conference on Preventing Violent Extremism* (H. Office, Ed.). Retrieved April 20, 2015, from http://tna.europarchive.org/20090120164241/http://press.homeoffice.gov.uk/Speeches/hs-speech-violent-extremism

Stanley, B. (2008). The thin ideology of populism. *Journal of Political Ideologies, 13*(1), 95–110.

Taggart, P. A. (2000). *Populism*. Buckingham, England: Open University Press.

UKIP. (2010). Manifesto. Retrieved May 15, 2015 from http://www.politicsresources.net/area/uk/ge10/man/parties/UKIPManifesto2010.pdf.

UKIP. (2012). The constitution. Retrieved May 4, 2015, from http://www.ukip.org/the_constitution

UKIP. (2013). What we stand for. Retrieved October 1, 2013, from http://www.ukip.org/issues/policy-pages/what-we-stand-for

UKIP. (2015). Believe in Britain: UKIP manifesto 2015. Retrieved May 4, 2015, from http://www.ukip.org/manifesto2015#

Wallis, R., Bruce, S., & Taylor, D. (1986). *'No surrender': Paisleyism and the politics of ethnic identity in Northern Ireland.* Belfast, Northern Ireland: Department of Social Studies, Queen's University of Belfast.

Worley, C. (2005), 'It's not about Race, it's about the community': New Labour and 'Community Cohesion'. *Critical Social Policy 25*(4), 483–496.

Zaslove, A. (2008). 'Here to Stay? Populism as a New Party Type'. *European Review, 16*, 319–336.

Index

Note: Page number followed by "n" refers to footnotes.

© The Editor(s) (if applicable) and The Author(s) 2016
G. Lazaridis et al. (eds.), *The Rise of the Far Right in Europe*,
DOI 10.1057/978-1-137-55679-0

universal Scandinavian welfare state, 114
universal welfare model, 114
Uomo Qualunque, 27, 27n6
'us' group, 91
  antagonistic relationship of, 91
  in Austria, 16, 19
  superiority and privileges of, 92

V
Venice, 36
Videnov, Zhan, 164
Vienna-based organisations, 84
Viennese anti-mosque movement, 15
Viennese Citizens' Initiatives, 94
Vilks, Lars, 119, 119n3
violence, 47–50
  acts of, 224–8
Volkish populist movements, 138
voluntary associations, types of, 127

W
Weber, Max, 11
welfare chauvinism, socio-economic policy of, 258
welfare national chauvinism, 131
welfare nationalism, 16, 110, 113
Westergaard, Kurt, 119
Western Political Movement, 35
Wilders, Geert, 2, 62
Wodak, R., 10
Women's Front of Golden Dawn, 220–1

X
xenophobia, 257
  in Bulgarian political discourses, normalisation of, 180
xeno-racism, 92

Y
Ye'Or, Bat, 71
Yugoslav republics, 17

CPSIA information can be obtained
at www.ICGtesting.com
Printed in the USA
LVHW081810281221
707355LV00002B/251